Robert M.
Bohm
University of Central Florida

DEATHQUEST

An Introduction to the

Theory and Practice of

CAPITAL PUNISHMENT

in the United States

anderson publishing co.
2035 Reading Road
Cincinnati, OH 45202
800-582-7295

Deathquest: An Introduction to the Theory and Practice of Capital Punishment in the United States

Copyright © 1999
Anderson Publishing Co.
2035 Reading Rd.
Cincinnati, OH 45202

Phone 800.582.7295 or 513.421.4142
Web Site www.andersonpublishing.com

Library of Congress Cataloging-in-Publication Data

Bohm, Robert M.
    Deathquest : an introduction to the theory and practice of capital punishment
in the United States / Robert M. Bohm.
        p.   cm.
    Includes bibliographical references (p.   ) and index.
    ISBN 0-87084-212-9 (paperback)
    1. Capital punishment--United States.   I. Title.   II. Title: Death quest.
HV8699.U5B65   1999
364.66' 0973--dc21   98-50466
                                                                     CIP

Cover design by Tin Box Studio, Inc.
Cover photo credit: © Andy Whale/Tony Stone Images

EDITOR Kelly Grondin
ASSISTANT EDITOR Sharon L. Boyles
ACQUISITIONS EDITOR Michael C. Braswell

DEDICATION

To Lisa, Traci, Allison, Daniel, Kami, Blythe, and Weston

ACKNOWLEDGMENTS

I would like to thank all of my friends and colleagues for their support, help, understanding, and inspiration. Although there are too many people to list here by name, many of them are cited in the pages of this book. The others know who they are.

Foreword

<hr />

by Donald A. Cabana

Professor, University of Southern Mississippi
Author of *Death at Midnight: The Confession of
an Executioner*
Former warden at various correctional facilities
throughout the South

"Vengeance is mine, saith the Lord;
and that means that it is not the
Lord Chief Justice's."
— George Bernard Shaw, 1922

On an oppressively humid July night in 1987, I stood at the window of the gas chamber at the Mississippi State Penitentiary, staring at Connie Ray Evans. Strapped into a cold, steel chair nicknamed the "Black Death" by some forlorn, condemned prisoner many years before I became warden, I was preparing to give the order that would end Connie Evans's life. This was my second execution in just five weeks. Still numb from the first one, I realized as I gazed into the eyes of this next victim that my senses were all but dulled. This one, I knew, would be even more difficult than the first. I had permitted myself to become close to Connie Ray Evans. I came to recognize him as more than just a prison number waiting his turn on death row. In the end, standing there that hot summer night, I realized I was about to execute a friend. My mind was haunted by questions: How had Connie Ray Evans and I gotten there? What goes so wrong that a normal eighteen–year–old kid spends the last seven years of his life awaiting a date with the executioner?

At a 1790's meeting of the American Philosophical Society held at the home of longtime friend Benjamin Franklin, Dr. Benjamin Rush delivered a paper condemning the young nation's embrace of capital punishment. Rush, signer of the Declaration of Independence, father of American psychiatry, and social reformer, asked the same question: How had America arrived at the use of such a barbaric sanction? He dared to believe that we could be better than that.

Two centuries later, on a sweltering August day in Boston, champion libertarian and death penalty opponent Henry Schwarzschild delivered a message eerily similar to Rush's earlier admonition. Insisting that it is useless to discuss a hypothetical society that applies capital punishment in a fair, rational, consistent manner, Schwarzschild asserted that such an idyllic society is nonexistent. It is necessary, then, to remember that people are not infallible, therefore rendering the legal system imperfect. For that reason alone, he concluded, the use of capital punishment should be relegated to the writings of historical scholars.

Deathquest would win the wholehearted approval of both Rush and Schwarzschild, indeed no small achievement. Professor Bohm has crafted an exhaustive introductory work that should be required reading, not just for students of criminal justice but for any thoughtful, enlightened citizenry as well. Absent the emotional histrionics that characterize so much capital punishment literature, this work forges a detailed, fact-based discussion of what many believe to be the most contentious social issue in America today. While the quality of Professor Bohm's book is unassailable, of even greater importance to the reader is the manner in which he "tells the story." This is not a textbook filled with charts, graphs and data, however impressive and necessary we perceive such material to be. It is, in the final analysis, a book about people—people not so very different from the rest of us. America's death rows are filled with hope and despair, dreams and nightmares, optimism and resignation. While the purpose of this work is not to beatify death row prisoners, it does force the reader to come to grips with the stereotypical images that we so often assign to them.

As any thoughtful reader will quickly conclude, Professor Bohm has skillfully succeeded in painting the death penalty issue in realistic hues and shades of gray. Very rarely can we attribute consummate good or evil to any particular individual or community, and so it is with those on death row.

The death penalty has been a force in every major civilization since the dawn of history. So has the debate and controversy that surrounds it. For our part, executions are not new to the American scene. They have been part of our machinery of justice since the pre-colonial era, brought to Jamestown, Plymouth and Boston by the earliest European settlers. Capital punishment is not a topic of discussion that falls within the purview of researchers or policymakers alone. The major religious denominations, civil rights organizations and other social- and reform-minded groups have all focused attention on the troublesome issues that arise from the capital punishment debate.

This book will foster renewed, vigorous examination of the multiple realities that are capital punishment, and the impact the execution process has each time America leads one of its citizens to the execution chamber. Whether discussing the early history of executions in this country, or retributive arguments, or our present enthrallment with sanitized lethal injection, Professor Bohm writes with acuity and a forcefulness that compels the reader to revisit longheld beliefs. This is not, after all, a book of abstract ideas or fictitious characters. Rather, when Professor Bohm forces us to confront the stark reality of the gallows, the grisly nature of the electric chair, or the sterility of the lethal injection table, he engages us in a self-examination of who we are as a society. The calculated, methodical, politically convenient approach to justice that has long been part of the execution protocol is laid bare in this book, in all of its disturbing reality.

This work will ensure that we never view state-ordered killing in quite the same way again.

Table of Contents

Chapter 8:   Arbitrariness and Discrimination
in the Administration of the Death Penalty   143

Introduction

At one level, the death penalty is a minor issue. The media keep the public aware of all sorts of horrible crimes, but relatively few people are directly affected by those crimes, either as perpetrators or victims, or as family and friends of perpetrators and victims. Very few people are sentenced to die for their crimes, and fewer people, still, are ever executed. The 3,000-plus inmates currently on death rows throughout the United States represent only one-tenth of one percent of the approximately 1.7 million inmates in all prisons and jails. Moreover, the only reason there are as many as 3,000 death row inmates is that some of them have been awaiting execution for more than 20 years.

Certainly, for me, the death penalty was a minor issue prior to the mid-1980s, and I am a criminal justice professor! I had not given much thought to the issue because other subjects, such as the causes and prevention of crime, were more important to me. (I suppose that even then I did not believe that the death penalty was an important tool in preventing crime.) Then, one day, an article in the local newspaper caught my eye. It mentioned a Gallup poll that showed that 75 percent of the American public supported the death penalty. What struck me as interesting was that such a large percentage of the public agreed about anything. Soon thereafter, I began my effort to understand why the death penalty in the United States was so strongly supported. I wanted to know what was motivating the "deathquest" of the American people.

I became aware, not long into my investigation, that, at another level, the death penalty represents two profound concerns of nearly everyone: the value of human life and how best to protect it. I also discovered that people differ greatly in the ways they believe those concerns should be addressed. For most people who support the death penalty, the execution of killers (and people who commit other horrible acts) makes sense. Death penalty supporters frequently state that executions do prevent those executed from committing heinous crimes again, and that the example of executions probably prevents most people who might contemplate committing appalling crimes from doing so. In addition, many death penalty supporters simply believe that people who commit such crimes deserve to die, that they have earned their ignominious fate.

For opponents, the death penalty issue is about something else entirely. It is a benchmark of the "developing moral standards" of American civilization.[1] As Winston Churchill once said, "The mood and temper of the public with regard to the treatment of crime and criminals is one of the most unfailing tests of the civilization of any country." Put somewhat differently, for many opponents, the level of death penalty support in the United States is a rough estimate of the level of maturity of the American people. The not-so-subtle implication is that a mature, civilized society would not employ the death penalty. Opponents maintain that perpetrators of horrible crimes can be dealt with effectively by other means, and that it makes little sense to kill some people, however blameworthy they are, to teach other people not to kill. These opponents argue that although the perpetrators of terrible crimes may deserve severe punishment, that punishment need not be execution.

The death penalty issue can be and has been addressed on many different levels. Only superficially is it a minor issue. Rather, it is a complex concern that encompasses fundamental questions of who we are as a people and how we deal with some of our most vexing social problems.

One of the more unexpected findings of my research is that most people have a relatively strong opinion about the death penalty, even though they know little about it. What they think they know, moreover, is often wrong. For those reasons, I decided to prepare and teach a college class on the death penalty. Not only did I believe that such a class would be a good vehicle for teaching critical-thinking skills in general, but also I was curious to know whether information about the death penalty (an entire semester's worth) would have any effect on people's opinions about it.

This book is a product of more than a decade of preparing and teaching my class. My principal goal, both in teaching and in writing this book, is to educate students so that whatever their death penalty opinions are, they are informed ones.

I believe it only fair to admit that I am an opponent of the death penalty. Years of study have convinced me that it is a penal practice we can do without. However, as I do in my classes, I will present in this book, as best I can, both sides of all issues. I will let the reader decide whether I have succeeded in the effort and interpret what I write in light of my biases. The reader should be forewarned that most of the literature and research on the death penalty has been produced by its opponents. For the most part, supporters have not felt the need to justify their position. As noted previously, for most of them, supporting the death penalty is just common sense.

The book is divided into 10 chapters. The first four are the least controversial, as they present only facts about the death penalty in the United States. The first chapter traces the history of the death penalty in the United States from 1608 until 1972—which may be called the pre-modern death penalty era, referring to the era prior to *Furman v. Georgia* (1972). The second chapter focuses on the role of the U.S. Supreme Court in the practice of capital punishment. Many of the Court's decisions that have shaped death penalty jurisprudence are described. The third chapter addresses the death penalty systems of the federal government and the military. Similarities and differences between those two systems and the systems of the 38 death penalty states are highlighted. The fourth chapter provides a detailed analysis of execution methods employed in the United States and outlines the legal history of the concept of "cruel and unusual punishment."

Chapters five through nine examine the arguments and counterarguments employed by proponents and opponents of the death penalty. The fifth chapter addresses the issue of general deterrence. People who believe in the general deterrent effect assume that either the threat of executions or executions themselves prevent other people from committing capital crimes. Incapacitation and the costs of capital punishment are the subjects of the sixth chapter. Incapacitation refers to the goal of execution preventing convicted murderers or other capital offenders from committing other crimes. In the second section of this chapter, the costs of capital punishment are compared to the costs of alternative punishments, especially life imprisonment without opportunity of parole, or LWOP. The seventh chapter explores the subject of miscarriages of justice in capital cases. Incidents of wrongful arrests, wrongful charges or indictments, wrongful convictions, wrongful sentences, and wrongful executions are discussed, as are the reasons for those miscarriages of justice. The eighth chapter addresses two of the major problems the Supreme Court found with pre-modern death penalty statutes: that they did not prevent the death penalty from being imposed arbitrarily and in a discriminatory fashion. The major focus of the chapter is the modern record and whether the procedural reforms that have been implemented since *Furman v. Georgia* was decided in 1972 have, indeed, eliminated arbitrary and discriminatory application of the death penalty. The ninth chapter examines the subjects of retribution and religion in relation to the death penalty. Emphasized in the section on retribution are the effects of capital punishment on the families of murder victims and death row and executed inmates.

The tenth and final chapter of the book focuses on American death penalty opinion. This chapter is divided into three major sections. The first section provides the history of death penalty opinion, describing what is called here "the too simple and, therefore, misleading death penalty opinion question period." The second section surveys the present period and chronicles "the more complex and revealing death penalty opinion question period." This section begins with a description of research that tested the hypothesis that death penalty support is largely a product of ignorance about the way capital punishment is actually administered. The final section, and the conclusion to the book, addresses the future of American death penalty opinion and the effect it may have on the practice of capital punishment in the United States.

Three remarks about terminology should prove helpful. First, the terms "death penalty" and "capital punishment" are used interchangeably. They refer to the same thing. Second, frequent use is made of the terms "pre-*Furman*" (pre-modern) and "post-*Furman*" (modern) to denote different historical periods. *Furman* refers to the 1972 landmark Supreme Court decision, *Furman v. Georgia*—the first time that capital punishment was held to be unconstitutional. The pre-*Furman* era, for purposes of this book, spans the period from 1608, the year the first person in America was executed by legal authority, to June 29, 1972, the day *Furman* was decided. The "modern" era of capital punishment, the post-*Furman* period, covers everything about the death penalty in the United States that has occurred since June 29, 1972. Third, the term "death-eligible" is used frequently. The definition provided by law professors Baldus and Woodworth is employed: "A death-eligible case refers to one in which the facts are sufficient under state law to sustain a capital murder conviction and death sentence, whether or not the state actually seeks a death sentence or the jury actually imposes a death sentence in the case."[2]

Notes

[1] See, for example, Kohlberg and Elfenbein, 1975.
[2] Baldus and Woodworth, 1998:386.

CHAPTER 1

History of the Death Penalty in the United States: The Pre-*Furman* Period (1608–1972)

The Death Penalty in Colonial Times

Captain George Kendall, a councilor for the Virginia colony, was executed in 1608 for being a spy for Spain—and so began America's experience with capital punishment. Besides being the earliest recorded lawful execution in America,[1] and an execution for a relatively unusual offense, there is nothing particularly noteworthy about Kendall's execution itself. The death penalty was just another one of the punishments brought to the New World by the early European settlers.

Death Penalty Laws. The crimes for which the death penalty was legally imposed varied from colony to colony. At one extreme was the law of the Puritans of the Massachusetts Bay Colony, which listed 12 death-eligible crimes: (1) idolatry, (2) witchcraft, (3) blasphemy, (4) murder, (5) manslaughter, (6) poisoning, (7) bestiality, (8) sodomy, (9) adultery, (10) man-stealing, (11) false witness in capital cases, (12) conspiracy and rebellion.[2] Each of these capital crimes, except conspiracy and rebellion, was accompanied by a Biblical quotation as justification. For example, following murder was this Biblical passage, in the language of the statute: "If any person committt any wilfull murther, which is manslaughter, committed upon premeditated mallice, hatred, or Crueltie, not in a mans necessarie and just defence, nor by meere casualtie against his will, he shall be put to death."[3]

At the other extreme was the law of the Quakers who were far less punitive than their neighbors to the north. In the Royal Charter of South Jersey (1646), capital punishment was originally forbidden altogether, but the prohibition ended in 1691.[4] William Penn's Great Act of 1682 (Pennsylvania) allowed capital punishment only for treason and murder.[5] The Quakers, however, were the exception. Most of the British colonies had statutes similar to those of the Massachusetts Bay Colony.

1

Today it may seem as if the statutes of the colonies listed too many capital crimes (crimes for which death could be imposed), but for colonial times, the number was relatively modest. In Great Britain, death could be imposed for more than 50 crimes, including burglary, robbery, and larceny. Later, during the reign of George II (1727-1760), the number of capital crimes was increased to nearly 100, and under George III (1760-1820), the death penalty could be imposed for almost 150 capital crimes.[6] The main reason for the relatively small number of capital crimes in colonial America was the great need for able-bodied workers. It made little sense to execute people at a time when workers were so scarce, and people could be made to work. The British colonies might have had even fewer capital crimes if long-term confinement facilities had been available.[7] (The first prison was not established until 1790.)

The Death Penalty Imposed. Since Kendall's execution in 1608, more than 19,000 executions, performed in the United States under civil (as opposed to military) authority, have been confirmed by M. Watt Espy, the leading historian of capital punishment in the United States. Espy estimates that between 20,000 and 22,500 people have been executed by legal authority since 1608.[8] This estimate does not include the approximately 10,000 people lynched in the nineteenth century.[9] Only 1,553 of the 19,000 executions—less than one percent of the total—occurred during this country's first two centuries. Compared to more recent times, colonial Americans used the death penalty sparingly. More executions were conducted in the 1930s (1,676) than in the entire 1600s (162) and 1700s (1,391).[10]

> *M*ore than 19,000 executions, and perhaps as many as 20,000 to 22,500, have been performed in the United States under civil (as opposed to military) authority since 1608.

Nearly all of the people executed during the past four centuries in America have been adult men; only about two percent (approximately 380) have been women. Ninety percent of the women were executed under local, as opposed to state, authority, and the majority (87 percent) was executed prior to 1866.[11] About 40 percent of all women executed met their fates during the 1600s (42) and 1700s (100).[12] The first woman executed in America was Jane Champion in the Virginia colony in 1632 (offense unknown).[13]

> *N*early all of the people executed during the past four centuries in America have been adult men.

About 1.8 percent (approximately 346) of the people executed have been juveniles; that is, individuals who committed their capital crimes prior to their 18th birthdays.[14] Most of them (69 percent) were black, and nearly 90 percent of their victims were white.[15] The first juvenile executed in America was Thomas Graunger in Plymouth colony in 1642 for the crime of bestiality.[16] He was 16 at the time of his crime and execution.[17] The youngest nonslave executed in the United States was Ocuish

Hannah, who was hanged for a murder she committed when she was 12 years old. Hannah was executed in New London County, Connecticut, on December 20, 1786.[18] Juveniles in America have been executed for sodomy with animals, arson, robbery, assault, rape, and murder.

Death Penalty Abolitionists. There have probably always been people opposed to capital punishment, but even though their numbers have often been small, they have not been without influence. Quakers, for example, have always opposed capital punishment, and, because of their early presence and influence in Pennsylvania, that state, and especially the city of Philadelphia, may be considered the birthplace of the American death penalty abolitionist effort.

Among the first people in the United States to organize others against the death penalty was Dr. Benjamin Rush (1747-1813), a Philadelphia physician and signer of the Declaration of Independence.[19] Rush was among the founders (in 1787) of the Philadelphia Society for Alleviating the Miseries of Public Prisons.[20] (In 1833, the Philadelphia Society changed its name to the Pennsylvania Prison Society. That same organization exists under the changed name today.) Rush questioned the Biblical support for capital punishment and the belief that it was a general deterrent to crime. He did not believe that the example of executions dissuades people from carrying out crimes they have contemplated committing. To the contrary, he thought that capital punishment might increase crime.[21] This made Rush one of the first Americans to suggest that the death penalty might have a counterdeterrent or "brutalizing effect" (more about this in Chapter 5). Reflecting Enlightenment philosophy, Rush maintained that the social contract was violated whenever the state executed one of its citizens. He was greatly influenced by Cesare Beccaria's argument against the death penalty in *On Crimes and Punishments*, first published in 1764.[22] People had opposed the death penalty for centuries, but Beccaria gave abolitionist sentiment an authoritative voice and renewed energy.[23]

In the late eighteenth century, Dr. Rush attracted the support of such dignitaries as Benjamin Franklin and William Bradford, who was Pennsylvania and later United States Attorney General. It was at Franklin's home in Philadelphia that Rush became one of the first Americans to propose confinement in a "House of Reform" as an alternative to capital punishment.[24] According to one commentator, the paper delivered by Rush at Franklin's home was "the first reasoned argument in America favoring the abolition of capital punishment."[25] The houses of reform envisioned by Rush would be places where criminals could learn to be law–abiding citizens through moral education. At least in part because of the efforts of Rush and his colleagues, in 1790, the Walnut Street Jail in Philadelphia was converted into the world's first penitentiary— an institution devoted primarily to reform.[26]

Pennsylvania became the first state in legal proceedings to consider degrees of murder based on culpability, largely as a result of Bradford's efforts.[27] Before this change, the death penalty was mandated for anyone convicted of murder, regardless of circumstance. Like Rush, Bradford did not believe that capital punishment deterred crime, citing the example of horse stealing, which at the time was a capital offense in Virginia and the most frequently committed crime in the state. Because of the severity of the penalty, convictions for the crime were hard to obtain.[28] Pressure from abolitionists also caused Pennsylvania to repeal the death penalty for all crimes except first-degree murder.[29] Many people were drawn to Rush's ideas, and petitions to abolish the death penalty were introduced in several state legislatures, but half a century would pass before the first state abandoned capital punishment.

It is important to keep in mind that the histories of the death penalty and the death penalty abolitionist movement in the United States are the same in many places because all of the significant changes in the practice of capital punishment—culminating in its complete abolition in some jurisdictions—are the result of abolitionist efforts. Those efforts created: (1) degrees of murder, which distinguish between murders heinous enough to warrant death and those murders that do not, (2) a reduction in the number of offenses warranting the death penalty (except for the federal government, as described in Chapter 3), (3) the hiding of executions from public view, and (4) a decreased annual number of executions (but that trend may be changing). Although abolition of the death penalty has been their unremitting goal, abolitionists have been far more successful reforming its practice.

The Death Penalty in the Nineteenth Century

Between 1800 and 1865, use of the death penalty increased significantly. The number of executions rose almost 60 percent over the number from the entire seventeenth and eighteenth centuries (from 1,553 to 2,443). Although after the Civil War, and until 1880, the number of executions dropped by two-thirds (to 825), from 1880 until the turn of the century, the number of executions increased to about a thousand each decade.[30]

The period between 1825 and 1850 was a time of reform in America. The increase in the number of executions, plus general abolitionist sentiment, spurred anti-death penalty activity, resulting in the organization of several abolitionist socieities (especially along the eastern seaboard) and the founding of the American Society for the Abolition of Capital Punishment in 1845.[31] By 1850, death penalty abolitionist societies were likewise working in Tennessee, Ohio, Alabama, Louisiana, Indiana, and Iowa.[32] Two other reform movements—anti-saloon and anti-slavery—also gave a boost to the death penalty abolitionists.

Hiding Executions from the Public. Pennsylvania became the first state, in 1834, to hide executions from the public by requiring them to be conducted in jails or prisons.[33] Only a few authorized officials and the relatives of the condemned were allowed to attend. New York, New Jersey, and Massachusetts enacted similar policies the following year.[34] Apparently, legislators were willing to sacrifice any general deterrent effect of witnessing executions to escape the "public disorder, rioting,

> *P*ennsylvania became the first state, in 1834, to hide executions from the public by requiring them to be conducted in jails or prisons. The last public execution was held in Galena, Missouri, in 1937.

and even murder" that sometimes accompanied the public spectacles, especially the botched executions and last-minute reprieves.[35] The last public execution was held in Galena, Missouri, in 1937.[36]

From Mandatory to Discretionary Capital Punishment Statutes. In 1838, Tennessee became the first state to enact a discretionary death penalty statute for murder; Alabama did the same, three years later.[37] All states before then employed mandatory death penalty statutes that required anyone convicted of a designated capital crime to be sentenced to death. Between the Civil War and the end of the nineteenth century, at least 20 additional jurisdictions changed their death penalty laws from mandatory to discretionary ones. Mandatory capital punishment laws were removed from all penal codes by 1963, except for a few rarely committed crimes in a handful of jurisdictions.[38]

This change from mandatory to discretionary death penalty statutes, which introduced unfettered sentencing discretion into the capital-sentencing process, was considered, at the time, a great reform in the administration of capital punishment. Ironically, it was unfettered sentencing discretion that the Supreme Court declared unconstitutional in its *Furman* decision in 1972.[39] (The *Furman* decision is discussed in detail in Chapter 2.)

States Abolish the Death Penalty. In 1846, the state of Michigan abolished the death penalty for all crimes, except treason, and replaced the penalty with life imprisonment. The law took effect the next year, making Michigan, for all intents and purposes, the first English-speaking jurisdiction in the world to abolish capital punishment.[40] The first state to outlaw the death penalty for all crimes, including treason, was Rhode Island, in 1852; Wisconsin was the second state to do so a year later.[41] Although no other states abolished the death penalty during this period, most states outside of the South began reducing the number of death-eligible crimes, generally to murder and treason.[42]

> *In* 1846, the state of Michigan abolished the death penalty for all crimes, except treason, and replaced the penalty with life imprisonment. The law took effect the next year, making Michigan, for all intents and purposes, the first English-speaking jurisdiction in the world to abolish capital punishment.

Opponents of the death penalty, who initially benefited from general abolitionist sentiment, saw concern with capital punishment wane as the Civil War approached, and attention shifted to the growing anti-slavery movement.[43]

Not until well after the Civil War did Iowa, in 1872, and Maine, in 1876, become the next states to abolish the death penalty. Legislatures in both states reversed themselves, however, and reinstated the death penalty in 1878, in Iowa, and in 1883, in Maine. Maine reversed itself again in 1887 and abolished capital punishment and, to date, has not reinstated it.[44] Colorado abandoned capital punishment in 1897, but the move apparently was unpopular with many of its citizens. At least partially in response to three lynchings of blacks by whites within two years of abolition, the death penalty was restored in 1901.[45]

From Local to State–Authorized Executions. A major change took place in the legal jurisdiction of executions during the time of the Civil War. Before the war, all executions were conducted locally—generally in the jurisdiction in which the crime was committed—but on January 20, 1864, Sandy Kavanagh was executed at the Vermont State Prison. He was the first person executed under state, as opposed to local, authority.

This shift in jurisdiction was not immediately adopted by other states. After Kavanagh, there were only about two state- or federally-authorized executions per year well into the 1890s; the rest were locally authorized.[46] That pattern would shift dramatically during the next 30 years. In the 1890s, about 90 percent of executions were imposed under local authority, but by the 1920s, about 90 percent were imposed under state authority.[47] Today, all executions are imposed under state authority, except those conducted in Delaware, Montana, the federal government, and the military.

The Death Penalty in the First Half of the Twentieth Century

As the United States entered the twentieth century, a new age of reform began. It was called the "Progressive Period."[48] Death penalty abolitionists benefited from the critical examination of American society that characterized the era and achieved a series of successes, albeit in most cases, temporary ones.[49]

States Abolish and Reinstate the Death Penalty. Between 1907 and 1917, six states outlawed capital punishment entirely (Kansas, 1907; Minnesota, 1911; Washington, 1913; Oregon, 1914; South Dakota, 1915; Missouri, 1917), and three states (Tennessee, 1915; North Dakota, 1915; Arizona, 1916) limited the death penalty to only a few rarely committed crimes, such as treason or the first-degree murder of a law enforcement official or prison employee. Tennessee also retained capital punishment for rape. The momentum, however, failed to last. By 1920, five states had reinstated the death penalty (Arizona, 1918; Missouri, 1919; Tennessee, 1919; Washington, 1919; Oregon, 1920).[50]

It has been argued that the reinstatement of capital punishment in the five states was at least partly the result of a media–inspired panic about the threat of revolution.[51] The Russian Revolution occurred in 1917, the same year the United States entered World War I. Just before the war, the United States had experienced intense class conflict as socialists, and especially the IWW or Industrial Workers of the World ("Wobblies"), increased in number and mounted the first serious challenge to capitalist dominance.[52] Within this frenzied atmosphere, a crime in 1920 involving two foreign anarchists received unprecedented worldwide media coverage. Nicola Sacco and Bartolomeo Vanzetti maintained their innocence but nevertheless were convicted of a robbery and murder. They were electrocuted in 1927. Surrounding circumstances and the trial record suggest that Sacco and Vanzetti were indeed innocent, and that they were sentenced to death because they were anarchists and foreigners.[53]

According to at least one observer, the threat of the death penalty has been used to terrify and subdue dissidents,[54] and that may have been a motivating factor in the case against Sacco and Vanzetti.

The death penalty abolitionist movement fell on hard times during Prohibition and the Great Depression (roughly 1920 to 1940). Only the determined efforts of members of the American League to Abolish Capital Punishment, founded in 1925, and a few high–profile abolitionists, such as attorney Clarence Darrow and Lewis E. Lawes, the abolitionist warden of New York's Sing Sing State Prison, kept the movement alive.[55] Despite their efforts, more capital offenders were executed during the 1930s than in any other decade in American history; the average was 167 executions per year.[56] The most executions in any single year occurred in 1935 when 199 offenders were put to death.[57] Furthermore, of the 10 states that abolished capital punishment for all crimes after 1850, only three—Minnesota, Maine, and Wisconsin—had not restored the death penalty entering the 1950s.[58] No state abolished the death penalty between 1918 and 1957. In contrast, after World War II, most of the advanced western European countries abolished the death penalty or severely restricted its use. Great Britain did not join them until 1969.[59]

> $\mathcal{M}$ore capital offenders were executed during the 1930s than in any other decade in American history; the average was 167 executions per year. The most executions in any single year occurred in 1935 when 199 offenders were put to death.

The Death Penalty from 1950 to 1972

Beginning in the 1950s, partly as a result of the lingering horrors of World War II and the movement by many allied nations either to abolish the death penalty or to restrict its use, the number of executions in the United States began to drop precipitously—from 1,289 in the 1940s to 715 during the 1950s[60]—and there were only 191 executions from 1960 through 1976.[61] The American abolitionist movement was able to claim some modest achievements in the late 1950s. Besides resurrecting debate in some state legislatures, the (then) territories of Alaska and Hawaii abolished the death penalty in 1957.[62] Delaware did the same in 1958, only to reinstate it three years later in 1961.[63]

Also during the 1950s, because of the extraordinary media attention devoted to them, two cases in particular influenced the ways in which many Americans viewed capital punishment. What is interesting is that the two cases had very different effects. The Rosenberg case, involving alleged treason, seemed to influence the public toward favoring capital punishment. The Chessman case, on the other hand, had the opposite and, for the time, the more sustained effect.

The Case of Ethel and Julius Rosenberg. Ethel and Julius Rosenberg were prosecuted for espionage during the summer of 1950 in an atmosphere of anti–Communist hysteria,[64] allegedly having given atomic bomb secrets to Soviet agents. Their guilt, and especially the evidence against them, continues to be the subject of much debate. There was a worldwide campaign of protest following their convictions. Among the notables who championed their cause were Albert Einstein, Jean–Paul Sartre, Pablo Picasso, and the sister of Bartolomeo Vanzetti. Appeals to both President Truman, just before he left office in 1953, and President Eisenhower were turned down. At the last moment, Supreme Court Justice Douglas granted a stay of execution, and Chief Justice Vinson sent out special jets to return the vacationing justices to Washington. The full Court canceled Douglas's stay, and the Rosenbergs were executed on June 19, 1953.

The paradox of the Rosenberg executions is reflected in American death penalty opinion of 1953. Between the first and fifth of November, 1953, Gallup queried the public about the death penalty for the first time in 16 years.[65] Results of the poll indicated that 70 percent of Americans favored the death penalty, 29 percent opposed it, and 1 percent had no opinion. The 70 percent figure was the highest level of support for the death penalty in the United States to that date, and it remained the highest level until the 1980s. To what extent the Rosenberg executions influenced that opinion can only be speculated. What seems clear is that the executions did not generate immediate and overwhelming sympathy for the Rosenbergs or have a dampening effect on American death penalty opinion.

The Case of Caryl Chessman. The decade–long case of Caryl Chessman began in 1948 when, at age 26, he was convicted on 17 counts, including robbery, kidnapping, sexual abuses, and attempted rape. Under California's "Little Lindbergh" law, capital punishment was mandatory for kidnapping "with bodily harm."[66] Chessman was "self–taught in law" and defended himself. He admitted committing many crimes, but he denied guilt in the kidnappings for which he was sentenced to death.[67]

Chessman had an unusually long stay on death row, due to the death penalty post–conviction process. A relatively large segment of the public found this well–publicized experience with capital punishment objectionable and turned against the death penalty.

For purposes of this account, Chessman's story begins on May 3, 1954, a day that held both good and bad news for him. The good news was that his book, *Cell 2544, Death Row*, was published. The book was the first of four and would receive critical acclaim, become a best seller (more than 500,000 copies sold), be translated into many languages, and bring to Chessman's situation unprecedented worldwide attention. The bad news was that California Governor Goodwin J. Knight denied Chessman a reprieve from his execution, scheduled for May 14.[68] The day before he was scheduled to die in San Quentin's gas chamber, however, Chessman won a writ of habeas corpus "on grounds that a false transcript of his first trial had been presented to an appeals court."[69] A writ of habeas corpus claims that a federal constitutional right has been violated and, thus, the claimant is being held illegally.[70] The writ was subsequently denied, and Chessman was rescheduled to die on July 30. The day before this execution, to allow the U.S. Supreme Court the opportunity to act on

Chessman's petition for a writ of review, California Supreme Court Justice Jesse W. Carter granted him a stay.

On March 3, 1955, San Quentin Warden Harley O. Teets impounded the manuscript of Chessman's second prison-written book, *Trial by Ordeal*. Teets charged that Chessman violated regulations when he attempted to send the book out of the prison without official clearance.[71] The book nevertheless was published by Prentice-Hall on July 11.[72] Criminologist Robert Johnson relates that the book was a study of "the media distortion of capital offenders, particularly of the type likely to enrage decent citizens."[73] Chessman was "branded the 'Red Light Bandit' during his lengthy tenure on San Quentin's death row, [and] he summarized [in the book] the public image of the condemned fostered by sensationalist journalism."[74]

The Supreme Court granted Chessman a new hearing in San Francisco's U.S. District Court on October 17, 1955. The Court ruled five to three that "Chessman's plea that his 1948 trial records had been 'fraudulently prepared' should not have been summarily dismissed."[75] Nearly a year later, on November 22, 1956, to prevent the setting of an execution date and to allow Chessman to make another appeal to the U.S. Supreme Court, the U.S. Circuit Court of Appeals in San Francisco granted Chessman a stay of mandate.[76]

State authorities had banned Chessman's writing for publication.[77] When a manuscript of his third book, *The Face of Justice*, was found in his cell on February 14, 1957, Chessman, then 35, was placed in solitary confinement. Another copy of the manuscript, however, was smuggled out of prison to his literary agent.

On April 8, 1957, the Supreme Court granted Chessman another hearing, to be held on May 13. This hearing would decide whether Chessman had been denied due process of law, as guaranteed by the Fourteenth Amendment, on the issue of his alleged fraudulent trial transcript. Then, on June 10, the U.S. Supreme Court granted him another stay of execution so that a lower court could review Chessman's lack of representation by an attorney at a Federal District Court hearing the previous year.[78] (That was the hearing to determine whether the state court records of his first trial were fraudulent.) Superior Judge Walter R. Evans ruled in Los Angeles on February 28, 1958, that the record of Chessman's original trial was "adequate for purposes of appeal," and Chessman lost his chance for a new trial on this issue.[79]

By the time Chessman lost another appeal to the U.S. Supreme Court for release on a writ of habeas corpus on April 6, 1959, his execution had been stayed six times, and he was running out of legal maneuvers.[80] On July 7, the California Supreme Court upheld the 11-year-old death verdict by denying his latest appeal for a rehearing, and on August 10, Chessman was ordered to die on October 23.[81] California Governor Edmund G. Brown rejected Chessman's plea for clemency four days before the scheduled execution.

It looked like the end of the line for Chessman, but he had not yet run out of luck. Two days before his execution, the U.S. Supreme Court granted his seventh stay to allow him to file a petition challenging the California Supreme Court's decision on July 7 to affirm his conviction.[82] On December 14, though, the Supreme Court, by an eight to zero vote, rejected that petition. The Court also dismissed a November 30 appeal for a new trial filed by psychiatrist Karl Menninger, writer Aldous Huxley, and

21 others. In Los Angeles, on December 21, Judge Herbert V. Walker ordered Chessman to be executed on February 19, 1960. It was Chessman's eighth execution order.[83]

On February 19, just 10 hours before Chessman was to die, Governor Brown gave Chessman, then 38, a 60-day reprieve. Brown's reasons for granting an eighth stay in 12 years were twofold. First, Brown had received a telegram from Assistant Secretary of State Roy R. Rubottom, Jr., relaying a Uruguayan government warning that if Chessman were executed, President Eisenhower might encounter hostile demonstrations there during his upcoming visit. Second, as a death penalty opponent, Brown wanted the state legislature to consider abolishing capital punishment in California.[84]

Brown's action was decried. Senator Clair Engle and others protested that "justice to an individual should be based on the facts of the case and 'not rest on international reaction'." But throughout the United States, Latin America, and Western Europe, opponents of the death penalty continued to protest on Chessman's behalf, and the Vatican newspaper, *L'Osservatore Romano*, pleaded for Chessman's life—but to no avail. Appeals for a stay of execution were rejected by U.S. Supreme Court Justice Hugo L. Black on February 13, the U.S. Circuit Court of Appeals in San Francisco on February 15, and the California Supreme Court on February 17-18.[85] Chessman was finally executed in the gas chamber at San Quentin on May 2, 1960.[86]

> *In each of Gallup's death penalty polls following Caryl Chessman's execution in 1960, the percentage of Americans in favor of the death penalty declined (and the percentage opposed increased) until, in 1966, public support for capital punishment reached an all-time low of 42 percent.*

Denying his guilt to the end, Chessman won the support of death penalty opponents universally. Pleas to save his life were made not only by Menninger and Huxley, but also by Albert Schweitzer, Pablo Casals, Brigitte Bardot, and thousands of others.[87] The execution cost California around half-a-million dollars, and it prompted anti-United States demonstrations throughout the world.[88] Additionally, in each of Gallup's death penalty polls following Chessman's execution, the percentage of Americans in favor of the penalty declined (and the percentage opposed increased) until, in 1966, public support for capital punishment reached an all-time low of 42 percent.[89]

In addition to the case of Caryl Chessman, the civil rights movements of the 1960s also helped galvanize abolitionist sentiment, as protests against the misuse of government authority continued to grow. Four states abolished the death penalty (Michigan, in 1963, for treason; Oregon, 1964; Iowa, 1965; and West Virginia, 1965), and two states (New York, 1965 and Vermont, 1965) sharply reduced the number of death-eligible crimes.[90]

Challenging the Legality of Capital Punishment. Although specific methods of execution had been legally challenged as early as 1890, the fundamental legality of capital punishment itself was not subject to challenge until the 1960s.[91] It had long been argued that the Constitution or, more specifically, the Fifth Amendment, authorized capital punishment and that a majority of the framers of the Constitution did not object to it. The Fifth Amendment reads as follows:

No person shall be held to answer for a *capital*, or otherwise infamous *crime*, unless on a presentment or indictment of a grand jury, except in cases arising in the land or naval forces, or in the militia, when in actual service in time of war or public danger; nor shall any person be subject for the same offense to be twice put in *jeopardy of life* or limb; nor shall be compelled in any criminal case to be a witness against himself, nor be *deprived of life*, liberty, or property, without due process of law, nor shall private property be taken for public use without just compensation (emphasis added).

The three explicit references to capital punishment in the amendment have not only been taken as prima facie evidence that the framers of the Constitution did not object to its use, but they also show that the framers expected it to be used because of the guidelines they provided (that is, "with due process of law").

Referral to capital punishment and the aforementioned guidelines is repeated in the Fourteenth Amendment, which was ratified shortly after the Civil War. The Fourteenth Amendment states in part:

No State shall make or enforce any law which shall abridge the privileges or immunities of citizens of the United States; nor shall any State *deprive any person of life*, liberty, or property, without due process of law; nor deny to any person within its jurisdiction the equal protection of the laws (emphasis added).

Given such evidence, it made little sense to argue that capital punishment violated the Constitution. That conventional wisdom was challenged in 1961.

In an article published in the *University of Southern California Law Review*, law professor Gerald Gottlieb suggested that "the death penalty was unconstitutional under the Eighth Amendment because it violated contemporary moral standards, what the U.S. Supreme Court in *Trop v. Dulles* (356 U.S. 86, 1958) referred to as 'the evolving standards of decency that mark the progress of a maturing society.'"[92] In *Trop* and in *Weems v. United States* (217 U.S. 349), the latter decided in 1910, the Court departed from the fixed or historical meaning it had always used in deciding whether a particular punishment was cruel and

> In 1961, in an article published in the *University of Southern California Law Review*, law professor Gerald Gottlieb suggested that "the death penalty was unconstitutional under the Eighth Amendment because it violated contemporary moral standards, what the U.S. Supreme Court in *Trop v. Dulles* (356 U.S. 86, 1958) referred to as 'the evolving standards of decency that mark the progress of a maturing society.'"

unusual in violation of the Eighth Amendment. The Court opined in *Weems* that the cruel and unusual punishment provision "would only offer paper, illusory protection if it was restricted solely to the intent of the Framers."[93] The Court consequently declared that the meaning of the Eighth Amendment is not limited by the Framers' intent, but that it changes with evolving social conditions—specifically, "the evolving standards of decency that mark the progress of a maturing society."[94] Neither *Trop* nor *Weems* were death penalty cases. Professor Gottlieb applied to the practice of capital punishment the Court's logic from two cases not concerned with the death penalty. The key question raised by Gottlieb's interpretation, of course, was whether the United States, in fact, had evolved or progressed to the point where standards of decency no longer permitted capital punishment.

Professor Gottlieb took an extreme position toward the death penalty, calling for its complete abolition. Most of the other attacks on the penalty during this period were more moderate, seeking only its reform. A 1961 *University of Texas Law Review* article by Professor Walter Oberer criticized the common practice of "death qualifying," a process that eliminates death penalty opponents from capital juries.[95] Professor Oberer argued that death qualification "purged the jury of its more compassionate members and produced a homogenous jury more likely to convict."[96]

Two years earlier, in 1959, drafters of the American Law Institute's Model Penal Code suggested two legal reforms in the way capital punishment was administered.[97] The first was a bifurcated (two-part) trial consisting of a guilt phase, where guilt or innocence was the principal issue to be determined, and a penalty phase, where the imposition of either a life or death sentence was the sole issue. The second reform was the use of enumerated aggravating and mitigating circumstances to guide and restrict the sentencing authority's (judge or jury) discretion during the penalty phase of the bifurcated trial. Both of those procedural reforms would later be incorporated into the new, that is, post-*Furman*, death penalty statutes (examined in detail in Chapter 2).

Problems with the administration of capital punishment had long been a focus of attack by death penalty opponents, but they were also a source of consternation to proponents of the penalty who wanted it "done right." By the 1960s, some reform in the process of putting capital offenders to death seemed necessary, as at least three members of the Supreme Court agreed. As criminologist Raymond Paternoster relates:

> In a rare and published dissent from a denial of certiorari in an Alabama rape case, *Rudolph v. Alabama*, 375 U.S. 889 (1963), Justice Arthur Goldberg (concurred in by Justices Brennan and Douglas) suggested that the entire Court ought to determine whether or not the death penalty for a rapist who has not taken a life was unconstitutional under the Eighth Amendment.[98]

(A writ of certiorari is an order from a higher court to a lower court whose decision is being appealed to send the records of the case forward for review. It is a dominant avenue to the U.S. Supreme Court.)

Rudolph's attorneys chose not to challenge the constitutionality of capital punishment for rape, but Justice Goldberg felt compelled to comment, anyway. In his written dissent from the certiorari denial—a rare occurrence in its own right—he listed three reasons why the death penalty may be an inappropriate sentence in rape cases where the victim does not die:

1. Prevailing standards of morality both in the United States and other "peer" countries may have progressed to the point where punishing rape by death is no longer acceptable,

2. punishing by death the crime of rape where no life was taken may be constitutionally impermissible because it is excessively severe, and

3. if the legitimate purposes for punishing rape (deterrence, rehabilitation, and retribution) can be effectively secured by a punishment less than death, the infliction of the death penalty may be unconstitutional because it is unnecessarily cruel.[99]

Goldberg's ruminations had little immediate effect, but they did hearten a small group of abolitionist lawyers by suggesting that the Supreme Court might be ready to consider the constitutionality of the death penalty for rape where the victim does not die. It seemed the appropriate time for a test case on the matter.

The defendant selected for the test case was William L. Maxwell, a 22–year–old black man who in 1961 was charged in Arkansas with the rape of a white woman.[100] Maxwell was convicted of the crime and sentenced to die the following year. His initial appeal to the Arkansas Supreme Court claimed that there was a pattern of racial discrimination in the way Arkansas juries handled rape cases. The appeal was denied. Maxwell's attorney, with the help of lawyers from the NAACP Legal Defense Fund, then drafted a writ of habeas corpus for review by the federal courts. In each of the courts—first the U.S. District Court, then the Court of Appeals for the Eighth Circuit, and, finally, the U.S. Supreme Court—the writ was rejected. This all occurred during 1964 and 1965.

In 1966, a second writ of habeas corpus was presented to the U.S. District Court on Maxwell's behalf and, this time, the court agreed to a hearing. Although his lawyers were able to show, using social scientific evidence, that there was a pattern of racial discrimination in death cases for rape in some Arkansas counties, the result was the same. The court rejected all of Maxwell's claims and refused his request for a stay of execution. The court's ruling was affirmed by the Court of Appeals for the Eighth Circuit. Maxwell, however, was not finished. In 1967, he won a stay of execution from the U.S. Supreme Court, and the Court sent the case back to the Eighth Circuit appellate court for further review. In 1968, the appellate court again denied Maxwell's claim and upheld his death sentence.

One of the consequences of the *Maxwell* case, as well as two other death penalty cases decided by the Supreme Court in 1968 (*Witherspoon v. Illinois* and *United States v. Jackson*—both discussed in the next chapter), was the unofficial suspension of all executions until some of the more problematic issues with the death penalty could be resolved. The last execution in the United States was held in June of 1967, when Luis Jose Monge was executed in Colorado's gas chamber.[101] The moratorium on executions would last 10 years until 1977, when Gary Gilmore requested to be executed by the state of Utah (more about this in Chapter 4).

Conclusion

William Maxwell's fate was finally determined by the U.S. Supreme Court on June 1, 1970 (*Maxwell v. Bishop*, 398 U.S. 262). The Court, however, did not directly address Maxwell's principal claim that racial discrimination on the part of jurors, who had total discretion in the sentencing decision, infected death cases for rape in at least some Arkansas counties. Instead, the Court vacated Maxwell's death sentence on the more narrow grounds that several prospective jurors in Maxwell's case were improperly removed during voir dire because of their general opposition to the death penalty. As for the problem of juror discretion and, presumably, the racial discrimination that it sometimes allowed, the Court, in footnote four of the *Maxwell* decision, announced that it would address that issue early in the 1970 term. The Court had already granted certiorari in the two test cases: *Crampton v. Ohio* and *McGautha v. California*. What the Court could not know at this time was that it was embarking on a road that would eventually lead to the complete abolition of capital punishment in the United States.

Discussion Questions

1. What general lessons can be learned from the history of the death penalty in the United States?

2. Why do people oppose capital punishment? How could they be so wrong?

3. Why do people support capital punishment? How could they be so wrong?

4. Should the public be allowed to view executions? Why or why not?

5. Which are fairer: mandatory or discretionary death penalty laws?

6. Should executions be carried out in the local jurisdictions where capital defendants are convicted and sentenced or at some other location in the state? Defend your answer.

7. Is the threat of the death penalty in the United States used to terrify and subdue political dissidents? Explain.

8. Why is the United States the only western industrialized nation to routinely employ capital punishment?

9. What can be learned from the cases of Ethel and Julius Rosenberg and Caryl Chessman?

10. Do you agree or disagree with Professor Gottlieb's argument that the death penalty is unconstitutional under the Eighth Amendment if it violates contemporary moral standards, or "the evolving standards of decency that mark the progress of a maturing society"? Why?

11. Is the death penalty inappropriate for rape? Why or why not?

Notes

[1] Espy and Smykla, 1987.

[2] Vila and Morris, 1997:8-9; Bedau, 1982:7.

[3] Exodus 21.12; Numbers 35.13, 14, 30, 31 (cited in Vila and Morris, ibid., p. 8).

[4] Bedau, op. cit., p. 7.

[5] Ibid.

[6] Vila and Morris, op. cit., p. 8; Thompson, 1975:22-23; Bedau, op. cit., p. 6.

[7] Filler, 1967:105.

[8] Updated from personal correspondence.

[9] Bedau, op. cit., p. 3.

[10] Schneider and Smykla, 1991:6, Table 1.1.

[11] Ibid., p. 14.

[12] Ibid., Table 1.7.

[13] Ibid., p. 14.

[14] Streib, 1998:206.

[15] Streib, 1989:39.

[16] Streib, 1988:251.

[17] Streib, 1989:39.

[18] Schneider and Smykla, op. cit., p. 15.

[19] Bedau, op. cit., p. 13.

[20] Filler, op. cit.

[21] Gorecki, 1983:85; also see Filler, op. cit., p. 106.

[22] Filler, op. cit., p. 105.

[23] Ancel, 1967:5-6.

[24] Bedau, op. cit., p. 13; Ralph, 1996:413.

[25] Filler, op. cit., p. 106.

[26] See Grimes, 1996:494; Bedau, op. cit.

[27] Paternoster, 1991:6; Filler, op. cit., p. 107.

[28] Filler, op. cit., pp. 106-107.

[29] Bedau, op. cit., p. 4; Bowers, 1984:7.

[30] Schneider and Smykla, op. cit., p. 6, Table 1.1.

[31] Bedau, op. cit., p. 21.

[32] Filler, op. cit., p. 112.

[33] Bowers, 1984: 8; Filler, op. cit., p. 109.

[34] Bowers, ibid.

[35] Bowers, ibid.; Denno, 1994:564.

[36] Bedau, op. cit., p. 13.

[37] Acker and Lanier, 1998:83.

[38] Ibid.

[39] Ibid., p. 85.

[40] Bedau, op. cit., p. 21; Bowers, op. cit., p. 9; Filler, op. cit., p. 113.

[41] Bedau, ibid.; Bowers, ibid.

[42] Gorecki, op. cit., p. 86.

[43] Bowers, op. cit., p. 10.

[44] Ibid.

[45] Bedau, op. cit., p. 24.

[46] Bowers, op. cit., pp. 43 and 50.

[47] Ibid., pp. 54-5.

[48] Zinn, 1990:341.

[49] For one of the most comprehensive examinations of the history of capital punishment in a single state (Texas, 1923-1990), see Marquart et al., 1994.

[50] Bedau, op. cit., p. 23, Table 1-2; Bowers, op. cit., p. 10.

[51] See, for example, Filler, op. cit., p. 119.

[52] Zinn, op. cit., p. 350.

[53] Ibid., p. 367.

[54] Ancel, op. cit., pp. 13-14.

[55] See Filler, op. cit., pp. 119-20.

[56] Schneider and Smykla, op. cit., p. 7; Gorecki, op. cit., p. 92.

[57] Paternoster, op. cit., p. 10, Table 1-2.

[58] See Bedau, op. cit.

[59] Zimring and Hawkins, 1986:12.

[60] Schneider and Smykla, op. cit., p. 6, Table 1-1.

[61] Bedau, op. cit., p. 25, Table 1-3.

[62] Bowers, op. cit., p. 10; Bedau, op. cit., p. 23, Table 1-2.

[63] Bowers, ibid.; Bedau, ibid.

[64] See Zinn, op. cit., pp. 424-426.

[65] See Bohm, 1991:116, Table 8.1.

[66] Facts on File, hereafter abbreviated FOF, 1961:156.

[67] FOF, ibid.; 1955:152.

[68] Ibid.

[69] FOF, 1955: 168.

[70] Bohm and Haley, 1997:234.

[71] FOF, 1956: 80.

[72] FOF, op, cit., p. 243.

[73] Johnson, 1989: 23. Chessman was arrested on suspicion of being Los Angeles's "Red Light Bandit"—a man who impersonated a police officer and used a red spotlight as he robbed couples parked at a "lovers' lane."

[74] Ibid.

[75] FOF, 1956: 345.

[76] FOF, 1957: 400.

[77] FOF, 1958: 60.

[78] Ibid., p. 192.

[79] FOF, 1959: 76.

[80] FOF, 1960: 123.

[81] Ibid., p. 308.

[82] Ibid., p. 348.

[83] Ibid., p. 439.

[84] Ibid., p. 68.

[85] Ibid.

[86] FOF, 1961: 156.

[87] Ibid.

[88] On the cost of the execution, see Bedau, 1982: 193 fn. 21; on the demonstrations, see FOF, ibid.

[89] See Bohm, op, cit.

[90] Bedau, op. cit., p. 23, Table 1-2.

[91] The challenges to specific methods of execution addressed whether such methods as electrocution violated the "cruel and unusual punishment" standard of the Eighth Amendment. See Chapter 2.

[92] Gottlieb, 1961:101; Paternoster, 1991:41.
[93] Paternoster, ibid., p. 51.
[94] Ibid., p. 52.
[95] Ibid., p. 41.
[96] Ibid.
[97] Ibid.
[98] Ibid., p. 42.
[99] Ibid.
[100] See ibid., pp. 42-5.
[101] Coyne and Entzeroth, 1994:95.

CHAPTER 2

Capital Punishment
and the Supreme Court

Before 1968, the only issue relating to capital punishment considered by the
Supreme Court concerned the methods used in administering the death penalty after a
valid death sentence had been imposed. The one exception was the case of *Powell v.
Alabama* (287 U.S. 45, 1932), in which the Court held that failure to provide counsel
in a capital case violates "due process" as required under the Fourteenth Amendment.

Pre–1968 Death Penalty Cases

Powell v. Alabama. The *Powell* case involved the so-called "Scottsboro Boys"—
nine young black men, ranging in age from 13 to 21, arrested for the alleged rapes of
two white women.[1] One remarkable aspect of the case was that it took only one
week to arrest, indict, arraign, try, convict, and sentence the defendants to death.[2]
Another conspicuous aspect was that none of the defendants was represented by
counsel until the day of the trial. Even then, it was not until the morning of the trial
that a reluctant Scottsboro attorney offered to represent the young men.

On appeal, the Alabama Supreme Court reversed the conviction of one of the
defendants but affirmed the convictions of the other seven (see Note 2). Those defendants appealed their convictions to the U.S. Supreme Court, which reversed all seven
convictions, holding that because of the special circumstances involved ("the ignorance and illiteracy of the defendants, their youth, the circumstances of public hostility, the imprisonment and the close surveillance of the defendants by the military
forces, the fact that their friends and families were all in other states and communication with them necessarily difficult, and above all they stood in deadly peril of their
lives"), the defendants were denied their right to the effective assistance of counsel
required by the due process clause of the Fourteenth Amendment.

The *Powell* decision was narrowly drawn—it applied only to cases in which defendants were indigent, incapable of defending themselves because of their ignorance, illiteracy, or other similar handicap, and the death penalty was a possible sentence—but it
was still important for two reasons. First, it was the first case in which the U.S. Supreme
Court applied the Fourteenth Amendment's due process clause to capital cases adjudicated in state courts. Second, it was the first in a series of cases that would extend the
Sixth Amendment right to the effective assistance of counsel.

Permissible Methods of Execution. As noted earlier, except for *Powell v. Alabama* (1932), all other capital punishment cases considered by the Supreme Court prior to 1968 concerned the methods of actually carrying out the death sentence. Following is a brief description of those other pre-1968 cases. It must be noted that the Eighth Amendment, which prohibits "cruel and unusual punishment," was not incorporated and made applicable to the states until 1962 (*Robinson v. California* [370 U.S. 660]). For that reason, in none of the pre-1968 cases (nor in any case since) was a particular execution method declared cruel and unusual.[3] Neither, as law professor Deborah Denno observes, did the Court *review any evidence* regarding whether a particular punishment was cruel and unusual.[4]

The first case involving the constitutionality of execution methods was *Wilkerson v. Utah* (99 U.S. 130, 1878), wherein the Court declared that shooting is not a cruel and unusual punishment. However, as Denno points out, the Court did not examine any evidence as to whether or not shooting was cruel because the plaintiff did not raise the issue. Wilkerson instead challenged the application of Utah's death penalty statute on the grounds that the statute did not specify the method of execution. The Court emphasized that for a punishment to be considered cruel and unusual in violation of the Eighth Amendment it had to involve torture or unnecessary cruelty, something that the Court apparently opined shooting did not.

> *In Wilkerson v. Utah* (99 U.S. 130, 1878), the Supreme Court emphasized that for a punishment to be considered cruel and unusual in violation of the Eighth Amendment it had to involve torture or unnecessary cruelty.

Electrocution as a permissible form of execution was the subject of *In re Kemmler* (136 U.S. 436, 1890)—the next method-of-execution case considered. Although admitting that electrocution was unusual, since it had never been used before, a unanimous Court decided that: "The punishment of death is not cruel, within the meaning of that word as used in the Constitution."[5] The Court's decision specified what constitutes "cruelty" in connection with legal punishments. According to the Court, "punishments are cruel when they involve torture or lingering death. . . . [i]t implies there [is] something inhuman and barbarous, something more than the mere extinguishment of life."[6] The Court also provided examples of punishments it would consider as manifestly cruel and unusual: "burning at the stake, crucifixion, breaking on the wheel, or the like."[7]

> *In In re Kemmler* (136 U.S. 436, 1890), a unanimous Supreme Court opined that "punishments are cruel when they involve torture or lingering death . . . something inhuman and barbarous, something more than the mere extinguishment of life."

In a related case, *Louisiana ex rel. Francis v. Resweber* (329 U.S. 459, 1947), the Court held that a second electrocution, conducted after the first one had failed to kill the defendant, is not in violation of the Eighth Amendment's prohibition. The case involved the botched execution of Willie Francis, a 16–year–old black youth sentenced to die in Louisiana's electric chair for the murder of a popular white druggist.[8] Francis was strapped into the state's portable electric chair, but when the switch was thrown, the device malfunctioned (it did not produce enough current) and death did not result. Francis was removed from the chair and returned to his prison cell. The chair was fixed and his execution rescheduled. Francis stated:

> [T]he experience was in all "plumb miserable." His mouth tasted "like cold peanut butter," and he saw "little blue and pink and green speckles." Added Francis: "I felt a burning in my head and my left leg, and I jumped against the straps."[9]

Francis challenged Louisiana's plan for a second attempt, arguing that it would constitute both torture and the degradation of a human being. The Court denied Francis's claim and maintained that the botched execution was "an unforeseeable accident," "an innocent misadventure," and unintentional on the part of the state—and therefore not a form of torture prohibited by the Eighth Amendment. Justice Burton dissented, seeming to agree with Francis that executing a person after a first attempt had failed was nothing less than imposing "death by installments."[10]

The last of the pre–1968 cases was *Andres v. U.S.* (333 U.S. 740, 1948). In this case, the Court upheld hanging, the traditional and, until the last decade of the nineteenth century, the primary method of execution in the United States.

1968 Cases: *U.S. v. Jackson* and *Witherspoon v. Illinois*

The Supreme Court decided two cases in 1968 that dealt with the discretionary roles of the prosecutor and the jury in the processing of a capital case. By agreeing to hear the cases, the Court embarked on a mission, perhaps unknowingly, to "fine tune" the way the death penalty was administered. The Court's effort in this regard continues to this day and occupies a considerable amount of its time.

The problem addressed in the first case, *U.S. v. Jackson* (390 U.S. 570, 1968), was the provision in the federal kidnapping statute that required a jury recommendation to impose the death penalty.[11] Under the statute, a defendant could escape a death sentence by waiving the right to a jury trial or by entering a guilty plea. By being able to dangle the prospect of a death sentence before a defendant, prosecutors gained considerable leverage in the plea bargaining process. The Court opined that the provision impermissibly encouraged defendants, particularly innocent defendants, to waive their right to a jury trial to escape the chance of a death sentence. The Court ruled the provision unconstitutional.

In *Witherspoon v. Illinois* (391 U.S. 510, 1968), the Court rejected the common practice of excusing prospective jurors simply because they were opposed to capital punishment.[12] Witherspoon argued that such a practice—referred to as "death qualification"—deprived him of his right to a jury that was representative of the community. Research shows that death-qualified juries are more conviction-prone.[13] The Court agreed with Witherspoon's argument and held that prospective jurors could be excused only for cause. That is, jurors could be excused only if they would automatically vote against imposition of the death penalty, regardless of the evidence presented at trial, or if their attitudes toward capital punishment prevented them from making an impartial decision on the defendant's guilt. The *Witherspoon* decision was especially important because it drew attention to the composition of capital juries. The discretion exercised by such juries was frequently identified as a principal source of the arbitrariness and discrimination that occurred in the imposition of the death penalty.[14] During the 1980s, the Supreme Court would reconsider its *Witherspoon* decision three different times.

Death Penalty Cases: 1969–1977

By 1969, opponents of capital punishment, and especially the NAACP Legal Defense Fund lawyers, believed that the time was right for an assault on the death penalty's constitutionality. The Supreme Court had announced, in footnote four of *Maxwell v. Bishop* (1970), that it would address early in the 1970 term the issue of juror discretion in capital cases and the problems it created. The Court had already granted certiorari in the two test cases: *Crampton v. Ohio* and *McGautha v. California* (both cases were consolidated under 402 U.S. 183).

McGautha v. California **and** *Crampton v. Ohio.* Dennis McGautha was sentenced to death for killing a store owner's husband during an armed robbery; James Crampton, for the first-degree murder of his wife.[15] Oral arguments in the cases were heard before the full Supreme Court in November of 1970. A final decision was rendered on May 3, 1971.

The defendants' lawyers argued that unfettered jury discretion in imposing death for murder resulted in arbitrary or capricious sentencing (that is, sentences not governed by principle; fickle or fanciful sentencing) and, hence, violated the Fourteenth Amendment right to due process of law. McGautha's trial–court judge, following the procedure used in California at the time, instructed the jury as follows: "Now, beyond prescribing the two alternative penalties [death or life imprisonment], the law itself provides no standard for the guidance of the jury in the selection of the penalty, but, rather, commits the whole matter of determining which of the two penalties shall be fixed to the judgment, conscience, and absolute discretion of the jury."[16]

Jurors in Crampton's case were instructed to "consider all the evidence and make your finding with intelligence and impartiality, and without bias, sympathy, or prejudice, so that the State of Ohio and the defendant will feel that their case was fairly and impartially tried."[17] They were also instructed that, unless they recommended mercy, a conviction for first–degree murder would result in a death sentence. The importance of Crampton's case to the issue at hand was not so much the jury instructions, though they provided little guidance on how to arrive at a decision, but, rather, whether bifurcated trials were required in capital cases. McGautha's trial was bifurcated; Crampton's was not.[18]

McGautha's claim, which was joined for decision with *Crampton*, was rejected by a vote of six to three. In rejecting the claim, the Court tacitly approved (1) unfettered jury discretion in death sentencing, and (2) capital trials in which guilt and sentence were determined in one set of deliberations. Regarding unfettered jury discretion, Justice Harlan, for himself, Chief Justice Burger, and Justices Stewart, White, Black, and Blackmun, reasoned that: "In light of history, experience, and the present limitations of human knowledge, we find it quite impossible to say that committing to the untrammeled discretion of the jury the power to pronounce life or death in capital cases is offensive to anything in the Constitution."[19] That conclusion was based on the underlying belief that it was impossible to adequately guide capital sentencing discretion:

> Those who have come to grips with the hard task of actually attempting to draft means of channeling capital sentencing discretion have confirmed the lesson taught by . . . history. . . . To identify before the fact those characteristics of criminal homicides and their perpetrators which call for the death penalty, and to express these characteristics in language which can be fairly understood and applied by the sentencing authority, appear to be tasks which are beyond present human ability.[20]

Furman v. Georgia. In 1972, about a year after the *McGautha* decision, William Henry Furman's lawyers also argued to the Supreme Court that unfettered jury discretion in imposing death for murder resulted in arbitrary or capricious sentencing. Furman was sentenced to die on September 20, 1968, in Savannah, Georgia, for the murder of William J. Micke, Jr. Micke was a 30-year-old white male Coast Guard petty officer, and the father of four children and the stepfather of six others. Furman, a 25-year-old black man with an IQ of 65, shot Micke during a burglary attempt at Micke's home.[21] However, Furman's lawyers, unlike McGautha's, claimed that unbridled jury discretion violated both their client's Fourteenth Amendment right to due process and his Eighth Amendment right not to be subjected to cruel and unusual punishment. Furman's challenge proved successful and, on June 29, 1972, the U.S. Supreme Court set aside death sentences for the first time in its history. Furman's sentence was commuted to life imprisonment. He was paroled in 1984 and was a construction worker in Macon, Georgia, as of 1997.

In its decision in *Furman v. Georgia*, *Jackson v. Georgia*, and *Branch v. Texas* (all three cases were consolidated under 408 U.S. 238, 1972, and are referred to here as the *Furman* decision)—the longest decision in Supreme Court history—the Court held that the capital punishment statutes in the three cases were unconstitutional because they gave the jury complete discretion to decide whether to impose the death penalty or a lesser punishment in capital cases.[22] Although nine separate opinions were written (a very rare occurrence), the majority of five justices (Douglas, Brennan, Stewart, White, and Marshall) pointed out that the death penalty had been imposed arbitrarily, infrequently, and often selectively against minorities. The majority agreed that the statutes provided for a cruel and unusual punishment in violation of the Eighth and Fourteenth Amendments. (The four dissenters were Chief Justice Burger and Justices Blackmun, Powell, and Rehnquist).

An interesting question is why the Supreme Court entertained the *Furman* challenge to unbridled jury discretion in capital cases in the first place, having just the year before rejected the same claim made in *McGautha*. The answer lies in the constitutional right that was challenged. As Professor Raymond Paternoster relates:

> The position that the plurality in *Furman* appeared to be taking . . . was that while *the process* of having defendants sentenced to death by juries lacking formal guidance is consistent with the Fourteenth Amendment's requirement of due process, *the product*, an arbitrary and freakish pattern of death sentencing, is condemned by the Eighth Amendment (emphasis in original).[23]

A practical effect of *Furman* was the Supreme Court's voiding of 40 death penalty statutes and the sentences of 629 death row inmates.[24] It is important to note that the Court did not declare the death penalty itself unconstitutional. It held as unconstitutional only the statutes under which the death penalty was then being administered. (Actually, the five justices in the majority split on this issue. Justices Brennan and Marshall maintained that capital punishment itself violated the Eighth and Fourteenth Amendments. Justices Douglas, Stewart, and White, on the other hand, rejected the position that capital punishment was inherently unconstitutional and argued that only the way it was being applied under current statutes made it unconstitutional.) The Court seemed to be implying that if the process of applying the death penalty could be changed to eliminate the problems cited in *Furman*, then it would pass constitutional muster. Taking the hint, 36 states proceeded to adopt new death penalty statutes designed to meet the Court's objections. Florida was the first jurisdiction to reinstate the death penalty after *Furman*. The Florida legislature met in special session to approve the new law in December of 1972, only five months after the *Furman* decision.[25] (Currently, 40 jurisdictions, which includes 38 states, the federal government, and the military, have death penalty statutes; 13 jurisdictions, including 12 states and the District of Columbia, do not.)

On June 29, 1972, in Furman v. Georgia, Jackson v. Georgia, *and* Branch v. Texas (all three cases were consolidated under 408 U.S. 238, 1972), the Supreme Court set aside death sentences for the first time in its history. The Court held that the capital punishment statutes in the three cases were unconstitutional because they gave the jury complete discretion to decide whether to impose the death penalty or a lesser punishment in capital cases. The majority of five justices pointed out that the death penalty had been imposed arbitrarily, infrequently, and often selectively against minorities.

The new death penalty laws took two forms. Some states removed all discretion from the process by mandating capital punishment upon conviction for certain crimes ("mandatory" death penalty statutes).[26] Other states provided specific guidelines that judges and juries were to use in deciding if death were the appropriate sentence in a particular case ("guided discretion" death penalty statutes).

> *C*urrently, 40 jurisdictions, which includes 38 states, the federal government, and the military, have death penalty statutes; 13 jurisdictions, including 12 states and the District of Columbia, do not.

Woodson v. North Carolina and Gregg v. Georgia. The constitutionality of the new death penalty statutes was quickly challenged, and on July 2, 1976, the Supreme Court announced its rulings in five test cases. In *Woodson v. North Carolina* (428 U.S. 280) and *Roberts v. Louisiana* (428 U.S. 325), the Court rejected, by a vote of five to four, mandatory statutes that automatically imposed death sentences for defined capital crimes. However, in *Gregg v. Georgia* (428 U.S. 153), *Jurek v. Texas* (428 U.S. 262), and *Proffitt v. Florida* (428 U.S. 242) (hereafter referred to as the *Gregg* decision), the

> *I*n 1976, in *Gregg v. Georgia* (428 U.S. 153), *Jurek v. Texas* (428 U.S. 262), and *Proffitt v. Florida* (428 U.S. 242), the Court, by a vote of seven to two, approved guided discretion statutes that set standards for juries and judges to use when deciding whether to impose the death penalty.

Court, by a vote of seven to two (Justices Marshall and Brennan dissented), approved guided discretion statutes that set standards for juries and judges to use when deciding whether to impose the death penalty. The guided discretion statutes struck a reasonable balance between giving the jury some direction and allowing it to consider the defendant's background and character and the circumstances of the crime. In doing so, they would respect the defendant's basic human dignity, as required by the Eighth Amendment, and prevent jury nullification—the practice of a jury's refusal to convict guilty defendants to avoid imposing unjust death sentences.[27]

The Court also approved three other major procedural reforms in *Gregg*: bifurcated trials, automatic appellate review of convictions and sentences, and proportionality review. Proportionality review is a process whereby state appellate courts compare the sentence in the case before it with sentences imposed in similar cases in the state. Its purpose is to identify sentencing disparities and aid in their elimination.[28]

The primary justification for the unique procedural safeguards approved in *Gregg* was the "death is different" principle created by Supreme Court Justice William Brennan and first articulated in *Furman v. Georgia*.[29] In *Furman*, the Court observed that death is "an unusually severe punishment, unusual in its pain, in its finality, and in its enormity."[30] Later, in *Gardner v. Florida* (420 U.S. 349, 1977), the Court elaborated:

> [F]ive Members of the Court have now expressly recognized that death is a different kind of punishment from any other which may be imposed in this country. From the point of view of the defendant, it is different both in its severity and its finality. From the point of view of society, the action of the sovereign in taking the life of one of its citizens also differs dramatically from any other legitimate state action. It is of vital importance to the defendant and to the community that any decision to impose the death sentence be, and appear to be, based on reason rather than caprice or emotion.[31]

As a result of those decisions, the death penalty, unlike any other punishment prescribed by law, requires special procedures that ensure its lawful application. Law professor Margaret Jane Radin refers to those special procedures as "super due process."[32]

Professor Paternoster has noted that the Court in *Gregg* and *Woodson* attempted to cleverly reconcile two seemingly irreconcilable goals: consistency in application and consideration of individual circumstances.[33] Whereas in *Woodson*, mandatory statutes would guarantee consistency in application; they would preclude "individualized" sentencing decisions. In *Gregg*, guided discretion statutes would allow for the consideration of factors peculiar to the case but would necessarily produce disparities in sentencing. If one of the two goals had to be sacrificed for the other, the Court apparently opted (if it ever considered the dilemma) for the consideration of individual circumstances over consistency in application. Inconsistency in application, however, was one of the problems cited by the Court in *Furman*.

It is also noteworthy that the Court approved the guided discretion statutes on faith, assuming that the new statutes and their procedural reforms would rid the death penalty's administration of the problems cited in *Furman*. Because guided discretion statutes, automatic appellate review, and proportionality review had never been required or employed before in death penalty cases, the Court could not have known whether they would make a difference. Now, more than 20 years later, it is possible to evaluate the results. Law professors Steiker and Steiker claim the statutes have not made much (positive) difference:[34]

> The Supreme Court's death penalty law, by creating an impression of enormous regulatory effort, while achieving negligible effects, effectively obscures the true nature of our capital sentencing system. The pre-*Furman* world of unreviewable sentencer discretion lives on, with much the same consequences in terms of arbitrary and discriminatory sentencing patterns.[35]

(Much of the death penalty research that has been conducted over the past 20–plus years on this matter is presented in subsequent chapters of this book.)

In any event, the Court actually accepted several different types of guided discretion statutes that varied in the restrictions placed on judges and juries. Some of those statutes were modeled after ones proposed in the American Law Institute's Model Penal Code of 1959.[36] The three most common types of guided discretion statutes are: (1) aggravating versus mitigating, (2) aggravating only, and (3) structured discretion.[37] Aggravating circumstances (or factors) refer "to the particularly serious features of a case, for example, evidence of extensive premeditation and planning by the defendant, or torture of the victim by the defendant."[38] Mitigating circumstances (or factors) refer "to features of a case that explain or particularly justify the defendant's behavior, even though they do not provide a defense to the crime of murder" (e.g., "youth, immaturity, or mental retardation of the defendant").[39] An example of each type of statute is presented next.

Aggravating versus Mitigating Death Penalty Statutes. Florida's current death penalty statute is an example of the "aggravating versus mitigating" type. It is the most widely used type of death penalty statute.[40] Under it, at least one aggravating factor must be found before death may be considered as a penalty. If one or more aggravating factors are found, they are weighed against any mitigating factors. If the aggravating factors outweigh the mitigating factors, then the sentence is death. If the mitigating factors outweigh the aggravating factors, the sentence is life imprisonment without possibility of parole.

> *The* most widely used type of death penalty statute is the aggravating versus mitigating type.

Following are the aggravating and mitigating circumstances listed in Florida's death penalty statute:

Aggravating Circumstances

1. The capital felony was committed by a person under sentence of imprisonment or placed on community control.

2. The defendant was previously convicted of another capital felony or of a felony involving the use or threat of violence to the person.

3. The defendant knowingly created a great risk of death to many persons.

4. The capital felony was committed while the defendant was engaged, or was an accomplice, in the commission of, or an attempt to commit, or flight after committing or attempting to commit, any robbery, sexual battery, arson, burglary, kidnapping, or aircraft piracy or the unlawful throwing, placing, or discharging of a destructive device or bomb.

5. The capital felony was committed for the purpose of avoiding or preventing a lawful arrest or effecting an escape from custody.

6. The capital felony was committed for pecuniary gain.

7. The capital felony was committed to disrupt or hinder the lawful exercise of any governmental function or the enforcement of laws.

8. The capital felony was especially heinous, atrocious, or cruel.

9. The capital felony was a homicide and was committed in a cold, calculated, and premeditated manner without any pretense of moral or legal justification.

10. The victim of the capital felony was a law enforcement officer engaged in the performance of his official duties.

11. The victim of the capital felony was an elected or appointed public official engaged in the performance of his official duties if the motive for the capital felony was related, in whole or in part, to the victim's official capacity.

Mitigating Circumstances

1. The defendant has no significant history of prior criminal activity.

2. The capital felony was committed while the defendant was under the influence of extreme mental or emotional disturbance.

3. The victim was a participant in the defendant's conduct or consented to the act.

4. The defendant was an accomplice in the capital felony committed by another person and his participation was relatively minor.

5. The defendant acted under extreme duress or under the substantial domination of another person.

6. The capacity of the defendant to appreciate the criminality of his conduct or to conform his conduct to the requirements of law was substantially impaired.

7. The age of the defendant at the time of the crime.[41]

Two issues about Florida's death penalty statute in particular, and aggravating versus mitigating death penalty statutes in general, are worthy of note. First, Florida is one of only four death penalty states (the others are Alabama, Delaware, and Indiana) where a jury's sentencing recommendation is only advisory.[42] In other words, a judge is legally entitled to ignore the jury's recommendation and impose the sentence (either life or death) that he or she believes is most appropriate.[43]

> *In* Alabama, Delaware, Florida, and Indiana, a jury's sentencing recommendation in capital cases is only advisory.

Second, the weighing of aggravating versus mitigating factors was not intended as a simple exercise in adding and subtracting. Jurors are not supposed to count the number of aggravating factors and then subtract them from the number of mitigating factors, or vice versa. Not all factors necesssarily count equally. It is conceivable that a single aggravating factor could outweigh several mitigating factors, or, again, vice versa.

Aggravating Only Death Penalty Statutes. Georgia's post–*Furman* capital statute is an example of the "aggravating only" type. In Georgia, if a jury finds at least one statutory aggravating factor, then it may, but need not, recommend death. Two exceptions are the offenses of aircraft hijacking or treason, for which the death penalty may be imposed without finding at least one of the statutory aggravating factors. In all capital cases, the jury may also consider any mitigating factor, although mitigating factors are not listed in the statute as they are in some states. The judge must follow the jury's recommendation.[44] The aggravating factors listed in Georgia's death penalty statute are similar to those in Florida's death penalty statute.

Structured Discretion Statutes. Texas's current death penalty statute is an example of the "structured discretion" type. It is the most unusual type of guided discretion statute, employed only in Texas, Oregon, and Virginia.[45] In Texas, aggravating or mitigating factors are not listed in the statute. Instead, during the sentencing phase of the trial, the state and the defendant or the defendant's counsel may present evidence as to any matter that the court deems relevant to sentence, that is, any aggravating or mitigating factors. The court then submits the following issues to the jury:

1. whether there is a probability that the defendant would commit criminal acts of violence that would constitute a continuing threat to society; and

2. (if raised by the evidence) whether the defendant actually caused the death of the deceased or did not actually cause the death of the deceased but intended to kill the deceased or another or anticipated that a human life would be taken.

During penalty deliberations, juries in Texas must consider all evidence admitted at the guilt and penalty phases. Then, they must consider the two aforementioned issues. To answer "yes" to the issues, all jurors must answer "yes"; to answer "no" to the issues, 10 or more jurors must answer "no". If the two issues are answered in the affirmative, jurors are then asked if there is a sufficient mitigating factor (or factors) to warrant that a sentence of life imprisonment rather than a death sentence be imposed. To answer "no" to this issue, all jurors must answer "no"; to answer "yes", 10 or more jurors must agree. If the jury returns an affirmative finding on the first two issues and a negative finding on the third issue, then the court must sentence the defendant to death. If the jury returns a negative finding on either of the first two issues or an affirmative finding on the third issue, then the court must sentence the defendant to life imprisonment.[46]

Answering the first issue in the affirmative might prove difficult for many people. Despite decades of trying, social scientists remain incapable of predicting, with a reasonable degree of accuracy (a debatable standard), future human behavior, criminal or otherwise. Given what might seem the difficulty in getting all 12 jurors to answer "yes" to the two issues of aggravation and "no" to the issue of mitigation, one might surmise that states with structured discretion statutes would have a hard time sentencing offenders to death. That conclusion, however, would be wrong: Texas has executed more people than any other state under its structured discretion statute, executing three times more people than any other state.[47] Apparently, getting all members of a jury to answer in the ways necessary to return a death sentence can be relatively easy.

Automatic Appellate Review. Each of the guided discretion statutes approved in *Gregg* also provided for automatic appellate review of all convictions and death sentences. This reform was added to ensure that death sentences were applied in a constitutionally acceptable manner. Prior to *Furman*, many death row inmates did not take advantage of the appellate process. During the 1960s, for example, one-quarter of the prisoners executed had no appeals at all, and two-thirds of their cases were never reviewed by a federal court.[48]

> *During the 1960s, one-quarter of the prisoners executed had no appeals at all, and two-thirds of their cases were never reviewed by a federal court.*

The review is typically conducted by the state's highest appellate court. In some states, the duties of the reviewing court are specified by statute, while in other states they are not. Georgia is an example of a state whose death penalty statute explicitly outlines the obligations of the Georgia Supreme Court in reviewing death sentences. The statute specifies that the reviewing court must determine:

1.   Whether the sentence of death was imposed under the influence of passion, prejudice, or any other arbitrary factor; and

2.   Whether, in cases other than treason or aircraft hijacking, the evidence supports the jury's or judge's finding of a statutory aggravating circumstance . . . ; and

3.   Whether the sentence of death is excessive or disproportionate to the penalty imposed in similar cases, considering both the crime and the defendant.[49]

At year-end 1996, 36 of the 38 states with capital punishment statutes provided for an automatic review of all death sentences, regardless of the defendant's wishes.[50] Arkansas has no specific provisions for automatic review, and South Carolina allows the defendant to waive sentence review if the court deems the defendant competent; also, the federal jurisdiction does not provide for automatic appellate review. Most of the 36 states automatically review both the conviction and the sentence. Idaho, Indiana, Oklahoma, and Tennessee review only the death sentence. The rationale for not allowing defendants to waive the automatic review is that the state has an independent interest in making sure that the death penalty is administered lawfully. On the other hand, the rationale for waivers is that the defendant's autonomy and freedom of choice ought to prevail. In either case, the automatic review is generally conducted by the state's highest appellate court. If either the conviction or the sentence is overturned, then the case is sent back to the trial court for additional proceedings or for retrial. It is possible that the death sentence may be reimposed as a result of this process. Although the Supreme Court does not require it (*Pulley v. Harris*, 1984), some states, as noted previously, provide for proportionality review during the review process.

Post–1976 Death Penalty Cases

This section of the chapter is devoted to many (but not all) of the Supreme Court cases decided after capital punishment was reinstated in 1976. Since that time, the Court has been engaging in a time-consuming effort to fine tune the way capital punishment is applied. Some of the issues have been so controversial that the Court has changed positions on them several times. The cases address eight basic and, frequently, interrelated issues: (1) the constitutionality of death penalty statutes, (2) what crimes are capital, (3) mitigating circumstances, (4) aggravating circumstances, (5) the appellate process, (6) capital juries, (7) who may or may not be executed, and (8) other procedural issues. Note that some of the cases address more than one issue. For the most part, cases in each subsection are presented in chronological order, only brief descriptions of the Court's holdings are provided, and case citations are omitted.

The Constitutionality of Death Penalty Statutes. Not long after the Supreme Court rendered its decisions in *Woodson* and *Gregg*, the constitutionality of the new death penalty statutes was challenged in *Harry Roberts v. Louisiana* (1977). The Supreme Court had rejected mandatory death penalty statutes as unconstitutional in *Woodson v. North Carolina* (1976) and *Roberts v. Louisiana* (1976), but the new rewritten Louisiana statute still mandated the death penalty for the killing of a special category of victim: a police officer. Consistent with its earlier ruling, the Court held that even mandatory death penalty statutes that are confined to a special category of victim are unconstitutional.

Ten years later, in *Sumner v. Shuman* (1987), the Court considered the death penalty mandated for a special category of offender. The Nevada legislature had (1) established the punishment of life imprisonment without possibility of parole, and (2) amended its death penalty statute to require the penalty for a murder committed by an inmate serving a life sentence without possibility of parole. In *Sumner v. Shuman*, the Court declared the provision unconstitutional. The Court's decisions in *Harry Roberts v. Louisiana* and *Sumner v. Shuman* seem to confirm the Court's opposition to mandatory death penalty statutes, even if they are confined to a special category of victim or offender.

Still, the Court is not necessarily opposed to mandatory provisions in otherwise nonmandatory statutes. In *Blystone v. Pennsylvania* (1990), for example, the Court upheld Pennsylvania's statute that mandates a death sentence if the jury finds at least one aggravating circumstance and no mitigating circumstance.

The most sweeping challenge to the constitutionality of the new death penalty statutes was *McCleskey v. Kemp* (1987) wherein the Court considered evidence of racial discrimination in the application of Georgia's death penalty statute. Recall that in the *Furman* decision, racial discrimination was cited as one of the problems with the pre-*Furman* statutes. The most compelling evidence was the results of an elaborate statistical analysis of post-*Furman* death penalty cases in Georgia. That analysis showed that Georgia's new statute produced a pattern of racial discrimination based on both the race of the offender and the race of the victim. In *McCleskey*, the Court opined that evidence such as the statistical analysis—which showed a pattern of racial discrimination—is not enough to render the death penalty unconstitutional. By a vote of five to four, it held that state death penalty statutes are constitutional even when statistics indicate they have been applied in racially biased ways.[51] The Court ruled that racial discrimination must be shown in individual cases—something McCleskey did not show in his case. For death penalty opponents, the *McCleskey* case represented the best, and perhaps last, chance of having the Supreme Court again declare the death penalty unconstitutional.

What Crimes are Capital. The Supreme Court has repeatedly emphasized that the death penalty should be reserved for the most heinous crimes. In two cases decided in 1977, the Court, for all intents and purposes, limited the death penalty to only "aggravated" or capital murders. (To date, all post-*Furman* executions have been for that type of murder.) The Court ruled in *Coker v. Georgia* that the death penalty is not warranted for the crime of rape of an adult woman in cases in which the victim is not killed. Likewise, in *Eberheart v. Georgia*, the Court held that the death penalty is not warranted for the crime of kidnapping in cases in which the victim is not killed. Traditionally, both rape and kidnapping have been capital crimes, regardless of whether the victim died.

The federal 1994 Violent Crime Control and Law Enforcement Act expanded the death penalty to about 50 crimes—46 of which involve murder. The four exceptions are treason; espionage; drug trafficking in very large amounts; and attempting, authorizing or advising the killing of any public officer, juror, or witness in a case involving a continuing criminal enterprise—regardless of whether such a killing actually occurs.

As of 1996, seven states had death penalty statutes that listed capital crimes which do not necessarily involve murder. They were:

- California: train-wrecking, treason, and perjury causing an execution

- Florida: capital drug-trafficking

- Kentucky: kidnapping with aggravating factors

- Louisiana: aggravated rape of victim under age 12 and treason

- Mississippi: aircraft piracy

- New Jersey: solicitation by command or threat in furtherance of a narcotics conspiracy

- Utah: aggravated assault by a prisoner serving a life sentence if serious bodily injury is intentionally caused.[52]

So far, no one has been sentenced to death for any of those crimes. If and when the statutory provisions are challenged, though, it seems unlikely that the Supreme Court would allow the execution of offenders convicted of any of the crimes.

> $\mathcal{T}$he federal 1994 Violent Crime Control and Law Enforcement Act expanded the death penalty to about 50 crimes.

Mitigating Circumstances. One of the changes to death penalty statutes approved by the Court in *Gregg* was the requirement that sentencing authorities (either juries or judges) consider mitigating circumstances before determining the sentence. That requirement has been the subject of several challenges. The first test was in 1978 in the cases of *Lockett v. Ohio* and *Bell v. Ohio*. In those cases, the issue was whether defense attorneys could present only mitigating circumstances that were listed in the death penalty statute. The Court held that trial courts must consider any mitigating circumstances that a defense attorney presents, and not just those listed in the statute.

The issue before the Court in *Skipper v. South Carolina* (1986) was the admissibility of a specific mitigating circumstance: the defendant's good behavior in jail while awaiting trial. Consistent with its earlier ruling in *Lockett* and *Bell*, the Court held that convicted murderers trying to escape a death sentence in favor of life in prison may present such evidence and it must be considered a legitimate mitigating circumstance in sentencing deliberations.

A year later, in *Hitchcock v. Dugger* (1987), the Court again revisited *Lockett* and *Bell* when a Florida court refused to consider evidence of nonstatutory mitigating circumstances. The Court reemphasized that the sentencing authority may not refuse to consider any relevant mitigating evidence. Also in 1987, the Court heard *California v. Brown*, in which the petitioner challenged the trial judge's instruction that the jury not be swayed by "mere sympathy, passion, prejudice or public opinion." The petitioner argued that such an instruction undermined his ability to present mitigating evidence and, hence, violated both his Eighth and Fourteenth Amendment rights. The Court rejected the argument.

In 1988, in *Mills v. Maryland*, the Court considered jury instructions that required the jury to be unanimous in its finding of a mitigating circumstance. In other words, before a Maryland juror (and jurors in other "weighing" states as well) could weigh a mitigating circumstance against aggravating circumstances, all 12 members of the jury had to agree that the mitigating circumstance did exist. If they did not, the mitigating circumstance could not be used in sentencing deliberations. The Court ruled that jury unanimity on the presence of a mitigating circumstance is not required before an individual juror may weigh it against aggravating factors. The issue arose again in 1990 in the case of *McKoy v. North Carolina*, and the Court held that sentencing instructions, which prevent the sentencing jury from considering any mitigating factor that the jury does not unanimously find, violates the Eighth Amendment.

In *Parker v. Dugger* (1991), the issue, in part, was whether appellate courts must independently (of trial courts) consider mitigating circumstances. The Florida Supreme

Court reviewed Parker's death sentence and disallowed two of the aggravating circumstances on which the trial judge based his sentencing decision. However, relying on the trial court's finding of no mitigating circumstances and the existence of other aggravating circumstances, the Florida Court upheld Parker's death sentence. The Florida Court would have found that the trial record supported a showing of non-statutory mitigating circumstances had it independently reviewed the evidence. The U.S. Supreme Court held that the Florida Supreme Court and, by implication, other reviewing courts, must conduct an independent reweighing of mitigating (and aggravating) evidence before rendering a decision.

In *Delo v. Lashley* (1993), the Court considered a Missouri case in which no evidence was presented to support the existence of a mitigating circumstance—the defendant's lack of prior criminal activity. The trial court judge refused to instruct the jury about the mitigating circumstance following the penalty phase of the trial because defense counsel provided no supporting evidence. The Supreme Court denied relief, holding that without supporting evidence, the Missouri trial court is not required to instruct the jury of the mitigating circumstance.

In sum, this line of cases clearly shows that the U.S. Supreme Court requires trial courts to consider any mitigating circumstances that a defense attorney presents, whether or not a mitigating circumstance is listed in a state's death penalty statute. The only qualification to this requirement is that the mitigating circumstance must be supported by evidence. Although the requirement serves the desired purpose of narrowing death eligibility, it also "invites arbitrary and even invidious decision-making."[53]

> *The* Supreme Court requires trial courts to consider any mitigating circumstances that a defense attorney presents, whether or not a mitigating circumstance is listed in a state's death penalty statute. The only qualification to this requirement is that the mitigating circumstance must be supported by evidence.

The problem, according to Steiker and Steiker, is that the "unconstrained consideration of any kind of mitigating evidence . . . gives those with a mind to discriminate the opportunity to discriminate."[54] They further claim that, "although such discretion cannot be used to render a defendant death-eligible contrary to community standards, it can be used to exempt favored defendants from the death penalty or to withhold severe punishment for crimes against despised victims."[55]

Aggravating Circumstances. The "trigger" for any death sentence is the finding of at least one aggravating circumstance. Without such a finding, death may not be imposed. Death penalty states vary in the number of aggravating circumstances listed in their statutes. Connecticut has the fewest with 7; Delaware has the most with 22.[56] Most death penalty statutes list between 8 and 12 aggravating circumstances.[57] It is important to note that aggravating circumstances differ widely in their significance; therefore, their content is more important than how many there are in determining the number of death-eligible offenses.[58] There are three broad types of aggravating circumstances: (1) those that focus on offender characteristics, (2) those that focus on the manner in which the murder was committed, and (3) those that focus on victim characteristics.[59]

As was the case with mitigating circumstances, the aggravating circumstance requirement has generated a series of constitutional challenges. Ironically, although the aggravating circumstance requirement, like the mitigating circumstance requirement, was intended to narrow death–eligibility, it has not done so very well. Steiker and Steiker state, "States have adopted, and the Court has sustained, aggravating circumstances that arguably encompass every murder."[60] Research shows that "virtually all persons sentenced to death in Georgia before *Furman* would have been deemed death eligible under Georgia's post-*Furman* statute."[61]

One of the first tests involving aggravating circumstances was *Godfrey v. Georgia* (1980). The Court held that the aggravating factor under which Godfrey had been sentenced to death (his offense, in the language of the statute, was "outrageously or wantonly vile, horrible or inhuman in that it involved torture, depravity of the mind, or an aggravated battery to the person") was too broad and vague, and as a result, it reversed Godfrey's death sentence. It is worth noting that the Court did not rule that the statutory aggravating factor was unconstitutional on its face (many other states have similar aggravating circumstances in their statutes), only in the way it was applied in Godfrey's case. The problem was twofold. First, the trial judge did not explain the meaning of the aggravating circumstance to the jury, and second, the Georgia Supreme Court did not apply a clarifying interpretation of the meaning it had developed in earlier cases. Thus, in the words of the Court, "There is no principled way to distinguish this case, in which the death penalty was imposed, from the many cases in which it was not." For such a statutory aggravating circumstance to withstand constitutional challenge, a state high court must adequately clarify its meaning and that meaning must be applied independently to the facts of the case (see *Walton v. Arizona*, 1990).

In *Barefoot v. Estelle* (1983), the Court addressed the issue of using psychiatric evidence to predict future dangerousness. Such a prediction was a component (and aggravating circumstance) in Texas's post-*Furman* death penalty statute. Barefoot claimed that (1) "psychiatrists, individually and as a group, are incompetent to predict with an acceptable degree of reliability that a particular criminal will commit other crimes in the future and so represent a danger to the community," (2) "psychiatrists should not be permitted to testify about future dangerousness in response to hypothetical questions and without having examined the defendant personally" (as they did in Barefoot's case), and (3) "in the particular circumstances of this case, the testimony of the psychiatrists was so unreliable that the sentence should be set aside." The Supreme Court rejected all three claims and held that such psychiatric evidence predicting future dangerousness is admissible.

The Court considered two other cases in 1983 involving aggravating circumstances. In *Zant v. Stephens*, the issue was whether a death sentence must be vacated if one of the three statutory aggravating circumstances found by the jury was subsequently held to be unconstitutional, even though the two other aggravating circumstances were valid. The Court noted that the answer depended on the function of aggravating circumstances in a particular state's death penalty statute. In Georgia, for example, where the case originated, the jury is instructed not "to give any special weight to any aggravating circumstance, to consider any multiple aggravating circumstances any more significant than a single such circumstance, or to balance aggravating against mitigating circumstances pursuant to any special standard." Consequently, "in Georgia, the finding of an aggravating circumstance does not play any role in guiding the sentencing body in the exercise of its discretion, apart from its function of narrowing the class of persons convicted of murder who are eligible for the death penalty." For those and other reasons, the Supreme Court did not vacate the death sentence in the Georgia case. The outcome likely would have been different had the case occurred in a state in which aggravating circumstances played a more important role.

In *Barclay v. Florida* (1983), the principal issue was whether a nonstatutory aggravating circumstance was admissible. The nonstatutory aggravating factor in this case was racial hatred. Barclay was a member of the Black Liberation Army, whose avowed purpose was "to kill white persons and to start a revolution and a racial war." The Court upheld Barclay's death sentence, implying that the sentencing authority may consider virtually any factor in aggravation (that would be properly before it) once it has found at least one statutory aggravating circumstance.

In 1987, the Court addressed for the first time the use of victim–impact statements in death penalty cases. The case was *Booth v. Maryland*. Victim–impact statements typically describe the harm done to and the suffering of victims and their family members. In accordance with Maryland law, victim–impact information was contained in the presentence investigation report. Booth's defense attorney moved to suppress the victim–impact statement, claiming it was both irrelevant and unduly inflammatory and, thus, its use violated the Eighth Amendment. The trial court judge denied the motion. The Supreme Court ruled five to four to vacate Booth's death sentence, holding that the introduction of victim–impact statements at the sentencing phase of a capital trial violated the Eighth Amendment. Two years later, in *South Carolina v. Gathers* (1989), the Court, again by a five to four decision, reversed Gathers's death sentence. It reasoned that the prosecutor's argument that the death penalty should be imposed because of the personal characteristics of the victim—that he was a religious person and a registered voter—violated *Booth v. Maryland*. By 1991, however, the composition of the Court had changed and so too had the position of some of the remaining justices. Consequently, in *Payne v. Tennessee* (1991), this time by a six to three decision, the Court reversed itself in both *Booth v. Maryland* and *South Carolina v. Gathers*. The Court ruled that the introduction of victim–impact evidence and prosecutorial argument on that subject at the sentencing phase of a capital trial does not violate the Eighth Amendment. The Court decided that "evidence about the victim and about the impact of the murder on the victim's family is relevant to the jury's decision as to whether or not the death penalty should be imposed."

The Appellate Process. Many of the capital cases that address the appellate process involve the Court's effort to reduce the amount of time between imposition of sentence and execution. That time interval currently averages more than 10 years. The Court first signaled its intention in *Barefoot v. Estelle* (1983). Not only did *Bare-*

foot allow psychiatric evidence predicting future dangerousness, it also approved acceleration of the appeals process in capital cases. Specifically, it allowed courts of appeal to deny an application for a stay of execution on habeas appeal—something they rarely did before *Barefoot*. The Court also provided detailed procedural guidelines for handling such appeals.

The following year, in *Pulley v. Harris* (1984), the Court decided that there was no constitutional obligation for state appellate courts to provide, upon request, proportionality review of death sentences. Recall that proportionality review, as required in Georgia's post-*Furman* death penalty statute, and as recommended in *Furman* as a desirable reform, is a means by which the appellate court can compare the sentence in the case before it with penalties imposed in similar cases in the state. Its purpose is to reduce discrimination in death sentencing. Since *Pulley*, many states have eliminated the proportionality review requirement from their statutes, while some states simply no longer conduct the reviews. Other states continue to conduct proportionality reviews but never find a death sentence to be disproportionate.[62] For example, the Georgia Supreme Court has found only one death sentence to be disproportionate in the more than 300 it has reviewed, and it has not found any death sentences to be disproportionate since *Pulley*.[63]

Further streamlining was accomplished in two more 1984 cases: *Woodward v. Hutchins* and *Antone v. Dugger*. In these cases, the Court announced that it would no longer consider issues raised for the first time pursuant to last-minute pleas for stays of execution when the issues could have been raised on previous petitions for habeas relief. The Court's ruling was aimed at the popular practice employed by some appellate attorneys of stalling executions by raising constitutional issues one at a time.

In 1989, in *Murray v. Giarratano*, the Court hastened the process by ruling that neither the Eighth nor the Fourteenth Amendment requires the appointment of counsel to indigent death row inmates seeking state post–conviction relief. Chief Justice Rehnquist, writing for the majority, explained that the right to counsel at the trial stage and for an initial appeal of the judgment and sentence of the trial court does not carry over to discretionary appeals. He reasoned that "the additional safeguards imposed by the Eighth Amendment at the trial stage of a capital case are . . . sufficient to assure the reliability of the process by which the death penalty is imposed."

Finally, in 1993, in *Herrera v. Collins*, the Court decided that a claim of actual innocence based on newly discovered evidence is not grounds for granting a further hearing in federal court. Chief Justice Rehnquist said that judges are not empowered "to correct errors of fact," even if a mistake could lead to the execution of an innocent person, and that the federal courts should intervene only when state courts violate constitutional procedures. The proper procedure for making claims of actual innocence after the "judicial process has been exhausted," is by filing a request for executive clemency. Clemency, wrote Rehnquist, "is the historic remedy for preventing miscarriages of justice"; it has "provided the 'fail safe' in our criminal justice system."

In dissent, Justice Blackmun, who was joined, in part, by Justices Stevens and Souter, responded that "nothing could be more contrary to contemporary standards of decency, or more shocking to the conscience, than to execute a person who is

In 1993, in *Herrera v. Collins*, Chief Justice Rehnquist said that judges are not empowered "to correct errors of fact," even if a mistake could lead to the execution of an innocent person. The proper procedure for making claims of actual innocence after the "judicial process has been exhausted," is by filing a request for executive clemency. Clemency, wrote Rehnquist, "is the historic remedy for preventing miscarriages of justice"; it has "provided the 'fail safe' in our criminal justice system."

actually innocent." Justice Blackmun argued that to rely on executive clemency to correct miscarriages of justice is to "make judicial review under the Eighth Amendment meaningless." He further suggested that "to obtain relief on a claim of actual innocence, the petitioner must show that he probably is innocent." Justice Blackmun ended his dissent with a warning to those who would reduce procedural safeguards to speed up the process:

> Of one thing, however, I am certain. Just as an execution without adequate safeguards is unacceptable, so too is an execution when the condemned prisoner can prove that he is innocent. The execution of a person who can show that he is innocent comes perilously close to simple murder.

Capital Juries. Challenges involving capital juries have occupied a considerable amount of the Court's time. Among the first was *Beck v. Alabama* (1980), in which the issue was whether a conviction–minded jury must be allowed to consider a verdict of guilt of a lesser included noncapital offense. Under Alabama's death penalty statute, the trial judge was prohibited from giving the jury this option. Instead, the jury was given the choice of either convicting the defendant of the capital crime, in which case it was required to impose the death penalty, or acquitting the defendant. (In Alabama, if the defendant is convicted and the death penalty is imposed, the trial judge must hold a hearing to consider aggravating and mitigating circumstances. After hearing the evidence, the judge may refuse to impose the death penalty and, instead, may sentence the defendant to life imprisonment without possibility of parole.) The Court held in *Beck* that the death penalty may not be constitutionally imposed after a jury verdict of guilt of a capital offense when the jury was not permitted to consider a verdict of guilt of a lesser included noncapital offense when the evidence would have supported such a verdict. In *Hopper v. Evans* (1982), the Court qualified its ruling in *Beck,* holding that *Beck v. Alabama* applies only when the evidence supports a verdict of a lesser sentence and not in the case where the defendant makes it crystal clear that he or she killed the victim, intended to kill the victim, and would do the same thing again in similar circumstances.

The Court revisited its *Witherspoon* decision in a series of cases. Recall that in *Witherspoon v. Illinois* (1968) the Court held that during the voir dire, prospective jurors may not be removed from the jury for cause simply because they voiced general objections to the death penalty or expressed conscientious or religious scruples against its imposition. In the first case, *Adams v. Texas* (1980), the Court decided that prospective jurors can be excluded from capital juries if their views on capital punishment would not allow them to obey their oath and follow the law of Texas without conscious distortion or bias. Texas law at that time required prospective jurors to state under oath that the mandatory penalty of death or life imprisonment would not affect their deliberations on any issue of fact. The law mandated a sentence of life imprisonment or death on conviction of a capital felony.

In *Wainwright v. Witt* (1985), the Court reconsidered its decisions in *Witherspoon* and *Adams* and held that potential jurors in capital cases should be excluded from jury duty in a manner no different from how they are excluded in noncapital cases. The Court opined that no longer does a juror's automatic bias against imposing the death penalty have to be proved with unmistakable clarity. Instead, the question of exclusion from a jury should be determined by the interplay of the prosecutor and the defense attorney and the decision of the judge based on his or her first-hand observations of the prospective juror. If the judge determines that a prospective juror's beliefs would bias the juror's ability to impose the death penalty, then the juror should be excluded.

The Court's final word on this issue (so far) came in *Lockhart v. McCree* (1986). In this case, the Court ruled that prospective jurors whose opposition to the death penalty is so strong that it would prevent or substantially impair the performance of their duties as jurors at the sentencing phase of the trial may be removed for cause. Stated differently, as long as jurors can perform their duties as required by law, they may not be removed for cause because they are generally opposed to the death penalty.

This series of cases modifying the Court's *Witherspoon* decision addressed the issue of what to do with prospective jurors who are opposed to capital punishment. Another interesting issue is what to do with prospective jurors who would automatically impose the death penalty following a defendant's conviction in a capital case. That issue was considered in *Morgan v. Illinois* (1992). During jury selection, Morgan's attorney requested the judge to ask all prospective jurors the following question: "If you found Derrick Morgan guilty, would you automatically vote to impose the death penalty no matter what the facts are?" The judge refused to ask the jurors this "life qualifying" or "reverse-*Witherspoon*" question. The jury found Morgan guilty and sentenced him to death. Morgan appealed the court's refusal to ask the reverse-*Witherspoon* question, and the Supreme Court reasoned that "a juror who will automatically vote for the death penalty in every case will fail in good faith to consider the evidence of aggravating and mitigating circumstances as the instructions require him to do." Thus, ruled the Court, a prospective juror who would automatically vote for the death penalty may be challenged for cause.

In *Bullington v. Missouri* (1981), the Court considered the issue of whether a death sentence could be imposed following a retrial when a jury had imposed life imprisonment at the first trial. The Court held that it could not because to do so would violate the Fifth Amendment's prohibition of double jeopardy.

In *Spaziano v. Florida* (1984), the jury override provision of Florida's death penalty statute was challenged. Recall that in Florida (as well as in Alabama,

Delaware, and Indiana), a trial judge is allowed to overrule the jury and impose a death sentence, even if all jurors voted for a life sentence, or impose a life sentence, even if all jurors voted for a death sentence. A majority of jurors in Spaziano's case recommended life imprisonment after he was found guilty of first-degree murder. The trial judge, however, who conducted his own independent weighing of the aggravating and mitigating circumstances in the case, overrode the jurors' recommendation and sentenced Spaziano to death. On appeal, the Supreme Court upheld Florida's override provision, maintaining that a sentencing judge may disregard the jury's recommendation of life imprisonment and impose the death penalty.

The issue in *Caldwell v. Mississippi* (1985) was whether a death sentence is valid when the sentencing jury is led to believe that responsibility for determining the appropriateness of a death sentence rests not with the jury but with the appellate court which later reviews the case. The prosecutor at Caldwell's trial urged the jury not to view itself as determining whether the defendant would die, because a death sentence would be reviewed for correctness by the state supreme court. The Supreme Court vacated the petitioner's sentence, arguing that the prosecutor's suggestion to the sentencing jury that the appellate court would correct an inappropriate death sentence created an intolerable risk of unreliable sentencing.

Another series of cases in this area deals with procedures that may contribute to unacceptable forms of juror discrimination in the imposition of the death penalty. In *Batson v. Kentucky* (1986), the Court considered the relatively common prosecutorial practice of using peremptory challenges to eliminate black people from trial juries in capital cases involving black defendants. This practice resulted in black defendants frequently being tried by all-white juries. In *Batson*, the Court held that "the Equal Protection Clause forbids the prosecutor to challenge potential jurors solely on account of their race or on the assumption that black jurors as a group will be unable impartially to consider the State's case against a black defendant." Thus, under *Batson*, once the defendant establishes a prima facie case showing race was a factor in a prosecutor's decision to exercise a peremptory challenge, the burden shifts to the prosecutor to provide a neutral, legitimate explanation to justify his or her striking of the juror.

The Court applied a similar logic to the selection of grand juries. In *Vasquez v. Hillery* (1986), the Court ruled that indictment by an all-white grand jury from which black individuals were systematically excluded created an intolerable risk that a defendant's indictment was a result of discrimination, thereby violating the Equal Protection Clause. The Court added that even though a defendant is subsequently lawfully convicted, that fact does not cure the taint attributed to a grand jury selected on the basis of race.

At issue in the case of *Turner v. Murray* (1986) was whether a defendant in an interracial murder case has a right to question prospective jurors about racial prejudice. In this case, the defendant was denied that opportunity. The Court ruled on appeal that failure to voir dire a jury about racial bias in an interracial murder case created an intolerable risk of discrimination.

In *J. E. B. v. Alabama* (1994), a noncapital case, the Equal Protection Clause was held to prohibit discrimination in jury selection on the basis of gender, or an assumption that an individual will be biased in a particular case solely because that person happens to be a woman or a man. The Court's decision suggests that the Court will not tolerate gender discrimination in capital jury selection for the same reason it will not tolerate racial discrimination.

The last case in this discussion is *Simmons v. South Carolina* (1994). At issue was South Carolina's new sentencing option in capital cases: life imprisonment without possibility of parole. Research shows that citizens are confused and skeptical about this sentencing option. Many citizens believe that even when offenders are sentenced to life imprisonment without possibility of parole, they may still be paroled. Concerned that the jury might not understand that "life imprisonment" did not carry with it the possibility of parole in Simmons's case, his defense attorney asked the trial judge to clarify the issue by defining the term "life imprisonment" in accordance with the South Carolina statute. The judge refused. On appeal, the Supreme Court ruled that a defendant has a right to inform the jury of the real consequences of a "life" sentence when the state argues that the defendant would be dangerous in the future (as the state did in Simmons's case), and "life" means life without possibility of parole, as a matter of state law.

Note that when a state does not argue that a defendant would be dangerous in the future, there is no obligation to explain to sentencing juries parole eligibility and minimum sentence requirements associated with life imprisonment sentences. Only a few death penalty statutes have such a requirement.[64]

Who May or May Not be Executed. The Supreme Court has established limits on who may or may not be executed and has established the principle that the Eighth Amendment requires at least a rough correspondence between the punishment imposed, the harm done, and the blameworthiness of the defendant.[65] In the extreme, this means that the Court would not allow an execution for jaywalking, however intentional. The cases that the Court has decided were not as easy. The first of the cases addressed the issue of whether a participant in a felony murder who did not kill, attempt to kill, or intend to kill may be executed. Many states include the crime of felony murder in their homicide statutes. In a felony murder, it is possible to find a defendant guilty of murder even though he or she did not intend to kill and may or may not have caused a death. Many states hold such a defendant guilty of first-degree murder because he or she committed a specified felony that caused a death. The Supreme Court first addressed the issue in *Enmund v. Florida* (1982). Enmund was the driver of the getaway car in a robbery in which the victims were murdered. Enmund did not himself kill and was not present at the killings, but the fact that he helped the killers escape was enough under Florida law to make him "a constructive aider and abettor and hence a principal in first-degree murder upon whom the death penalty could be imposed." Enmund was sentenced to death for his role in the crime. In addressing Enmund's blameworthiness, the Court ruled that to impose the death penalty on someone who did not kill or intend to kill violated the Eighth Amendment. The Court reversed the judgment, upholding Enmund's death penalty and remanded the case for further proceedings in light of its ruling.

The Court revisited its *Enmund* decision in 1987 in the case of *Tison v. Arizona*. As in *Enmund*, Raymond and Ricky Tison were participants in felony murders—in this case, involving robbery and kidnapping. Also like Enmund, the Tison brothers did not do the killing or intend to kill. Unlike Enmund, however, the Tisons were major participants in the crimes and showed a "reckless indifference to human life." The Court held that even though the killing and intent to kill were absent, the other circumstances were sufficient to support a judgment of death.

In 1986, in *Ford v. Wainwright*, the Court considered the issue of whether states may execute people who have literally gone crazy on death row. Writing for the majority, Justice Marshall noted that the Court had never decided whether the Constitution forbids the execution of the insane, even though for centuries no jurisdiction has approved the practice. This does not mean that insane persons have never been executed. To the contrary, as attorney Stephen Bright observes, "'insane' has been so narrowly defined as to allow people with severe mental illness to be put to death."[66] Justice Powell defined insanity for Eighth Amendment purposes as the condition under which people "are unaware of the punishment they are about to suffer and why they are to suffer it." Consistent with its common-law heritage, the Court held that states are barred from executing people who have developed mental illness while on death row. The implication is that death row inmates must first be cured of their mental illness before they are executed.[67]

> *In* 1986, in *Ford v. Wainwright*, Justice Powell defined insanity for Eighth Amendment purposes as the condition under which people "are unaware of the punishment they are about to suffer and why they are to suffer it."

In 1988 and 1989, the Supreme Court decided three cases that dealt with the age of the offender at the time the crime was committed. At issue was the question of whether the Constitution permits the execution of juveniles. The Court held in *Thompson v. Oklahoma* (1988) that the Constitution prohibits the execution of a person who is under 16 years of age at the time of his or her offense. In this particular case, the Court stipulated that the decision applies only when a state has not specifically legislated the death penalty for such minors. The next year, in the cases of *Stanford v. Kentucky* and *Wilkins v. Missouri*, the Court determined that the Eighth Amendment does not prohibit the execution of persons who are 17 (in *Stanford*) or 16 (in *Wilkins*) years of age at the time of their offenses. The three decisions together suggest that the Supreme Court will not allow the execution of persons who are under 16 years of age at the time of their offenses.

The Court also decided in 1989 the case of *Penry v. Lynaugh*. The issue in *Penry* was whether the Eighth Amendment categorically prohibits the execution of a capital offender who is mentally retarded. Court testimony indicated that Penry, who was 22 years old when he allegedly committed the brutal rape and murder for which he was convicted and sentenced to death, had the reasoning capacity of a 7-year-old. The Court provided the following rationale in upholding Penry's death sentence:

In sum, mental retardation is a factor that may well lessen a defendant's culpability for a capital offense. But we cannot conclude today that the Eighth Amendment precludes the execution of any mentally retarded person of Penry's ability convicted of a capital offense simply by virtue of his or her mental retardation alone. So long as sentencers can consider and give effect to mitigating evidence of mental retardation in imposing sentence, an individualized determination whether "death is the appropriate punishment" can be made in each particular case. While a national consensus against execution of the mentally retarded may someday emerge reflecting the "evolving standards of decency that mark the progress of a maturing society," there is insufficient evidence of such a consensus today.

Only 11 death penalty states prohibit the execution of the mentally retarded. It is estimated that 12 to 20 percent of the death row population is mentally retarded,

> *O*nly 11 death penalty states prohibit the execution of the mentally retarded.

and that at least 27 mentally retarded defendants have been executed under post–*Furman* statutes.[68]

Other Procedural Issues. Other procedural issues that do not fit well into any of the other categories are briefly described in this last section. In *Ake v. Oklahoma* (1985), the issue was whether the Constitution requires that an indigent defendant have access to psychiatric examination and assistance necessary to prepare an effective defense based on his or her mental condition, when sanity at the time of the offense is seriously in question. In *Ake*, the Court held that "when a defendant has made a preliminary showing that his insanity at the time of the offense is likely to be a significant factor at trial, the Constitution requires that a State provide access to a psychiatrist's assistance on this issue if the defendant cannot otherwise afford one."

In *Darden v. Wainwright* (1986), the Court decided that a Florida prosecutor's reference to a capital murder defendant as "an animal" at a sentencing trial did not violate the defendant's rights.

In *Powell v. Texas* (1989), the Court ruled that the Sixth Amendment is violated if a state psychiatrist conducts a pretrial evaluation without notice to defense counsel.

In *Minnick v. Mississippi* (1990), the Court held that once counsel is requested, police interrogation must cease, and any reinitiation of interrogation without presence of counsel, irrespective of whether the accused has consulted with counsel, is prohibited.

In *In Re Berger* (1991), the Court determined that appointed counsel representing a capital defendant before the U.S. Supreme Court is limited to $5,000 in fees, even though 21 U.S.C. § 848 (q) (10) prescribes no such limitation.

In *Arizona v. Fulminante* (1991), the Court decided that the petitioner's confession to a fellow inmate, who was really a government agent, as a result of a promise by the fellow inmate to protect the petitioner from other inmates, was coerced and therefore inadmissible. Although noting that the erroneous admission of a coerced confession may, in some cases, be a harmless error, under the circumstances of this case, it was not.

A Note on the Appellate Process under Post–*Furman* Statutes

In addition to automatic appellate review, defendants sentenced to death also have a dual system of collateral review; that is, they may challenge their convictions and/or sentences through both state post-conviction proceedings and federal habeas corpus petitions.[69] Steps in the dual system of collateral review in death penalty cases are:[70]

Stage 1:
  Step 1: Trial and Sentence in State Court
  Step 2: Direct Appeal to State Appeals Court
  Step 3: U.S. Supreme Court for Writ of Certiorari

Stage 2:
  Step 1: State Post-conviction
  Step 2: State Court of Appeals
  Step 3: U.S. Supreme Court for Writ of Certiorari

Stage 3:
  Step 1: Petition for Writ of Habeas Corpus in U.S. District Court
  Step 2: Certificate of Probable Cause and Request for Stay of Execution
  Step 3: U.S. Circuit Court of Appeals
  Step 4: U.S. Supreme Court for Writ of Certiorari
  Step 5: Request for a Stay of Execution

A state appellate court has three options when a conviction and/or death sentence has been appealed to it: (1) it can vacate the conviction (and therefore the sentence) and remand the case to the trial court for additional proceedings or for retrial, (2) it can affirm the conviction and remand the case to the trial court for resentencing, or (3) it can affirm both the conviction and sentence.[71] If the state appellate court affirms both the conviction and the sentence, an appeal may be made to the U.S. Supreme Court through a writ of certiorari. If the appeal to the Supreme Court is unsuccessful, the capital defendant may then return to state post-conviction proceedings and begin the appeals process anew. Even if the defendant's appeal is denied in the state appellate courts, because of the dual system of collateral review, the defendant may appeal to the appropriate U.S. District Court through a writ of habeas corpus. If the appeal is denied in the U.S. District Court, that decision may be appealed to the appropriate U.S. Circuit Court of Appeals. If denied there, a third appeal may be made to the U.S. Supreme Court.

Until recently, it was possible for people sentenced to death to employ this dual system of collateral review numerous times (see, for example, the case of Caryl Chessman). Now, however, because of Supreme Court decisions, the passage of the Antiterrorism and Effective Death Penalty Act of 1996, and similar measures by state legislatures, access to both the federal and state appellate courts has been made more difficult. Proponents of this type of legislation believe that most appeals are frivolous and are simply delaying tactics, and they hope that the new rules will greatly reduce the long delays in executions and the high costs associated with the entire capital punishment process. But what if many of the appeals are not frivolous and delaying tactics? What if the delays in executions are greatly reduced because death row inmates are unable to have their claims heard in the federal courts?

Many appeals filed by death row inmates may, indeed, be frivolous and delaying tactics, but the evidence shows that many of them are not. For example, as of April 1, 1998, 1,642 of the people sentenced to death in the United States since January 1, 1973, have had their convictions and/or sentences reversed by the appellate courts.[72] If, as estimated, there are 200 to 300 death sentences imposed each year, then for the period 1973-1998 there would have been 5,200 to 7,800 death sentences and 21 to 32 percent of them would have been found faulty by the appellate courts.

The percentage of death penalty cases overturned by the appellate courts since the reestablishment of capital punishment has far exceeded the percentage of appellate reversals of all other noncapital felony cases—in most states, this probably does not exceed one percent.[73] Trial courts seem to be doing better in recent years, however. For example, at the end of 1980, appellate courts had reversed the death sentences of 1,533 defendants: more than 60 percent of all defendants sentenced to death under post-*Furman* statutes at that time.[74] For the same period, extended to 1998, the reversal rate had fallen to an estimated 20 to 30 percent. The reversal rate during more recent years would have to be far below 20 to 30 percent for it to drop that much during the extended period. Still, compared to the reversal rate for all other noncapital felony cases, the reversal rate in capital cases is significantly higher.

> *If*, as estimated, there are 200 to 300 death sentences imposed each year, then for the period 1973-1998 there would have been 5,200 to 7,800 death sentences, and 21 to 32 percent of them would have been found faulty by the appellate courts.

Professor Paternoster provides an excellent summary of appellate court action in pre-1990, post-*Furman* capital cases:

1. Nationally, almost 30% of the initial convictions in capital cases are overturned on appeal.

2. [W]hile the reversal rate in non-capital federal *habeas corpus* petitions is low [estimates range from 1% to 7%], the reversal rate in capital *habeas* petitions was 60-75 percent as of 1982, 70 percent as of 1983, and 60 percent as of 1986.

3. [B]etween 1976 and 1983 federal appellate courts ruled in favor of the capital defendant in 73 percent of the habeas petitions heard while relief was granted in only 6 percent of non-capital cases.

4. [I]n the Eleventh Circuit Court of Appeals capital inmates were granted relief half the time in their habeas appeals.

5. [T]his level of success in federal *habeas corpus* petitions occurs *after* the state's supreme court has affirmed the case, thereby rejecting the defendant's claims, and *after* the U.S. Supreme Court has denied *certiorari* (emphasis in original).

6. This high reversal rate in capital cases has resulted from such fundamental constitutional errors as ineffective assistance of counsel, prosecutors' reference to defendants who refuse to testify, denial of the right of an impartial jury, and problems of tainted evidence and coerced confessions.[75]

In sum, despite a very elaborate process that includes guided discretion statutes and bifurcated trials, a large number of convictions and/or sentences in death penalty cases are reversed on appeal—a reversal rate many times higher than in noncapital cases. The errors that are discovered, moreover, are not insignificant legal technicalities but are the result of violations of fundamental constitutional protections. Under such circumstances, a likely result of restricting the access of death row inmates to the appellate process is miscarriages of justice. In other words, without the ability to challenge arrests, charges, indictments, convictions, sentences, and pending executions in the appellate courts, there likely will be an increase in the number of innocent people or people not legally eligible for execution involved in the capital punishment process. The subject of miscarriages of justice in capital cases is examined in detail in Chapter 7.

Conclusion

As the list of cases and appeals reversals indicate, over the past two decades the Supreme Court has been actively refining the procedures approved in *Gregg*. Its faith in its ability to make the system of capital punishment a just and constitutionally acceptable one remains strong. With Justices Marshall and Brennan no longer members of the Court, it is only on rarest of occasions that any doubts are expressed—but they *are* expressed. On February 22, 1994, for example, in a rare written dissent from the Court's refusal to hear the appeal of a Texas inmate scheduled to be executed the next day, Justice Harry A. Blackmun asserted that he had come to the conclusion that "the death penalty experiment has failed" and that it was time for the Court to abandon the "delusion" that capital punishment could be administered in a way that was consistent with the Constitution. Blackmun proclaimed, "From this day forward, I no longer shall tinker with the machinery of death." What is interesting is that, unlike Justices Marshall and Brennan, who always opposed capital punishment, Justice Blackmun had supported the administration of capital punishment for more than 20 years.[76]

Justice Blackmun is the exception. The majority of the current Court continues to make adjustments to the process. To summarize the general elements of that process:

Bifurcated trials are required in capital cases. Guided discretion statutes are constitutional; mandatory statutes of any kind are not. For practical purposes, capital punishment is permissible only in cases of aggravated murder. (At the state level it is also permissible for a few other rarely committed crimes, such as treason. At the federal level, it is authorized for about 50 crimes even though the federal government has not executed anyone since 1963.) It is not a permissible penalty unless there is at least one aggravating circumstance. A person who participated in a crime that resulted in death but who did not actually kill or plan to kill anyone may be found guilty of aggravated murder if he or she was a major participant and showed a reckless regard for the value of human life. Juries must be allowed to convict a capital defendant of an included noncapital offense instead of the capital one. During the penalty phase of bifurcated trials, courts must

In 1994, in a rare written dissent from the Court's refusal to hear the appeal of a Texas inmate scheduled to be executed the next day, Justice Harry A. Blackmun asserted that he had come to the conclusion that "the death penalty experiment has failed" and that it was time for the Court to abandon the "delusion" that capital punishment could be administered in a way that was consistent with the Constitution. Blackmun proclaimed, "From this day forward, I no longer shall tinker with the machinery of death."

allow the presentation of any mitigating evidence that is supported by evidence and victim–impact statements. The presentation of aggravating evidence is initially limited only to factors listed in the statutes. However, after one statutory aggravating factor has been found, any factor in aggravation can be considered. Automatic appellate and proportionality reviews, though desirable, are not required. Death penalty opponents may be excluded from juries in capital cases if they are opposed to the death penalty, no matter what the circumstances. Prospective jurors who would automatically vote for the death penalty may be challenged for cause. Executing people who have gone crazy on death row is not permitted, but execution of a mentally retarded capital offender is. Execution of persons who were under 16 years of age at the time of their offense generally is prohibited. Execution by lethal injection, firing squad, hanging, electrocution, or lethal gas is not cruel and unusual punishment and, thus, is allowable for capital crimes.

Discussion Questions

1. Are any of the current execution methods cruel and unusual punishments?

2. Do you agree with the Court's decision in *Louisiana ex rel. Francis v. Resweber*? Why or why not?

3. Do you agree with the Court's *Witherspoon* decision?

4. Do you agree with Justice Harlan in *McGautha* that it is impossible to adequately guide capital sentencing discretion?

5. Do you agree with the Court's *Furman* decision?

6. Which are fairer: mandatory or discretionary death penalty laws?

7. Do you agree with Justice Brennan that "death is different"?

8. Does the death penalty require "super due process"?

9. Do the guided-discretion death penalty statutes adequately reconcile the goals of consistency in application and consideration of individual circumstances?

10. Which type of guided-discretion death penalty statute is fairest?

11. Is automatic appellate review necessary?

12. Do you agree with the Court's decision in *McCleskey v. Kemp*?

13. Should any crimes besides aggravated murder be death-eligible?

14. Do you agree with Professors Steiker and Steiker that the "unconstrained consideration of any kind of mitigating evidence . . . gives those with a mind to discriminate the opportunity to discriminate . . . [by exempting] favored defendants from the death penalty or [by withholding] severe punishment for crimes against despised victims"?

15. Has the requirement of finding at least one statutorily enumerated aggravating circumstance adequately narrowed death-eligibility?

16. Can future dangerousness be accurately and adequately predicted?

17. Should a prediction of future dangerousness be a basis for sentencing someone to death?

18. Should victim-impact statements be admissible at the penalty phase of a capital trial?

19. Should proportionality review be required of all death penalty jurisdictions?

20. Should appointment of counsel be required for appeals beyond the automatic appeal?

21. Should a person's opinion about the death penalty (either in favor or opposed) affect whether he or she serves as a juror in a capital case?

22. Should a judge be allowed to overrule a jury sentence in a capital case (as is allowed in Alabama, Delaware, Florida, and Indiana)?

23. Should a participant in a crime in which a capital murder is committed be death-eligible, even though the participant did not kill or intend to kill?

24. Should inmates who have become insane while on death row be executed anyway?

25. At what age should a person be death-eligible? Should there be an age limit for death-eligibility?

26. Should mentally retarded offenders be death-eligible? At what IQ level, if any, should a capital offender be death-eligible?

27. What are the steps in the dual system of collateral review?

28. Should we be concerned about the reversal rate of convictions and death sentences in capital cases?

29. What, if anything, should be learned from Justice Blackmun's recent *mea culpa*?

30. What are the general elements of the capital punishment process in the United States?

Notes

[1] See Carter, 1969; Paternoster, 1991:68, fn. 3.
[2] Only eight of the suspects were indicted; the 13-year-old was not.
[3] Denno (1997) notes that courts have relied on *In re Kemmler* to dismiss challenges not only to electrocution but to the other four methods of execution as well. See the discussion of *In re Kemmler* below and in Chapter 4.
[4] Denno, 1997; 1998.
[5] *In re Kemmler*, 136 U.S. 436 at 447, 1890.
[6] Ibid.
[7] Ibid.
[8] See Denno, 1994:607-612; Paternoster, op. cit., p. 39.
[9] Andersen, 1983:32.
[10] *Louisiana ex rel. Francis v. Resweber*, 329 U.S. 459 at 474, 1947.
[11] See Nakell and Hardy, 1987:20.
[12] Ibid.
[13] Among studies that examine the effects of death-qualification are: Dillehay and Sandys, 1996; Thompson, 1989; Luginbuhl and Middendorf, 1988; Moran and Comfort,1986; Horowitz and Seguin,1986; Cowan et al.,1984; Fitzgerald and Ellsworth,1984; Gross, 1984; Haney, 1984; Jurow, 1971; Goldberg, 1970; Bronson, 1970.
[14] See Nakell and Hardy, 1987:20.
[15] Paternoster, op. cit., pp. 45-46.
[16] *McGautha v. California*, 602 U.S. 183 at 190, 1971.
[17] Ibid., at 195.
[18] Acker, 1996:143-4.
[19] *McGautha v. California*, op. cit., at 207.
[20] Ibid., at 204.

[21] *Savannah Morning News*, August 12, 1967, p. 8B; September 21, 1968, p. 1A.

[22] All three cases involved black defendants, two of whom—Lucious Jackson and Elmer Branch—were sentenced to death for raping white women. William Furman, as previously noted, was sentenced to death for murder. See Coyne and Entzeroth, 1994:96.

[23] Paternoster, op. cit., p. 54.

[24] Andersen, op. cit., p. 38.

[25] Cole, 1984.

[26] Nearly one-third of the states that adopted death penalty statutes between 1972 and 1976 enacted mandatory death penalty statutes, see Acker and Lanier, 1998:85.

[27] Acker, op. cit., p. 145.

[28] For a detailed examination of proportionality review, see Bienen, 1996.

[29] Also see Steiker and Steiker, 1998:55; Bedau, 1987.

[30] *Furman v. Georgia*, 408 U.S. 238 at 287-289,1972.

[31] *Gardner v. Florida*, 420 U.S. 349 at 357, 1977. Also see *Woodson v. North Carolina* 428 U.S. 280, 1976, and *Gregg v. Georgia*, 428 U.S. 153, 1976.

[32] Radin, 1980.

[33] Paternoster, op. cit., pp. 75-76; also see Steiker and Steiker, op. cit.

[34] Steiker and Steiker, ibid.; also see Acker, op. cit.; Mello, 1989.

[35] Steiker and Steiker, ibid., p. 70.

[36] Acker and Lanier, 1997; Nakell and Hardy, op. cit.

[37] Acker and Lanier relate, "It is futile in the post-*Furman* era to embark on a discussion of 'the death penalty' from a procedural standpoint, for there are almost as many variations on capital-sentencing laws as there are capital-punishment jurisdictions" (1998:89).

[38] Baldus and Woodworth, 1998:394.

[39] Ibid.

[40] Acker and Lanier, op. cit., p. 101.

[41] Florida Statutes Ann., ch. 921, sec. 921.141, 1993.

[42] See Acker and Lanier, op. cit., p. 98; Bowers and Steiner, 1998:309.

[43] In five states—Arizona, Colorado, Idaho, Montana, and Nebraska—juries are excluded entirely from the capital sentencing process. Only a few states (e.g., Kentucky and Texas) give juries sentencing responsibility in noncapital cases), see Acker and Lanier, ibid.; Bowers and Steiner, ibid.

[44] Coyne and Entzeroth, op. cit., pp. 264-265.

[45] Acker and Lanier, op. cit., p. 103.

[46] Coyne and Entzeroth, op. cit., pp. 261-262.

[47] See *Death Row, U.S.A.*, 1998.

[48] Andersen, op. cit.

[49] Ga. Code Ann. Sec. 27-2537, Supp. 1975; also see *Gregg v. Georgia*, 1976:212; Paternoster, op. cit., p. 63.

[50] See Snell, 1997.

[51] Justice Powell, who wrote the opinion in *McCleskey*, has since stated that his vote in *McCleskey* was his biggest and most regrettable mistake as a Supreme Court Justice. See Cavender, 1995:128.

[52] Snell, 1997:3, Table 1.

[53] Steiker and Steiker, op. cit., p. 63.

[54] Ibid.

[55] Ibid.

[56] Acker and Lanier, op. cit., p. 92.

[57] Ibid.

[58] Ibid.

[59] Ibid., pp. 92-3.

[60] Steiker and Steiker, op. cit., p. 57.

[61] Ibid., p. 58.

[62] Bright, 1997:14.

[63] Ibid.

[64] Acker and Lanier, op. cit., pp. 99–100.

[65] See Hoffmann, 1993:124, for the correspondence between the punishment and blameworthiness.

[66] Bright, op. cit., p. 19.

[67] For a detailed description of the Ford case, see Miller and Radelet, 1993.

[68] Bright, op. cit., p. 17.

[69] Paternoster, op. cit., p. 202.

[70] From Paternoster, ibid.; also see Cook and Slawson, 1993:19; Freedman, 1998:418)

[71] See Paternoster, ibid., pp. 202–204.

[72] *Death Row U.S.A.*, 1998.

[73] White, 1987:10.

[74] Ibid.

[75] Paternoster, op. cit., pp. 208–209; also see Freedman, 1998:427.

[76] Cited in Bohm and Haley, 1997:307.

CHAPTER 3

The Death Penalty
at the Federal Level
and in the Military

It is important to understand that there are 40 separate death penalty systems in the United States. Thirty-eight states have a death penalty system, as do the federal government and the military. No two systems are exactly alike. In this chapter, the death penalty systems of the federal government and the military are examined.

The Death Penalty at the Federal Level

Except for the judicial branch, the federal government (that is, the executive and legislative branches) historically has played a limited role in the administration of capital punishment in the United States. Its principal responsibility has been the execution of offenders found guilty of committing federal capital crimes. In addition, the president has granted an occasional pardon or commutation, and Congress has tinkered with federal death penalty legislation. Beginning in the 1990s, however, Congress has become much more active in death penalty matters. Two major initiatives have been the expansion of the number of federal crimes punishable by death and the changing of the ways capital crimes are handled. Those congressional initiatives will be examined following a brief description of the role of the federal courts in capital punishment.

Capital Punishment and the Federal Courts. The federal courts represent one-half of the dual court system in the United States.[1] The other half is the state court system. The federal court system consists of three levels of courts. At the bottom are 94 district courts. The U.S. district courts are further divided into 13 circuits, with at least one federal district court in each state, one each in the District of Columbia and the Commonwealths of Puerto Rico and the Northern Mariana Islands, and one each in the U.S. territories of the Virgin Islands and Guam. Violations of federal capital punishment statutes are first adjudicated in federal district courts, as are claims first made in federal post-conviction proceedings.

The middle level of the federal court system is comprised of 13 U.S. circuit courts of appeals. Twelve of them have jurisdiction over death penalty appeals from U.S. district courts in the particular geographic areas assigned to them. The Court of Appeals for the Federal Circuit is the only court of appeals that does not hear appeals in death penalty cases.

At the top of the federal court system is the United States Supreme Court—the "court of last resort." Under its appellate jurisdiction, the Court hears death penalty cases appealed from U.S. circuit courts of appeals or from the high court of a state. It hears appeals from the high court of a state only when claims under federal law or the Constitution are involved. This means that the Supreme Court rules only on death penalty cases in which (1) the constitutionality of a state or federal death penalty statute is challenged, or (2) a capital defendant claims that his or her constitutional rights were violated. Such violation might be improper guilt phase or penalty phase court procedures or improper procedures of the appellate court.

> The Supreme Court rules only on death penalty cases in which (1) the constitutionality of a state or federal death penalty statute is challenged, or (2) a capital defendant claims that his or her constitutional rights were violated. Such violation might be improper guilt phase or penalty phase court procedures or improper procedures of the appellate court.

For a case to be heard by the Supreme Court, at least four of the nine justices must vote to hear the case (the "rule of four"). (It takes five justices to stay, or stop, an execution.) The Court next issues a writ of certiorari to the lower court whose decision is being appealed, ordering it to send the records of the case forward for review. The Court will issue a writ of certiorari only if the defendant in the case has exhausted all other avenues of appeal and the case involves a substantial federal question as defined by the appellate court.

When the Supreme Court decides a case it has accepted on appeal, it can take one of four actions:

1. affirm the verdict or decision of the lower court and "let it stand";

2. modify the verdict or decision of the lower court, without totally reversing it;

3. reverse the verdict or decision of the lower court, requiring no further court action; or

4. reverse the verdict or decision of the lower court and remand the case to the court of original jurisdiction, for either retrial or resentencing.

Appeals to the Supreme Court are heard at the discretion of the Court, in contrast to appeals to the U.S. circuit courts, which review cases as a matter of right. The high Court's refusal to hear a case generally ends the process of direct appeal.

In some cases, a death row inmate whose appeal has been denied may still try to have the Supreme Court review his or her case on constitutional grounds by filing a writ of habeas corpus. A writ of habeas corpus is a court order directing a law officer to produce a prisoner in court to determine if the prisoner is being legally detained or imprisoned. The habeas corpus proceeding does not test whether the prisoner is guilty or innocent. Recent changes making it more difficult to get habeas petitions heard by the Court are discussed in a later section of this chapter.

Federal Capital Crimes. Prior to the 1990s, the most significant act of Congress regarding the death penalty may have been its effort to reduce the number of federal capital crimes. In the latter part of the nineteenth century, Congress reduced the number of federal crimes punishable by death from 60 to only 3 nonmilitary offenses: murder, rape, and treason.[2] A hundred years later, it has reversed course and added numerous new crimes. The 1994 federal crime bill (the Violent Crime Control and Law Enforcement Act), for example, expanded the number of federal crimes punishable by death to about 50. (Estimates vary depending on whether statutes or offenses are counted, and how offenses are counted.) The bill also reinstated the death penalty for federal crimes already on the books that likely would have been held unconstitutional had they been tested. The new law brings the earlier statutes into compliance with guidelines established by the Supreme Court (see the discussion in Chapter 2). The federal crimes for which the death penalty is now available as a sentencing alternative are: [3]

- aircraft hijacking (either domestic or international) where death results

- alien smuggling where death results

- assassination of the President or Vice President

- assassination of a member of Congress, cabinet member, Supreme Court justice, and major Presidential or Vice Presidential candidates

- attempting, authorizing, or advising the killing of any public officer, juror or witness in a case involving a continuing criminal enterprise—regardless of whether such a killing actually occurs

- carjacking where death results

- destroying federal property with explosives or by arson where death results

- destroying aircraft, motor vehicles, or their facilities where death results

- destroying property used in interstate commerce with explosives or by arson where death results

- drive-by shooting where death results

- drug trafficking in large quantities (even where no death results)

- espionage

- first–degree murder on federal land or property

- genocide

- gun murders during federal crimes of violence and drug trafficking crimes

- hostage–taking where death results

- kidnapping where death results

- killing or attempted killing by a drug kingpin of a public officer or juror to obstruct justice

- mailing injurious articles (e.g., explosives) where death results

- murder at a U.S. international airport

- murder by a federal prisoner serving a life sentence

- murder by an escaped federal prisoner

- murder for hire involving interstate travel or the use of interstate facilities

- murder in aid of racketeering activity

- murder involving firearms or other dangerous weapons during attack on federal facilities

- murder of a federal witness, victim, or informant

- murder of a state correctional officer by a federal prisoner

- murder of a U.S. citizen abroad

- murder by terrorism of a U.S. citizen abroad

- murder of federal jurors and court officers

- murder of federal law enforcement officials or employees

- murder of foreign officials or internationally protected people on U.S. soil

- murder of state or local officials assisting federal law enforcement officials

- murder within the special maritime and territorial jurisdiction of the United States

- robbery of a federally insured bank where death results

- sexual abuse committed within federal territorial jurisdiction where death results

- child molestation committed within federal territorial jurisdiction where death results

- torture where death results outside the United States

- train sabotage where death results

- transporting or receiving explosives with intent to kill where death results

- treason

- use of weapons of mass destruction (e.g., biological weapons or poison gas) where death results

- violating a person's federally protected rights based on race, religion, or national origin where death results

It is interesting to note that all but four of the crimes involve murder. The four exceptions are treason; espionage; drug trafficking in large quantities; and attempting, authorizing, or advising the killing of any public officer, juror or witness in a case involving a continuing criminal enterprise—regardless of whether such a killing actually occurs.

Federal Capital Punishment Procedures. When the Supreme Court in *Furman* (1972) invalidated existing death penalty statutes, it also invalidated the federal death penalty law. Procedures that would meet the requirements of *Furman* were not created by Congress until 1988 in a new statute that allowed the death penalty for murder in the course of a drug–kingpin conspiracy. Six people have subsequently been sentenced to death under this conspiracy law, although none of them, as of January 1, 1999, has been executed.[4] Using the long record of reforms summarized in Chapter 2, Congress incorporated into its new law many of the desirable features of state death penalty statutes already approved by the Supreme Court. Congress further refined federal death penalty procedures in the Federal Death Penalty Act of 1994. Among the features the current federal death penalty law shares with some states are:

- requiring a minimum of two attorneys be appointed to represent federal capital defendants (at least one of the attorneys must have experience in capital defense work)

- requiring the government to inform the defendant of its intention to seek death within a reasonable time before trial or before the court accepts a defendant's guilty plea

- requiring the government, before trial or plea, to list the aggravating circumstances that it proposes to prove to justify a death sentence

- the weighing of statutorily enumerated aggravating and mitigating circumstances (no method or standard for weighing is prescribed)

- giving the government the burden of establishing aggravating circumstances beyond a reasonable doubt

- requiring unanimity on the part of jurors in the finding of an aggravating circumstance

- requiring that a sentence other than death be imposed if no aggravating circumstance is found to exist

- requiring only a single juror to find a mitigating circumstance before it can be weighed

- allowing victim–impact evidence

- the right to appeal both the conviction and the death sentence*

- exempting from the federal death penalty persons less than 18 years of age at the time of the offense, mentally retarded and insane persons, and pregnant women (but only while they are pregnant)

A few features unique to the federal death penalty statute are:

- requiring authorization from the U.S. attorney general before federal prosecutors can file capital charges

- requiring the court to consider the federal public defender's recommendation about which attorneys are qualified for appointment in capital cases

- three different sets of aggravating circumstances: those for espionage and treason; those for homicide; and those for nonhomicide drug offenses

- requiring federal judges in capital sentencing proceedings to instruct the jury that "in considering whether a sentence of death is justified, it shall not consider the race, color, religious beliefs, national origin, or sex of the defendant or of any victim"

---

*There are three grounds for appeal: (1) the death sentence was imposed under the influence of passion, prejudice, or any other arbitrary factor, (2) the admissible evidence and information adduced does not support the special finding of the existence of the required aggravating factor, or (3) the proceedings involved any other legal error requiring reversal which was properly preserved for appeal under the rules of criminal procedure. No relief may be provided for any error that the government proves to be harmless beyond a reasonable doubt.

- requiring a jury that recommends death to furnish the court with a certificate signed by each juror swearing that discrimination played no part in the decision and that the same sentencing recommendation would have been made regardless of the race, color, religious beliefs, national origin, or sex of the defendant or any victim

- restricting the federal government's ability to impose the death penalty on Native Americans (capital prosecution of persons subject to the criminal jurisdiction of an Indian tribal government where federal jurisdiction is based solely on Indian country and where the offense occurred within the boundaries of Indian country is prevented, unless the governing body of the Indian tribe waives its sovereign immunity)

Federal Executions. Between 1927 and 1963, the U.S. government executed 34 people, two of whom were women.[5] Since March 15, 1963, when Victor H. Feguer was hanged at Iowa State Penitentiary for kidnapping,[6] no one else has been executed under any federal statute. Eighteen people were under federal death sentence as of April 1, 1998: twelve were black, four were white, one was Latino, and one was Asian.[7] Until recently, federal prisoners were usually executed in the state where the crime occurred because the federal government did not have its own site for executions. That practice will change because the Federal Bureau of Prisons has constructed the first national execution chamber in American history in Terre Haute, Indiana.[8] Death is by lethal injection.[9]

> *Until* recently, federal prisoners were usually executed in the state where the crime occurred, because the federal government did not have its own site for executions. That practice will change because the Federal Bureau of Prisons has constructed the first national execution chamber in American history in Terre Haute, Indiana.

The Racial Justice Act and the Fairness in Death Sentencing Act. Justice Powell suggested in the *McCleskey* decision (described in Chapter 2) that claims of racial discrimination would be best presented to legislative bodies for corrective action. Congress thereupon commissioned a review of research on racial discrimination in capital charging and sentencing. The resulting General Accounting Office (GAO) report confirmed that such discrimination was a problem—especially when it was based on the race of the victim.[10] (Findings of the GAO report are described in more detail in Chapter 8.) In an effort to rectify the situation, two pieces of legislation were proposed: the Racial Justice Act and the Fairness in Death Sentencing Act.

The legislation was intended to give offenders sentenced to death the right to challenge as racially discriminatory their individual death sentences, much in the same way that individuals may challenge racially discriminatory outcomes under federal employment or housing laws.[11] The two pieces of legislation would allow a black defendant or a defendant whose victim was white the opportunity to present evidence showing a pattern of racially discriminatory charging or sentencing. The State could rebut the evidence by showing, by a preponderance of the evidence, that the pattern of racially discriminatory charging or sentencing could be explained by identifiable and pertinent nonracial factors. If the State failed in its rebuttal, the defendant would be entitled to have his or her death sentence set aside.[12]

Both proposals were vigorously opposed by state attorneys general and by prosecutors who claimed that (1) racial discrimination did not exist, making legislation unnecessary, and (2) passage of the legislation would result either in the use of quotas or the de facto abolition of the death penalty.[13]

The Racial Justice Act stalled and was set aside. The House of Representatives passed the Fairness in Death Sentencing Act in 1990 and again in 1994, but the Senate in a House–Senate Conference Committee rejected the act both times.[14] When Congress enacted death penalty measures as part of the Violent Crime Control and Law Enforcement Act later in 1994, it included no provisions regarding racial discrimination in charging or sentencing.[15]

The Antiterrorism and Effective Death Penalty Act of 1996. Congress has recently turned its attention to what some of its members believe has been the abuse of the writ of habeas corpus in death penalty cases. Recall that a writ of habeas corpus claims that a federal constitutional right has been violated and, thus, the claimant is being held illegally. It is a primary avenue to the U.S. Supreme Court. In 1995, for example, 21 percent of death row inmates (648) had a habeas corpus petition active in the federal courts; this represented about 2 percent of all active habeas corpus petitions in the federal courts.[16] Critics maintain that abuse of the writ has contributed to the long delays in executions (currently averaging more than 10 years after conviction) and to the high costs associated with capital punishment.

In part to speed up the process and reduce costs, Congress passed the Antiterrorism and Effective Death Penalty Act of 1996, and President Clinton signed it into law on April 24. The law requires that second or subsequent habeas petitions be dismissed when the claim has already been made in a previous petition. It also requires that new claims be dismissed unless the Supreme Court hands down a new rule of constitutional law and makes it retroactive to cases on collateral review. Under the act, the only other way the Supreme Court will hear a claim made for the first time is when the claim is based on new evidence not previously available. Even then, the new evidence must be of sufficient weight, by a clear and convincing standard of proof, to convince a judge or jury that the capital defendant was not guilty of the crime or crimes for which he or she was convicted.

The act made the federal appellate courts "gatekeepers" for second or subsequent habeas corpus petitions. Now, to file a second or subsequent claim, a capital defendant must first file a motion in the appropriate appellate court, announcing his or her intention. A panel of three judges must hear the motion within 30 days and decide whether the petitioner has a legitimate claim under the act. If the claim is denied, the new law prohibits any review of the panel's decision, either by a rehearing or writ of certiorari to the Supreme Court. So far, the U.S. Supreme Court has upheld the constitutionality of the new law.[17]

The Death Penalty in the Military

Information on the military's use of the death penalty is scarce. What little is available suggests that, historically, the military has used the death penalty mostly for crimes committed during wartime.[18] In this section of the chapter, three topics are addressed: (1) the history of military executions, (2) military capital offenses, and (3) military capital punishment procedures.

Military Executions. Although there are no official records on the subject, it is believed that executions by the military were relatively common during both the American Revolution and in the early years of the nation. It is also believed that many death sentences were never carried out because of subsequent pardons. It is presumed that the crime for which most soldiers were sentenced to death during this period was desertion.

Official War Department records of military executions were first kept during the Civil War by the Union Army. Those records show 267 executions for the following offenses:

desertion	141
murder	72
rape	23
mutiny	20
theft	4
multiple offenses	4
spying	3

The list shows that more than half of the executions were for desertion. More Union soldiers would have been executed for desertion had President Lincoln not pardoned many of them, deciding "to take the risk on the side of mercy." There is no record of executions by the Confederate Army. Either no such records were kept, or they were destroyed before the war's end.

During World War I, the U.S. military executed 35 of the 145 soldiers sentenced to death. All of the soldiers executed were black. They were executed for murder and mutiny (19), rape (11), murder and rape (3), and murder (2). Ten of the executions were conducted in France and the remaining 25 in the United States. All executions took place at dawn following the day the trial ended. Because executions were carried out so quickly, there was no time to review the records of a case, as required by law, or enough time for condemned soldiers to petition the President for clemency or a pardon.

During World War II, the Army executed 147 soldiers. The Navy, the Air Force, and the Marine Corps executed none. The crimes for which soldiers were executed were murder (76), rape (52), murder and rape (18), and desertion (1). Although only one soldier was executed for desertion, 2,864 soldiers were tried for the offense and 49 of them were sentenced to death. All of those death sentences, except the one, were later commuted to life imprisonment. The one execution involved what has been called "the most widely publicized [case] of cowardice and desertion in modern times." The soldier violated Articles of War #52—desertion to avoid hazardous duty—and was executed by firing squad in France on January 31, 1945. In addition to American soldiers, 14 German prisoners of war were hanged at the United States Disciplinary Barracks, Fort Leavenworth, Kansas, in July and August 1945, for murdering other POWs.

Criminologist J. Robert Lilly has researched the records of 18 American soldiers executed by the U.S. Army in England from 1943 to 1945.[19] Eight of the executions were for murder, six were for rape, and four were for murder/rape.[20] Fifty-six percent (10) of the 18 soldiers executed, and 80 percent of all U.S. soldiers executed in the European Theater, were African-American even though African-Americans comprised no more than 10 percent of the soldiers in the European Theater and in the Army, generally.[21] Combined with the three Latinos executed, minorities accounted for 72 percent (13) of the 18 executions studied by Lilly. He found that only non-white soldiers were executed for rape. He also discovered evidence of racial discrimination at nearly every stage of the process.[22]

After World War II and until 1961, the military executed only 12 soldiers, although many more had been sentenced to death. All but the 12 had their sentences commuted. Eleven of the 12 executed were African-American.[23] The U.S. military's last execution was on April 13, 1961. Private John Bennett was hanged at the United States Disciplinary Barracks, Fort Leavenworth, Kansas, for the rape and attempted murder of an 11-year-old Austrian girl. Bennett was the 464th Army soldier executed since 1861. By contrast, the Navy has executed no more than 26 sailors during its history (not counting deaths from flogging which was outlawed in 1850). The last executions by the Navy were in 1849, when two sailors were hanged for mutiny. Similarly, the Air Force has executed only three airmen in its history: one in 1948 and two in 1954. The Coast Guard has carried out no executions, and no information is available on the Marines.

> The U. S. military's last execution was on April 13, 1961. Private John Bennett was hanged at the United States Disciplinary Barracks, Fort Leavenworth, Kansas, for the rape and attempted murder of an 11-year-old Austrian girl. Bennett was the 464th Army soldier executed since 1861.

As of April 1, 1998, eight soldiers occupied the military's death row: five were African-American, two were Asian, and one was white.[24] Because of the Supreme Court's recent decision in *Loving v. United States* (116 S. Ct. 1737, 1996), discussed later in this chapter, the first military execution since 1961 is likely to happen soon (if it has not already happened by the time this is read).

Military Capital Offenses. Offenses for which death is a potential punishment in the military can be divided into three general categories: (1) offenses that could be committed at any time, (2) offenses committed during time of war, and (3) offenses that are "grave breaches" of the law of war. There are 10 potentially capital offenses that could be committed at any time:

1. mutiny or sedition

2. misbehavior before the enemy

3. subordinate compelling surrender

4. forcing a safeguard

5. aiding the enemy

6. espionage

7. improperly hazarding a vessel

8. premeditated murder

9. felony murder

10. rape

The five potentially capital offenses committed during time of war are:

1. desertion

2. assaulting or willfully disobeying superior commissioned officer

3. improper use of countersign

4. spying

5. misbehavior of sentinel

For purposes of the military's death penalty, "time of war" refers to a period of war declared by Congress or the factual determination by the President that the existence of hostilities warrants a finding that a "time of war" exists (examples of the latter are the Korean and Vietnam wars). The death penalty is mandatory for soldiers convicted of spying in time of war; however, given the Supreme Court's consistent post-*Furman* record of rejecting mandatory death penalty statutes, it is doubtful the military's mandatory provision could withstand constitutional scrutiny if ever challenged.

The third category of offenses for which the death penalty is a possible sanction is "grave breaches" of the law of war. The law of war to which this provision refers is the Geneva Convention Relative to the Treatment of Prisoners of War. Potentially capital crimes under the law of war are:

1. willful killing, torture, or inhuman treatment, including biological experiments

2. willfully causing great suffering or serious injury to body or health

3. unlawful deportation or transfer or unlawful confinement of a protected person

4. compelling a protected person to serve in the forces of a hostile power

5. willfully depriving a protected person of the rights of fair and regular trial prescribed in the present Convention

6. taking of hostages and extensive destruction and appropriation of property, not justified by military necessity and carried out unlawfully and wantonly

Military Capital Punishment Procedures. The Supreme Court has recently upheld the military death penalty process in *Loving v. United States* (1996).[25] Private Loving had been sentenced to death in 1988 for the murder of two taxi drivers. He appealed, arguing that his death sentence violated the Eighth Amendment's prohibition against cruel and unusual punishment and the separation of powers doctrine. The latter requires that Congress, and not the President, set military death penalty policy. The statute under which Loving was convicted and sentenced contained a list of aggravating factors—at least one of which had to be found before a death sentence could be imposed—issued by President Reagan in 1985 by executive order. President Reagan was responding to the ruling of the Court of Military Appeals in *U.S. v. Matthews* (1983), wherein the court held the military's death penalty unconstitutional because it was imposed in an arbitrary manner. Specifically, the statute "failed to narrow effectively the class of defendants eligible for capital punishment." Recall that the Supreme Court reached the same conclusion about the civilian death penalty in *Furman v. Georgia* in 1972. President Reagan issued the aggravating factors to satisfy the Court on this issue. In *Loving*, the Court ruled nine to zero that Congress had granted the President that power in 1951 under the *Uniform Code of Military Justice,* and it denied Private Loving's claim.

> ■ *The* U.S. Supreme Court has recently upheld the military death penalty process in *Loving v. United States* (1996).

The military's death penalty process has much in common with some of the schemes approved by the Supreme Court in *Gregg*. Chief among them is that the members of the military court (the military's counterpart to the civilian jury) must unanimously find, beyond a reasonable doubt, at least one statutorily enumerated aggravating circumstance before it may consider a death sentence. Any aggravating circumstance that is found must be weighed against any mitigating circumstances that are presented at trial. Like its civilian counterpart, the military court must allow the presentation of any mitigating factor that is supported by evidence. If the members of the military court unanimously find that the aggravating circumstance or circumstances substantially outweigh any mitigating circumstances, then a death sentence may be imposed; if the mitigating circumstances are found to outweigh the aggravating circumstance or circumstances, then a death sentence may not be imposed.

The military's aggravating factors, many of which are unique to the military, are:

1. that the offense was committed before or in the presence of the enemy, except that this factor shall not apply in the case of a violation of Article 118 [premeditated murder and felony–murder] or 120 [rape];

2. that in committing the offense the accused—

    (A) knowingly created a grave risk of substantial damage to the national security of the United States; or

    (B) knowingly created a grave risk of substantial damage to a mission, system, or function of the United States, provided that this subparagraph shall apply only if substantial damage to the national security of the United States would have resulted had the intended damage been effected;

3. that the offense caused substantial damage to the national security of the United States, whether or not the accused intended such damage, except that this factor shall not apply in case of a violation of Article 118 [premeditated murder and felony–murder] or 120 [rape];

4. that the offense was committed in such a way or under circumstances that the life of one or more persons other than the victim was unlawfully and substantially endangered, except that this factor shall not apply to a violation of Articles 104 [aiding the enemy], 106a [espionage], or 120 [rape];

5. that the accused committed the offense with the intent to avoid hazardous duty;

6. that, only in the case of a violation of Article 118 [premeditated murder and felony–murder] or 120 [rape], the offense was committed in time of war and in territory in which the United States or an ally of the United States was then an occupying power or in which the armed forces of the United States were then engaged in active hostilities;

7. that, only in the case of a violation of Article 118(1) [premeditated murder]:

    (A) the accused was serving a sentence of confinement for 30 years or more or for life at the time of the murder;

    (B) the murder was committed: while the accused was engaged in the commission or attempted commission of any robbery, rape, aggravated arson, sodomy, burglary, kidnapping, mutiny, sedition, or piracy of an aircraft or vessel; or while the accused was engaged in the commission or attempted commission of any offense involving the wrongful distribution, manufacture, or introduction or possession, with intent to distribute, of a controlled substance; or, while the accused was engaged in flight or attempted flight after the commission or attempted commission of any such offense.

(C) the murder was committed for the purpose of receiving money or a thing of value;

(D) the accused procured another by means of compulsion, coercion, or a promise of an advantage, a service, or a thing of value to commit the murder;

(E) the murder was committed with the intent to avoid or to prevent lawful apprehension or effect an escape from custody or confinement;

(F) the victim was the President of the United States, the President–elect, the Vice President, or, if there was no Vice President, the officer in the order of succession to the office of President of the United States, the Vice-President-elect, or any individual who is acting as President under the Constitution and laws of the United States, any member of Congress (including a delegate to, or resident commissioner in, the Congress) or member–of–Congress elect, justice or judge of the United States, a chief of state or head of government (or the political equivalent) of a foreign nation, or a foreign official . . . if the official was on official business at the time of the offense and was in the United States or in a place described in Mil. R. Evid. . . . ;

(G) the accused then knew that the victim was any of the following persons in the execution of office: a commissioned, warrant, noncommissioned, or petty officer of the armed services of the United States; a member of any law enforcement or security activity or agency, military or civilian, including correctional custody personnel; or any firefighter;

(H) the murder was committed with intent to obstruct justice;

(I) the murder was preceded by the intentional infliction of substantial physical harm or prolonged, substantial mental or physical pain and suffering to the victim. For purposes of this section, 'substantial physical harm' means fractures or dislocated bones, deep cuts, torn members of the body, serious damage to internal organs, or other serious bodily injuries. The term 'substantial physical harm' does not mean minor injuries, such as a black eye or bloody nose. The term 'substantial mental or physical pain or suffering' is accorded its common meaning and includes torture;

(J) the accused has been found guilty in the same case of another violation of Article 118 [premeditated murder and felony-murder];

8. that only in the case of a violation of Article 118(4) [felony–murder], the accused was the actual perpetrator of the killing or was a principal whose participation in the burglary, sodomy, rape, robbery, or aggravated arson was major and who manifested a reckless indifference for human life;

9. that, only in the case of a violation of Article 120 [rape]:

    (A) the victim was under the age of 12; or

    (B) the accused maimed or attempted to kill the victim;

10. that, only in the case of a violation of the law of war, death is authorized under the law of war for the offense;

11. that, only in the case of a violation of Article 104 [aiding the enemy] or 106a [espionage]:

    (A) the accused has been convicted of another offense involving espionage or treason for which either a sentence of death or imprisonment for life was authorized by statute; or

    (B) that in committing the offense, the accused knowingly created a grave risk of death to a person other than the individual who was the victim.

Other key features of the military's capital punishment procedure are listed next. Some of the procedures are the same as those in other death penalty jurisdictions, and some of them are unique to the military.

- Before arraignment, the prosecution must provide written notice to the defense of aggravating factors that the prosecution intends to prove.

- Court members (the military's equivalent to civilian jurors) do not need to possess any specific requirements other than being the best qualified by reason of age, education, training, experience, length of service, and judicial temperament. They do not have to hold any particular rank.

- Although the UCMJ requires only five court members, including a military judge, defense counsel is likely to insist on a 12–person panel (because of Supreme Court decision, a panel should never be fewer than six). The accused may not elect to be tried by a military judge alone.

- Capital defendants are entitled to individual military counsel, preferably one with experience defending capital cases. They may also retain civilian counsel. The military is not required to appoint "ABA qualified" civilian defense counsel at government expense.[26]

- A guilty plea may not be accepted for an offense for which the death penalty may be adjudged.

- If death is adjudged, the president (military judge and one of the court members) shall announce which aggravating factors were found by the members.

- A death sentence includes a dishonorable discharge or dismissal, as appropriate. Confinement is a necessary incident of a death sentence but not part of it.

- Convictions and death sentences may be appealed first to the particular branches' court of criminal appeals (e.g., the Army Court of Criminal Appeals); next, to the United States Court of Appeals for the Armed Forces; and finally, to the United States Supreme Court.

- The President of the United States must approve all military executions. The President may also grant a commutation or pardon.

- Execution is by lethal injection.

Conclusion

With the exception of the federal courts, neither the federal government nor the military plays a significant role in the practice of capital punishment. Neither jurisdiction has executed anyone under post-*Furman* statutes—yet, together, they have made many more crimes death-eligible than has any of the states.

Discussion Questions

1. What are four actions the Supreme Court can take when it decides a case it has accepted on appeal?

2. Do you agree with the list of federal capital crimes? Should any of the crimes be removed from the list? Should any crimes be added to the list?

3. Do you agree with the changes in federal habeas corpus made in the Antiterrorism and Effective Death Penalty Act of 1996?

4. What are major procedural differences among the death penalty statutes of the death penalty states, the federal government, and the military?

5. What accounts for the differences identified in question four?

Notes

[1] Material in this section is from Bohm and Haley, 1999:Chap. 7.

[2] Gorecki, 1983:86; Filler, 1967:117.

[3] The list is from the published law itself—Public Law 103-322, September 13, 1994; Snell, 1997:4, Table 2; Coyne and Entzeroth, 1998:151-55.

[4] Death Penalty Information Center, January 1, 1999.

[5] Ibid.

[6] Montgomery, 1994; Death Penalty Information Center, ibid.

[7] *Death Row, USA*, 1998.

[8] Montgomery, op. cit.

[9] *Death Row, USA*, 1998.

[10] U.S. General Accounting Office, 1990.

[11] Baldus and Woodworth, 1998:410; Acker, 1996:150-1.

[12] Ibid.

[13] Baldus and Woodworth, op. cit., pp. 410-11.

[14] Baldus and Woodworth, 1998:410; Acker, 1996:150-1.

[15] Acker, op. cit., p. 151.

[16] Scalia, 1997:9.

[17] See *Felker v. Turpin*, 116 S. Ct. 2333, 1996.

[18] Unless indicated otherwise, information in this section is from Einwechter, 1998; Montgomery, 1994; Wyble, 1985.

[19] Lilly, 1996.

[20] Ibid., p. 497, Table 1.

[21] Ibid., p. 497; Lilly, Davies, and Ball, 1995:2.

[22] Lilly, 1993:13.

[23] Lilly, 1997:11.

[24] *Death Row, USA*, 1998.

[25] The following account of the *Loving* case is from Lilly, 1996:511-12.

[26] ABA (American Bar Association) guidelines require lead trial defense counsel in capital cases to have at least five years criminal defense experience, to have tried no fewer than nine jury trials of serious and complex cases (one of which was a capital case), or to have completed in the last year a CLE course in defending capital cases.

CHAPTER 4

Methods of Execution

Introduction: Cruel and Unusual Punishment

Human beings historically have been quite creative in the methods they have legally employed to put people to death. At one time or another, execution methods have included "flaying and impaling, boiling in oil, crucifixion, pulling asunder, . . . burying alive, and sawing in half."[1] None of those methods has ever been used legally in the United States, but beheading, pressing to death, drawing and quartering, breaking on the wheel, drowning, and burning at the stake were used as late as the 18th century.[2]

The death penalty was one of the punishments brought to the New World by the early European settlers, as were methods of execution. However, as Professor Hugo Adam Bedau points out, "It is curious that any of these barbarous and inhumane methods of execution survived so long, for the English Bill of Rights (1689) proscribed "cruel and unusual punishments."[3] Such punishments were also prohibited by several American state constitutions and by the Eighth Amendment of the United States Constitution.

A Fixed or Historical Meaning. For approximately 120 years after the adoption of the Bill of Rights, the Supreme Court employed a fixed or historical meaning for the concept of cruel and unusual punishment. The Court interpreted the concept's meaning in light of the practices authorized and used at the time that the Eighth Amendment was adopted in 1791. Thus, only the most barbarous punishments and tortures were prohibited. Capital punishment itself was not prohibited because there was explicit reference to it in the Fifth Amendment, and it was in use when the Eighth Amendment was adopted.

The Court, in *Wilkerson v. Utah* (1878), provided examples of punishments that were prohibited by the Eighth Amendment because they involved "torture" or "unnecessary cruelty." They included punishments in which the criminal "was embowelled alive, beheaded, and quartered." The Court expanded the meaning of cruel and unusual punishment in *In re Kemmler* (1890) to include punishments that "involve torture or lingering death . . . something more than the mere extinguishment of life," such as "burning at the stake, crucifixion, breaking on the wheel, or the like."

A New Meaning. In 1910, in the noncapital case of *Weems v. United States,* the Court abandoned its fixed or historical interpretation of cruel and unusual punishment and created a new one. Weems was a U.S. government official in the Philippines convicted of making two false accounting entries amounting to 616 pesos (about $13.25 in 1998 dollars).[4] He was sentenced to 15 years of hard labor and forced to wear chains on his ankles and wrists. After completing his sentence, he was to be under surveillance for the rest of his life, and he was to lose his voting rights as well. Weems argued that his punishment was disproportionate to his crime and, therefore, cruel and unusual.[5]

The Court agreed with Weems and broke with tradition, holding "(1) that the meaning of the Eighth Amendment is not restricted to the intent of the Framers, (2) that the Eighth Amendment bars punishments that are excessive, and (3) that what is excessive is not fixed in time but changes with evolving social conditions."[6] Thenceforward, the Court no longer used the fixed or historical interpretation; it chose instead to interpret the concept in the context of "evolving social conditions."

The Court further clarified its position nearly 50 years later in another noncapital case, *Trop v. Dulles* (1958). As punishment for desertion during World War II, Trop was stripped of his U.S. citizenship.[7] The Court reviewed the case on appeal and ruled that the punishment was cruel and unusual because it was an affront to basic human dignity. It noted that the "dignity of man" was "the basic concept underlying the Eighth Amendment," and it held that Trop's punishment exceeded "the limits of civilized standards." Referring to the earlier *Weems* case, the Court emphasized that "the limits of civilized standards . . . draws its meaning from the evolving standards of decency that mark the progress of

> *In* Weems v. United States *(1910), the Supreme Court held "(1) that the meaning of the Eighth Amendment is not restricted to the intent of the Framers, (2) that the Eighth Amendment bars punishments that are excessive, and (3) that what is excessive is not fixed in time but changes with evolving social conditions."*

a maturing society." Those evolving standards are, in turn, determined by "objective indicators, such as the enactments of legislatures as expressions of 'the will of the people,' the decisions of juries, and the subjective moral judgments of members of the Supreme Court itself."[8] In short, it appears that as long as a punishment has been enacted by a legislature, imposed by a jury, and approved of by the Supreme Court, it will not be considered cruel and unusual.

For a century after the ratification of the Eighth Amendment, hanging was the only legally authorized method of execution in the United States. The one exception was that spies, traitors, and deserters convicted under federal statutes could be shot.[9] Five methods of execution are currently authorized in various jurisdictions in the United States: (1) hanging, (2) firing squad, (3) electrocution, (4) lethal gas, and (5) lethal injection.

Hanging

Hanging was one of the first lawful execution methods used in the United States. Although its use declined dramatically after the introduction of the electric chair in 1890, more people—at least 70 percent of the total—have been executed by hanging than by any other method.[10]

The slow and agonizing deaths caused by hangings prior to the nineteenth century were meant to be instructive for the public and degrading to the person executed. Quicker and more dignified methods of execution were firing squad and beheading.[11] In the nineteenth century, British master hangmen discovered the "long drop"—a fall sufficiently long to break the neck and cause relatively quick and painless death.[12] The long drop proved a more humane technique than the previous strangulation method, but in some cases it still took up to 20 minutes to cause death.[13]

*F*ive methods of execution are currently authorized in various jurisdictions in the United States: (1) hanging, (2) firing squad, (3) electrocution, (4) lethal gas, and (5) lethal injection.

There were also numerous botched hangings. At least 170 legal hangings performed in the United States between 1622 and 1993 were botched.[14] Before routine use of the long drop, most of the flawed hangings resulted in slow and painful strangulation. An improperly administered long drop (that is, if the drop were too long) could cause decapitation. As late as the 1960s, for example, at the state prison in Walla Walla, Washington, a hanging resulted in the inmate's head nearly being torn off and witnesses to the execution being spattered with blood.[15]

Three states (Delaware, New Hampshire, and Washington) still allow hanging;[16] however, all three also authorize lethal injection. Delaware authorizes lethal injection for those sentenced after June 13, 1986; for those sentenced before that date, the condemned prisoner may select lethal injection or hanging. New Hampshire authorizes hanging only if lethal injection cannot be given (see note 45). In Washington, the choice is the condemned prisoner's to make. If the prisoner fails to choose, the method is hanging. The first person executed by hanging in the United States since 1965 was child-killer Westley Allan Dodd, on January 5, 1993, in the state of Washington.[17]

Firing Squad

Execution by firing squad currently remains an option in two states: Idaho and Utah.[18] The other method authorized in both states is lethal injection. In Idaho, the choice is made by the Director of the Department of Corrections; in Utah, the condemned prisoner makes the choice. If the prisoner refuses to choose, the method is lethal injection.

Firing squads in Utah consist of five volunteer marksmen. Four of them are given rifles with live rounds and one of them is given a rifle with blanks.[19] The rifle with blanks maintains the fiction that none of the shooters will know who fired the fatal shot. In reality, the kick produced by live rounds is easily distinguishable from the kick produced by blanks, and any firearms expert would have no trouble telling the difference. The inmate is seated and strapped to a chair with a hood over his head and a bull's-eye over his heart. Following a signal from the warden, the shooters fire at the bull's-eye. There is no solid evidence, but it is presumed that a competently performed execution by firing squad causes a quick death with little or no pain. When given a choice between death by firing squad and death by hanging, most inmates choose the former. Botched executions by firing squad are rare.

The most celebrated recent execution by firing squad was the January 17, 1977 execution of Gary Gilmore in Utah.[20] Gilmore was the first person executed in the United States in a decade and the first person executed under post-*Furman* statutes. Unlike most death row inmates, Gilmore had voluntarily waived his right to appeal and demanded that the state of Utah carry out his sentence. His case was appealed anyway without his consent, and he received three stays of execution. While in prison, he twice tried to commit suicide. His last words were "Let's do it."

> *The most celebrated recent execution by firing squad was the January 17, 1977 execution of Gary Gilmore in Utah. Gilmore was the first person executed in the United States in a decade and the first person executed under post-Furman statutes.*

Electrocution

Electrocution is the only legally authorized method of execution in four states, and it is an option in six others.[21] It is the only method in Alabama, Florida, Georgia, and Nebraska. Ohio and Virginia authorize a choice of electrocution or lethal injection. If an Ohio inmate refuses to choose, the method is electrocution; if a Virginia inmate refuses to choose, the method is lethal injection. Arkansas, Kentucky, South Carolina, and Tennessee offer the same choice to death row inmates whose offenses occurred before March 4, 1983, March 31, 1988, January 4, 1996, and January 1, 1999, respectively. For those whose capital offenses occur after those dates, there is no choice—execution is by lethal injection. Although many

> *During the twentieth century, more people have been executed by electrocution than by any other method.*

states have recently abandoned electrocution, between 1930 and 1972 it was the method employed by 25 states; hanging was employed in 13 states and lethal gas in 11.[22] During the twentieth century, more people have been executed by electrocution than by any other method.[23]

The history of electrocution as a method of capital punishment is both fascinating and instructive.[24] The electric chair is an American invention and an unintended product of a corporate battle between the Westinghouse and Edison companies. In the late 1880s, competition was fierce over which of the two companies would "electrify" American cities. Westinghouse was successfully touting its alternating current

(AC), while Edison was promoting, somewhat less successfully than Westinghouse, its direct current (DC). A problem with Edison's direct current was that low transmission voltages reduced its range to just a mile beyond the generator that produced it. There was no such problem with alternating current. In addition, alternating current proved cheaper than direct current to transmit. Trying to beat its competition, Edison staged public demonstrations during which animals were electrocuted with Westinghouse's alternating current to show how dangerous their competitor's product was.

The governor of New York, meanwhile, dissatisfied with hanging as the state's method of execution, appointed a three-member commission to determine and recommend to the legislature "the most humane and practical method [of execution] known to modern science." One of the commission members was Dr. Alfred P. Southwick, a dentist from Buffalo, who believed that electrocution would be preferable to hanging. Before his appointment to the commission, Dr. Southwick (later known as the "father of electrocution") had witnessed a man touch an electric generator and die what appeared to be a fast and painless death. Southwick also witnessed and conducted the electrocution of animals in demonstrations like those performed by the Edison company. Southwick enlisted the help of Edison, who already was an American hero, to persuade the other commission members to endorse electrocution as the new method of execution. Edison personally opposed capital punishment, but he agreed to help Southwick, who had convinced him that the issue was not whether capital punishment should be employed, but rather what form it should take.

The commission did recommend that hanging be replaced with electrocution. Interestingly, the commission also considered lethal injection (as well as the guillotine and the garrote) as an alternative to hanging but rejected injection because of protests from the medical profession. Doctors feared that people would associate death with the hypodermic needle and the practice of medicine. On June 4, 1888, the legislature, with little opposition, enacted New York's Electrical Execution Act. The act provided that anyone sentenced to die after January 1, 1889, would be electrocuted instead of hanged. The act did not, however, stipulate what type of current would be employed. That matter was left to the Medico-Legal Society of New York to decide. Following a number of experiments on animals, it was decided that Westinghouse's alternating current (AC) would be used.

William Kemmler became the first person to die by legally authorized electrocution on August 6, 1890. Kemmler had been convicted of the brutal first-degree murder of his girlfriend, who he believed was involved with another man. Although there was little doubt about his guilt, his appeals drew much public interest. In an effort to block the ultimate test of alternating current's lethality, Westinghouse retained for Kemmler one of the nation's leading lawyers, W. Bourke Cockran, and reportedly spent more than $100,000 on the appeals.

The case ultimately reached the Supreme Court. Kemmler's lawyer, however, failed to convince the Court that death by electrocution was cruel and unusual. The Court refused to decide Kemmler's claim, arguing that the Eighth Amendment did not apply to the states (*In re Kemmler* [1890]).[25] By taking that position, the Court did not have to scrutinize the New York state legislature's conclusion that electrocution produced "instantaneous, and, therefore, painless death."

Eyewitness reports of Kemmler's execution belie the legislature's conclusion. Kemmler did not die "instantaneously"[26]—a second jolt of electricity had to be administered four-and-a-half minutes after the first one. During the second jolt, witnesses observed Kemmler's hair and flesh burning and blood on his face. His body emitted a horrible stench. Whether his death was a "painless" one is uncertain. Electricians blamed faulty equipment for the botched execution. Among the problems were the failure to provide enough power, an uninterrupted current, and adequate contact between the electrodes and Kemmler's body. Reaction to the bungled execution was mixed. Some commentators argued that death by electrocution was worse than hanging; others believed it was not. It was even suggested that the execution was intentionally sabotaged to deter further use of the alternating current. Not surprisingly, Westinghouse stated that "[t]hey could have done better with an axe." Experts on electricity, such as Thomas Edison and Nikola Tesla, publicly debated whether electrocution was so horrible that it should never have been invented. Both proponents and opponents of capital punishment called for repeal of New York's Electrical Execution Act, but to no avail.

Nearly a year after Kemmler's execution, New York electrocuted four men in one day and a fifth man later that year. Despite continued reports of flawed electrocutions, numerous other states were quick to adopt the new method and, as noted at the beginning of this section, electrocution became the method used by a majority of executing states between 1930 and 1972.[27]

Botched electrocutions are not a thing of the past. Following are three more recent newspaper accounts.[28]

- The state's [Georgia's] first try at executing Alpha Otis Stephens in the electric chair failed today, and he struggled to breathe for eight minutes before a second jolt carried out his death sentence.[29]

- [In Michigan City, Indiana] five jolts of electricity instead of the prescribed two were needed today to execute William E. Vandiver. . . . A prison doctor said Vandiver, 37, was still breathing after the first round of 2,300 volts and second of 500 volts were applied at 12:03 a.m. Three more blasts of current were applied before he was pronounced dead 17 minutes later.[30]

- The replacement of a worn sponge in the headpiece of the electric chair by two maintenance workers at Florida State Prison led to the botched execution of Jesse Tafero. Their action triggered an eruption of smoke and flames from Tafero's head. . . . When the first jolt of 2,000-volt electricity hit Tafero, the sponge in the headpiece gave off a combustible gas, which shot smoke and flames from the top of the leather hood hiding Tafero's face. The flames—described as 3 inches to a foot long—horrified witnesses. Tafero's attorney described the flawed execution as torture. . . . Between the jolts, witnesses observed Tafero seemingly gasping for air.[31]

Lethal Gas

Seeking a more humane method of execution, in 1921 the Nevada legislature passed a "Humane Death Bill."[32] The legislation replaced hanging with death by lethal gas, which had gained attention because of its use in World War I. The condemned inmate was to be executed in his or her cell, while asleep and without any warning. Governor Emmet Boyle, who personally opposed the death penalty, nevertheless signed the legislation, believing that, upon challenge, it would be ruled unconstitutional as a cruel and unusual punishment.

The first person sentenced to die under the new legislation was Gee Jon, who was convicted of a gangland murder. Jon was a member of a "tong," in this case an organized Chinese crime association. Jon appealed his death sentence to the Nevada Supreme Court, which, to the surprise of Governor Boyle, upheld the constitutionality of lethal gas. When prison officials realized the impracticality of executing Jon in his cell while he slept, they quickly built a chamber for the purpose, and on February 8, 1924, Jon became the first person to be lawfully executed with a lethal dose of cyanide gas.

By 1927, Arizona, California, Colorado, North Carolina, and Wyoming had passed legislation requiring executions to be carried out using lethal gas. By 1970, 10 states (which, in addition to the aforementioned, included Maryland, Mississippi, Missouri, and New Mexico) used lethal gas as their sole method of execution, but by 1992, Maryland was the only state to do so.[33] Maryland abandoned lethal gas for lethal injection in 1994, except for inmates whose sentence was imposed before the change in statute. They have a choice between lethal gas and lethal injection.

Lethal gas is currently an option in only four states.[34] California and Missouri authorize both lethal gas and lethal injection.[35] If the condemned inmate refuses to choose, the method is lethal gas. Arizona authorizes lethal injection for persons whose capital sentence was imposed after November 15, 1992; for those who were sentenced before that date, the condemned prisoner may select lethal injection or lethal gas. If the condemned prisoner refuses to choose, the method is lethal injection. Maryland authorizes lethal injection for those sentenced after March 11, 1994; for those who were sentenced before that date, the condemned prisoner may select lethal injection or lethal gas.

A newspaper account of the 1979 execution of Jesse Bishop in Nevada describes death by lethal gas:

> After a metal door to the 10-by-10 death chamber clanged shut, three volunteer guards flipped switches to activate the device that lowered cyanide pellets into acid beneath the death seat. Only one of the switches was live, so none of the guards knew which one would kill Bishop. . . . [When the] cyanide pellets fell into the acid bath, unleashing deadly gas, Bishop wrinkled his nose, seemed to search the room and breathed deeply several times. His eyes rolled upward, his head fell on his chest and then snapped back. He took another deep breath and closed his eyes—for the last time. Bishop's face reddened, saliva ran from his mouth and his body shuddered. After a series of convulsive jerks, it was over.[36]

Lethal Injection

In the continuing quest to find more humane and publicly acceptable methods of execution, Oklahoma became the first jurisdiction in the United States to authorize lethal injection as an execution method.[37] The legislation, passed on May 11, 1977, replaced electrocution with the "continuous, intravenous administration of a lethal quantity of an ultrashort–acting barbiturate in combination with a chemical paralytic agent."[38] The three chemicals most commonly used in lethal injections are (1) sodium thiopental or sodium pentothal, a common anesthetic used in surgery, which is the ultrashort–acting barbiturate that is supposed to induce a deep sleep and loss of consciousness in about 20 seconds, (2) pancuronium bromide, a total muscle relaxant, and (3) potassium chloride, which induces cardiac arrest.[39]

Economic matters played a major role in Oklahoma's change to lethal injection. Legislators were concerned that the electric chair, which had not been used since 1966, would be too expensive to return to good working order. The cost of fixing the chair was estimated to be $62,000.[40] Execution by lethal gas was rejected because of the estimated $300,000 cost of a gas chamber.[41] Lethal injection was estimated to cost less than $15 per execution.[42] Also favoring the use of lethal injection was the argument that persons executed by this method could donate all of their bodily organs for medical transplants. Other execution methods limited this possibility.

Texas, Idaho, and New Mexico were quick to follow Oklahoma in adopting lethal injection as their method of execution. In Florida, however, a 1979 bill calling for the replacement of electrocution with lethal injection was defeated in the state legislature. Opposed to the legislation were medical doctors, and especially anesthesiologists, who argued that, among other things, no assurances could be given that the barbiturates would not wear off before death occurred, causing the condemned inmate to wake up and slowly suffocate to death. The 1980 annual meeting of the American Medical Association saw a resolution passed urging doctors not to be participants in executions by lethal injection. To participate would constitute a violation of the Hippocratic Oath and international medical principles, and would represent "a corruption and exploitation of the healing profession's role in society." The resolution was mostly symbolic, however, because no state's death penalty statute required that a licensed doctor perform the lethal injection. Nevertheless, a 1994 study by the American College of Physicians, Human Rights Watch, the National

> *In the continuing quest to find more humane and publicly acceptable methods of execution, Oklahoma became the first jurisdiction in the United States to authorize lethal injection as an execution method. The legislation, passed on May 11, 1977, replaced electrocution with the "continuous, intravenous administration of a lethal quantity of an ultrashort–acting barbiturate in combination with a chemical paralytic agent."*

Coalition to Abolish the Death Penalty, and Physicians for Human Rights found that 29 of the then 37 capital punishment states required the presence or participation of a physician at all executions, and that no licensing boards in any of the states were enforcing the prohibition.[43]

The first person executed by lethal injection was Charles Brooks, Jr., in Texas, on December 7, 1982. He was sentenced to die on December 14, 1976, for the murder of David Gregory in Forth Worth. Brooks was also the first black man to be executed in the United States since 1967 and the first person executed in Texas since 1964.[44]

The only challenge to lethal injection as an execution method that the Supreme Court has been willing to hear was *Heckler v. Chaney* (470 U.S. 821, 1985). In this case, inmates in Oklahoma and Texas claimed that the Food and Drug Administration (FDA) as required by law had not approved the drugs used in lethal injections for that purpose. The plaintiffs claimed that to use approved drugs for unapproved purposes violates the misbranding prohibition of the Federal Food, Drug, and Cosmetic Act. The plaintiffs wanted the FDA to approve the drugs for the purpose of human execution; the FDA refused to do so. The Court dodged the issue, maintaining that the FDA's discretionary authority in refusing the plaintiffs' demands was not subject to judicial review.

Theoretically, death by lethal injection should be a more humane method of execution than any of the other methods then or now in use. The popular image is one in which the condemned inmate painlessly falls asleep (forever) on a hospital gurney. Perhaps the New York legislature of 100 years ago, in its rejection of lethal injection as a less humane method of execution than electrocution,[45] showed an insight still valid today. Despite the creation of elaborate machines to administer the lethal drugs, problems still arise.[46] Consider, for example, the following newspaper account of the 1988 execution of Raymond Landry in Texas:

> Prison officials began administering the lethal dosage [to Landry] at 12:21 a.m. Landry was not pronounced dead until 24 minutes later. In between, a tube attached to a needle inside his right arm began leaking, sending the lethal mixture shooting across the death chamber toward witnesses. "There was something of a delay in the execution because of what officials called a 'blowout'. . . . The syringe came out of the vein and the warden ordered the (execution) team to reinsert the catheter into the vein." The leak occurred two minutes after the injections began.[47]

Another problem that could occur in lethal injections, although it would be nearly impossible to detect, is that an inadequate dose of sodium pentothal would cause the inmate to retain consciousness and suffer great pain during the injections of the second and third chemicals.[48] A similar problem would occur if the three chemicals were administered out of sequence.

Lethal injection is the method of execution provided by the most states (34), at least as an option, as well as by the U.S. military and the U.S. government.[49] For the military, the government, and in the following 19 states, it is the sole method of execution: Colorado, Connecticut, Illinois, Indiana, Kansas, Louisiana, Mississippi, Montana, Nevada, New Jersey, New Mexico, New York, North Carolina, Oklahoma, Oregon,

> ■ *L*ethal injection is the method of execution provided by the most states (34), at least as an option, as well as by the U.S. military and the U.S. government.

Pennsylvania, South Dakota, Texas, and Wyoming. In Arkansas, lethal injection is the authorized mode of execution for those convicted after July 4, 1983; for Arizona, after November 15, 1992; for Delaware, after June 13, 1986; for Kentucky, after March 31, 1998; for Maryland, after March 24, 1994; for New Hampshire, if it can be given; for South Carolina, after January 4, 1996; and for Tennessee, after January 1, 1999. Lethal injection is one of two options in the following seven states: California, Idaho, Missouri, Ohio, Utah, Virginia, and Washington.

Lethal injection is also the method by which the most people have been executed under post-*Furman* statutes (since 1976). As of August 19, 1998, 473 people had been executed in the United States under post-*Furman* statutes. The number of executions by method employed are as follows: lethal injection (318); electrocution (140); lethal gas (10); hanging (3); firing squad (2).[50]

Conclusion

Law professor Deborah Denno argues that if the Supreme Court were willing to hear Eighth Amendment challenges to all current execution methods, to consider available evidence demonstrating the cruelty of those methods, and to apply both the "death is different" and "evolving standards of decency" criteria, it would be forced to conclude that all current methods of execution are unconstitutional.[51] Denno believes that if the Court were to follow such a course, it would also have to declare the death penalty itself unconstitutional because no method of punishment could meet the required standards. Denno may be overly optimistic on the latter point.

In the future, death penalty jurisdictions may require executions to be conducted using methods designed (and possibly approved) for human euthanasia. For example, an execution during which the condemned prisoner dies by inhaling carbon monoxide from a mask and tank—a preferred method of euthanasia expert, Dr. Jack Kevorkian—might meet the required criteria. Criminal justice futurist Gene Stephens predicts that executions may one day be conducted using ultrasound which would literally "dematerialize" the condemned inmate. An added benefit to ultrasound is that it would eliminate the costs of disposing of the body.[52] If the death penalty continues to be employed, the future will likely bring execution methods which are now beyond imagination.

Discussion Questions

1. Do you agree with the Supreme Court's definition of "cruel and unusual punishment"?

2. Are any of the current execution methods cruel and unusual punishments?

3. Should execution methods be cruel (and unusual)?

4. Should we be concerned about botched executions? What should be done about them?

Notes

[1] Bedau, 1982:14; also see Denno, 1994:566, fn. 87.
[2] Bedau, ibid.; Denno, ibid., p. 563.
[3] Bedau, ibid., p. 15.
[4] Paternoster, 1991:51.
[5] Ibid.
[6] Ibid., p. 52.
[7] Ibid.
[8] Ibid., p. 53.
[9] Bedau, op. cit.
[10] Percentage calculated by dividing 16,000 hangings cited in Denno, op. cit., p. 680, by the more liberal 22,500 total execution estimate of Espy.
[11] Denno, op. cit., p. 679.
[12] Ibid.
[13] Ibid.
[14] Ibid., p. 686.
[15] Ibid., p. 682.
[16] Denno, 1997:Appendix 3; Stephan and Snell, 1996:Table 2; Death Penalty Information Center, January 25, 1999.
[17] Denno, 1994, op. cit., p. 683.
[18] Denno, 1997, op. cit.; Stephan and Snell, op. cit.
[19] See Denno, 1994, op. cit., pp. 687-88.
[20] See, for example, Mailer, 1979.
[21] Denno, 1997, op. cit.; Stephan and Snell, op. cit.; Death Penalty Information Center, January 25, 1999.
[22] Paternoster, op. cit., p. 23.
[23] Denno, 1994, op. cit., p. 557.
[24] The following account is from Denno, 1994, op. cit.; Bedau, 1982, op. cit., pp. 15-16; Paternoster, op. cit., pp. 14-15.
[25] The Court made the Eighth Amendment applicable to the states in 1962, see *Robinson v. California*, 370 U.S. 660.
[26] The specific cause of death from electrocution is presumed to be extensive electrical damage to the nervous system.
[27] It is interesting that electrocution is considered an acceptable method for human executions but unacceptable for animal euthanasia. According to the American Veterinarian Medical Association, "electrocution [is] an unacceptable method unless it is preceded by an injury inducing immediate unconsciousness, such as a blow to the head, because electrocution alone will not lead to unconsciousness

for 10-to-30 seconds or longer" (cited in Denno, 1997). For an explicit description of the execution by electrocution of John Evans in Alabama, see Canan, 1989.

[28] Denno ,1997, op. cit., Appendix 2A, provides descriptions of 14 botched electrocutions since 1976.

[29] *The Anniston (Alabama) Star*, December 12, 1984.

[30] Ibid., October 16, 1985. Heart death cannot be ensured with voltages of less than 2,000 volts. Current exceeding six amps can cause excessive burning of the flesh, see Denno, 1997, op. cit.

[31] *Charlotte (North Carolina) Observer*, May 10, 1990.

[32] See Bedau, op. cit., p. 16.

[33] Denno, 1997, op. cit.

[34] Denno, 1997, op. cit., Appendix 3; Stephan and Snell, op. cit.; Death Penalty Information Center, January 25, 1999.

[35] For detailed descriptions of executions by lethal gas at San Quentin in California, see Kroll, 1989.

[36] *The Anniston (Alabama) Star*, October 22, 1979. Because of the pain and agony experienced by Jesse Bishop, Nevada changed its method of execution from lethal gas to lethal injection. As was the case with electrocution, it is interesting that lethal gas is considered an acceptable method for human executions but unacceptable for animal euthanasia. Dr. Richard Traystman, Director of the Anesthesiology and Critical Care Medicine Research Laboratories at Johns Hopkins Medical School, states, "[W]e would not use asphyxiation, by cyanide gas or by any other substance, in our laboratory to kill animals that have been used in experiments—nor would most medical research laboratories in this country use it" (cited in Denno, 1997). For a description of eight botched executions by lethal gas since 1976, see Denno, 1997, op. cit., Appendix 2A.

[37] See Bedau, op. cit., pp. 17-19.

[38] Ibid., p. 17.

[39] Denno, 1997, op. cit.

[40] Ibid.

[41] Ibid.

[42] Currently, the cost of drugs used in lethal injections averages about $70 per execution. See ibid.

[43] Recer, 1994.

[44] Reinhold, 1982.

[45] In 1953, the British Royal Commission on Capital Punishment concluded that lethal injection as a method of capital punishment was deficient for four reasons: (1) it "could not be administered to individuals with certain 'physical abnormalities' that make veins impossible to locate, and that even 'normal' veins can be flattened by cold or nervousness, conditions oftentimes characteristic of an execution setting"; (2) it "is difficult unless the subject fully cooperates and keeps 'absolutely still'"; (3) "although a qualified [*sic*] injection requires medical skill, the medical profession was opposed to participating in the process"; and (4) "because of all such problems, the Commission concluded that it was likely that executioners would have to implement intramuscular (rather than intravenous) injection even though the intramuscular method would be slower and more painful." Cited in Denno, 1997, op. cit.

[46] Denno, 1997, op. cit., Appendix 2C, provides descriptions of 22 botched executions by lethal injection since 1976.

[47] *The Anniston (Alabama) Star*, December 13, 1988.

[48] Denno, 1997, op. cit.

[49] Denno, 1997, op. cit., Appendix 3; Stephan and Snell, op. cit.; Death Penalty Information Center, January 25, 1999.

[50] Death Penalty Information Center, August 19, 1998.

[51] Denno, 1997, op. cit.; 1998; also see Gottlieb, 1961.

[52] Stephens, 1990. Another possibility is the return to a method employed in antiquity. For example, in 399 B.C., Socrates was condemned to drink a cup of hemlock, an execution method that produced a relatively dignified and presumably painless death.

CHAPTER 5

General Deterrence
and the Death Penalty

The next several chapters consider rationales or justifications for capital punishment, as well as arguments against its use. Available evidence is presented and evaluated. This chapter examines general deterrence—the belief that people in general can be prevented from engaging in crime by punishing specific individuals and making examples of them. In the context of this book, the broad deterrence question is whether or not executions prevent people other than the person executed from committing capital crimes.[1]

Another type of deterrence is specific or special deterrence—the prevention of individuals from committing crime again by punishing them. Special or specific deterrence does not apply to capital punishment because execution precludes the determination of whether a punished individual returns to crime. When people want to forever prevent prisoners from reoffending, they desire incapacitation and not specific or special deterrence. Capital punishment ensures incapacitation, which is one of the most compelling rationales in support of the death penalty. Incapacitation is the subject of the next chapter. Subsequent chapters address the costs of capital punishment, miscarriages of justice, arbitrariness and discrimination in the death penalty's administration, retribution, and religious arguments. The last chapter is devoted to public opinion about the death penalty.

The Relative Importance of General Deterrence

Until recently, general deterrence was the reason cited most often when people were asked why they supported the death penalty.[2] This was a curious finding because other research found that retribution was the primary basis of death penalty support.[3] Professors Phoebe Ellsworth and Lee Ross contend that the reason for the paradox is that deterrence is more scientific or socially desirable than retribution: "people mention it [deterrence] first because its importance is obvious, not because its importance is real."[4] Ellsworth and Ross's contention is supported by their finding that compelling evidence of no deterrent effect would not have much effect on people's death penalty support. In other words, a majority of death penalty supporters would not change their opinion even if it were proven to them that their belief in general deterrence was wrong.

83

Deterrence no longer seems to be an important rationale for death penalty proponents. According to recent a Gallup poll, when asked their reasons for supporting the death penalty, only 13 percent of respondents chose "it is a deterrent,"[5] while 50 percent chose "a life for a life" (that is, retribution).

Arguments and Counterarguments

Philosopher Ernest Van den Haag explains why one should believe in the general deterrent effect of the death penalty. In the first place, he says, "our penal system rests on the proposition that more severe penalties are more deterrent than less severe penalties."[6] If this is true, he asserts, the corollary is that "the most severe penalty—the death penalty—would have the greatest deterrent effect."[7] He adds that "arguments to the contrary assume either that capital crimes never are deterrable (sometimes because not all capital crimes have been deterred), or that, beyond some point, the deterrent effect of added severity is necessarily zero."[8]

Professor Van den Haag's first assumption—more severe penalties are more deterrent than less severe penalties—is generally correct. Beyond a point, though, added severity may reduce deterrence. In England during the eighteenth century, for example, there were about 150 capital crimes. Many of the crimes were so petty that juries chose not to convict clearly guilty defendants rather than having to condemn them to die. The practice is called jury nullification.[9] Such a practice likely reduces any general deterrent effect.

Professor Van den Haag's corollary—the most severe penalty, the death penalty, would have the greatest deterrent effect—is based on a debatable assumption and a testable proposition with no scientific evidence to support it. Is the death penalty the most severe penalty? For many, it may be; but for others, it may not. The prospect of spending the rest of one's life in prison may be more terrifying to some people than death, as it apparently was for Gary Gilmore.

Taking the opposite position to Van den Haag, Cesare Beccaria, the eighteenth century philosopher whose ideas are the basis of much of the criminal justice process in the United States today, claimed that life imprisonment (he called it "perpetual servitude") is probably a greater deterrent than death:

> To anyone raising the argument that perpetual servitude is as painful as death and therefore equally cruel, I will reply that, adding up all the moments of unhappiness of servitude, it may well be even more cruel; but these are drawn out over an entire lifetime, while the pain of death exerts its whole force in a moment. And precisely this is the advantage of penal servitude, that it inspires terror in the spectator more than in the sufferer, for the former considers the entire sum of unhappy moments, while the latter is distracted from the thought of future misery by that of the present moment.[10]

Although Beccaria could never have imagined the prolonged process now operative in the United States—a process that takes an average of 10 years to complete[11]—he still may be correct that life imprisonment is a more severe punishment (and better deterrent) than execution. In any case, he did not think much of capital punishment, calling it a "useless prodigality of torments" that "never made men better."[12] He believed that "the death penalty cannot be useful, because of the example of barbarity it gives men."[13]

Abolitionists maintain that the important question is not whether capital punishment is the severest punishment, but rather what punishment should be the severest allowed by law. As noted in the last chapter, not all punishments are legally allowed. The United States Constitution prohibits cruel and unusual punishments. Interestingly, how a person answers the question of what punishment should be the severest allowed by law may be what ultimately divides people on the death penalty issue.

Even if it were agreed that the death penalty is the severest penalty (and that at least some capital crimes are deterrable), the problem remains that there is no scientific evidence showing conclusively that the death penalty has any marginal effect. There is no evidence that capital punishment deters more than an alternative noncapital punishment, such as life imprisonment without opportunity for parole.[14] Instead, statistics indicate that capital punishment makes no discernible difference on homicide or murder rates.

> *There* is no scientific evidence showing conclusively that the death penalty has any marginal deterrent effect. There is no evidence showing that capital punishment deters more than an alternative noncapital punishment, such as life imprisonment without opportunity for parole.

Evidence

When considering the deterrence question, it is useful to distinguish between pre- and post–1975 studies because, until 1975, there were no scientific data showing that capital punishment had a significant (or greater than a chance) effect on homicide or murder rates.[15] This finding held, despite more than 40 years of research and dozens of studies.

Pre–1975 Studies. The pre-1975 studies generally employed one of three basic research designs.[16] The first type compares murder rates of states with and without a capital punishment statute. For example, Professor Thorsten Sellin compared the average annual homicide death rates (per 100,000 population) in contiguous states with and without capital punishment for the years 1920 through 1963.[17] If capital punishment had a marginal deterrent effect, one would expect that states without capital punishment would have higher homicide rates than states with capital punishment—all other things being equal. States next to each other were compared in an effort to control for other possibly influential factors. Sellin found no persuasive evidence of deterrence. The following are among his findings:

- The average annual homicide death rates for Michigan (without capital punishment), Indiana (with capital punishment), and Ohio (with capital punishment) during the time period were all 3.5.

- Rates for Minnesota (without capital punishment), Wisconsin (without capital punishment), and Iowa (with capital punishment) were 1.4, 1.2, and 1.4, respectively; rates for North Dakota (without capital punishment), South Dakota (with capital punishment), and Nebraska (with capital punishment) were 1.0, 1.5, and 1.8, respectively.

- Rates for Maine (without capital punishment), New Hampshire (with capital punishment), and Vermont (with capital punishment) were 1.5, 0.9, and 1.0, respectively.

- Rates for Rhode Island (without capital punishment), Massachusetts (with capital punishment), and Connecticut (with capital punishment) were 1.3, 1.2, and 1.7, respectively.

Again, those data fail to reveal a marginal deterrent effect for the death penalty.[18]

Sellin also employed his comparative method to the specific cases of police killings and prison murders.[19] Regarding police killings, Sellin wanted to test whether or not capital punishment provided police officers an added measure of protection. It was (and still is) assumed by many people that the threat of execution deters criminals from carrying guns and using them when they face arrest.[20] Sellin examined rates of municipal police killings for contiguous states per 10 years and 100,000 population for the years 1919 through 1954. As with his previous comparisons of general homicide rates for contiguous states, Sellin did not find that the availability of capital punishment had any discernible effect on the rate of police killings. Specifically, he reported that the rate of police killings in 82 cities in abolition states was 1.2, while the rate in 182 cities in death penalty states was 1.3.[21] Sellin observed in an editorial postscript to his study that from 1961 through 1963, 140 police officers were killed in the United States: 9 in abolition states and 131 in death penalty states. When he computed the average annual risk for the three years per 10,000 police in abolition states and contiguous death penalty states, he found a rate of 1.312 in the abolition states and 1.328 for the bordering death penalty states—not a significant difference.[22]

With regard to prison murders, Sellin researched whether, if capital punishment were an effective deterrent to murder, it would be reasonable to assume that inmates and correctional staff in prisons in abolition states would be in greater jeopardy for their lives than inmates and correctional staff in prisons in death penalty states because in abolition states there is no death penalty threat to deter would-be killers. The answer he found was that the evidence did not support the intuitive belief.[23] To the contrary, in 1965, there were 61 prison killings in the 37 jurisdictions that responded to his survey—8 of the victims were staff members and 53 were inmates. All of the staff members and 85 percent of the inmates were killed in death penalty states. Wendy Wolfson, who examined prison killings in 52 jurisdictions in the United States in 1973, has reported similar findings.[24] Of the 124 prison killings in 1973,

11 of the victims were staff members and 113 were inmates. Ninety-one percent of the staff member victims and 95 percent of the inmate victims were killed in death penalty jurisdictions. These data clearly show that prison staff members and inmates are no safer in prisons in death penalty states than in prisons in abolition states. The threat of death does not seem to effectively deter prison killings.[25]

The principal criticism of studies such as Sellin's is that the comparative results are weak evidence of deterrence (or its absence), because contiguous states are not necessarily comparable in all important respects. In attempting to overcome the criticism, studies have been conducted that compare several important factors that could affect the murder rates in the contiguous states.[26] Examples of such factors include probability of apprehension, probability of conviction, labor force participation, unemployment rate, population aged 15 through 24, real per-capita income, nonwhite population, civilian population, per-capita government expenditures (state and local), and per-capita police expenditures (state and local).[27] When those factors are compared for the contiguous states, no apparent reason emerges for the absence of a deterrent effect for capital punishment. Still, the criticism remains that the early comparative studies fail to account for the simultaneous influence of the other possible influential factors. That criticism would later be addressed using new, more powerful statistical analytic techniques.

A second type of research design compares murder rates before and after the abolition and/or reinstatement of the death penalty.[28] If capital punishment has a deterrent effect, one would expect higher murder rates in states following abolition of the death penalty or lower rates following its reinstatement—all other things being equal. But before-and-after studies reveal no apparent deterrent effect for capital punishment.

A particularly interesting example of the "before-and-after" methodology using cross-national comparisons is a study by Professors Dane Archer, Rosemary Gartner, and Marc Beittel.[29] The researchers examined homicide rate changes for selected countries one year, five years (where possible), and the maximum possible years before and after abolition of the death penalty. The countries (dates of abolition, except for extraordinary crimes, are in parentheses) were: Austria (1968), Canada (1967), Denmark (1930), England and Wales (1965), Finland (1949), Israel (1954), Italy (1890), Netherland Antilles (1957), Norway (1905), Sweden (1921), and Switzerland (1942). In some countries, homicide rates increased following abolition, and in other countries, the rates decreased, but there were more decreases than increases. In short, these data do not show that capital punishment has a consistent or, for that matter, any deterrent effect. Fluctuations in homicide rates before and after abolition are probably a function of factors other than capital punishment. A problem with before-and-after studies is that they fail to control for other possibly influential factors.

The third type of research design examines short-term murder trends just before and just after highly publicized executions of convicted murderers.[30] If capital punishment has a deterrent effect, one would expect murder rates to decrease after these executions—all other things being equal. Some of the studies do reveal a short-term deterrent effect,[31] but in no case does the decrease in homicides last very long. Moreover, replications and reanalyses of these studies tend to show brutalizing, rather than deterrent, effects of execution publicity (more about brutalizing effects later).[32] This method does not provide any evidence of a long-term deterrent effect for capital punishment. The major problem with this method, like the other two, is the failure to adequately control for other possibly influential factors on homicides or murders.

In sum, none of the studies using any of the three research designs produced evidence to support a belief in the (long-term) deterrent effect of the death penalty. If the death penalty were an effective deterrent to homicides or murders (or any other crimes), one might expect to see at least some supportive evidence in at least some studies.

Ehrlich Finds a General Deterrent Effect. In 1975, economics professor Isaac Ehrlich published the first scientific study to report a deterrent effect for capital punishment.[33] Ehrlich began his article with two major criticisms of Sellin's research. The first was that Sellin compared different states on the basis of whether they had death penalty statutes rather than on whether they actually employed the death penalty. The second was that Sellin failed to control for a variety of factors that could influence homicide or murder rates.

Ehrlich used a sophisticated statistical analytic technique—multiple regression analysis—to examine the simultaneous effect of several variables on homicide rates during the years 1933 to 1969. Among the variables were arrest and conviction rates for murder, unemployment rates, labor force participation rates, per-capita incomes, and proportions of the general population between 14 and 24 years of age. His key variable—execution risk—was measured by dividing the number of executions by convictions for murder in the United States

> *In 1975, economics professor Isaac Ehrlich published the first scientific study to report a deterrent effect for capital punishment. Ehrlich concluded that "an additional execution per year over the period in question [1933 to 1969] may have resulted, on average, in seven or eight fewer murders."*

during the time period selected. Ehrlich concluded that "an additional execution per year over the period in question may have resulted, on average, in seven or eight fewer murders."[34]

Ehrlich's findings drew considerable attention. For example, the solicitor general of the United States introduced Ehrlich's prepublished results in *Fowler v. North Carolina* (428 U.S. 904, 1976) as evidence in support of the death penalty.[35] The study was cited in the majority's opinion in *Gregg v. Georgia* (1976), to support the more modest contention that scientific evidence concerning the death penalty's general deterrent effect was "inconclusive."[36] Ehrlich's research continues to inform the opinions of some Supreme Court members who believe that capital punishment deters many types of murder.[37] Finally, Ehrlich's research has inspired additional studies (see Yunker, 1976; Cloninger, 1977; Wolpin, 1978; Layson, 1985), including another one by Ehrlich himself (1977), that have found a statistically significant general deterrent effect for the death penalty.[38] Each of those studies, however, is considered methodologically inferior to Ehrlich's first study.

Most of the attention devoted to Ehrlich's first study was critical, and numerous methodological flaws with his research were cited.[39] Among the problems were: (1) the failure to compare the effectiveness of capital punishment with that of particular prison terms (the marginal effect issue), (2) his finding of a deterrent effect does not hold if the years between 1965 and 1969 are omitted from his statistical model, (3) his use of aggregate United States data ignores important regional differences, and (4) despite his criticism of Sellin's failure to control for possibly influential factors on homicide or murder rates, in accounting for the increase in homicides during the 1960s, Ehrlich fails to consider the possible influences of racial discord, the Vietnam conflict, the sexual revolution, and increased handgun ownership—to name only a few possible factors. Regarding the third and fourth problems, although the homicide rate in the United States did indeed increase during the 1960s, the increase was as great in those states with capital punishment as it was in those states without it. More generally, Ehrlich's model also omitted such variables as the decline in time served in prison for murder and the availability and quality of emergency medical care, both of which might significantly affect the murder rate.

One of the first and most forceful critiques of Ehrlich's research came from a panel established in 1975 by the National Academy of Sciences.[40] The panel's final report was based in part on several commissioned papers. One of the more influential was by Professor Lawrence R. Klein, a past president of the American Economic Association, and his colleagues, Professors Brian Forst and Victor Filatov.[41] Most of the problems listed earlier, as well as several others, were first described in this paper. Klein and his colleagues were more generous than the full panel would be in their assessment of Ehrlich's research. They wrote, "The deterrent effect of capital punishment is definitely not a settled matter, and this is the strongest social scientific conclusion that can be reached at the present time."[42] The panel's report emphasized that Ehrlich's research provides "no useful evidence on the deterrent effect of capital punishment" and that "the current evidence on the deterrent effect of capital punishment is inadequate for drawing any substantive conclusions."[43] Although not all members agreed, the report concluded on a pessimistic note: "research on this topic is not likely to produce findings that will or should have much influence on policy makers."[44]

Ehrlich's research also inspired numerous studies that failed to find a deterrent effect for the death penalty. Professors Peter Passell (1975), William J. Bowers and Glenn L. Pierce (1975), Brian Forst (1977), Scott H. Decker and Carol W. Kohfeld (1984, 1986, 1987, 1988, 1990), Carol W. Kohfeld and Scott H. Decker (1990), and William C. Bailey all used Ehrlich's multiple regression analytic approach, but none of them found a statistically significant deterrent effect. Professor Bailey, a sociologist at Cleveland State University and the most prolific researcher in this area, has conducted numerous studies on the possible deterrent effect of capital punishment using multiple regression analysis. His research on the possible deterrent effect on first-degree murder reviewed: (1) executions versus imprisonment (1974; 1977a), (2) the role of celerity or swiftness in the use of the death penalty (1980), (3) actual executions in each of five states—California, North Carolina, Ohio, Oregon, and Utah—(1979a; 1979d; 1979b; 1979c; 1978, respectively), (4) executions in Chicago and Washington, D.C. (1984a; 1984b, respectively), (5) executions during the 1950s (1983), (6) execution publicity (1990; and with Peterson, 1989), and (7) executions for assaults against the police (with Peterson, 1987; 1994). He also looked for a deterrent effect of executions on rape (1977b) and noncapital felonies (1991). In none of those studies did Bailey find a statistically significant deterrent effect.

Five Counterarguments to Studies that Show No General Deterrent Effect

The first three counterarguments to studies that show no general deterrent effect of capital punishment are from a 1980 report by the Committee on the Judiciary of the United States Senate: "[T]he value of these [deterrence] studies is seriously diminished by the unreliability of the statistical evidence used, the contrary experience of those in the field of law enforcement, and the inherent logic of the deterrent power of the threat of death."[45] The fourth counterargument that undermines the value of the deterrence studies is the observation that, from the mid–1960s through the 1970s, the homicide rate increased as the number of executions decreased.[46] A fifth counterargument is that the death penalty's deterrent effect has been reduced to nothing in recent years (and thus does not show up in the research) because it has not been imposed often or quickly enough to have the desired effect.

Regarding the first point—that "the value of the studies is seriously diminished by the unreliability of the statistical evidence used"—the report noted that "those who are, in fact, deterred by the threat of the death penalty and do not commit murder are not included in the statistical data."[47] It added that "even those favoring abolition agree that the available evidence on the subject of deterrence is, at best, inadequate."[48]

That the available evidence on the subject of deterrence is, at best, inadequate may have been true in 1980, but it is no longer, as the previous section makes clear. As Professor William J. Bowers explains:

> The evidence that capital punishment has no deterrent advantage over imprisonment is now stronger and more consistent than when the Court last considered this issue in *Gregg*. Indeed, a comprehensive review of previous studies and recent analyses of refined statistical data both support the contention that the death penalty has a "brutalizing" rather than a deterrent effect—that executions can be expected to stimulate rather than to inhibit homicides.[49]

In 1989, following a comprehensive review of death penalty research by a panel of distinguished scholars, the American Society of Criminology—the largest association of criminologists in the nation—passed a resolution condemning capital punishment and calling for its abolition. Among the reasons for the Society's position was the absence of "consistent evidence of crime deterrence through execution."[50] Additionally, a recent survey of 67 current and past presidents of the top three criminology professional organizations—the American Society of Criminology, the Academy of

Criminal Justice Sciences, and the Law and Society Association—found that about 90 percent of them believe that the death penalty "never has been, is not and never could be a deterrent to homicide over and above long imprisonment."[51]

The second counterargument is that most law enforcement officials continue to favor capital punishment because they believe it is an effective deterrent to violent crime.[52] Law enforcement officers, it is assumed, are in the best position to judge the utility of capital punishment because they are the people "most frequently called upon to deal with murderers and potential murderers."[53] The third counterargument, which simply generalizes the second, is that "[t]here is an inherent logic in the deterrent power of the threat of death."[54] The deterrent power of capital punishment, in short, makes intuitive sense.

*I*n 1989, following a comprehensive review of death penalty research by a panel of distinguished scholars, the American Society of Criminology—the largest association of criminologists in the nation—passed a resolution condemning capital punishment and calling for its abolition. Among the reasons for the Society's position was the absence of "consistent evidence of crime deterrence through execution."

Defense attorney Anthony Amsterdam agrees with the third point—that "the real mainstay of the deterrence thesis . . . is not evidence but intuition"—but argues that the intuitive belief is misguided:

> You and I ask ourselves: Are we not afraid to die? Of course! Would the threat of death, then not intimidate us to forbear from a criminal act? Certainly! *Therefore,* capital punishment must be a deterrent. The trouble with this intuition is that the people who are doing the reasoning and the people who are doing the murdering are not the same people. You and I do not commit murder for a lot of reasons other than the death penalty.[55]

In addition, there are intuitive reasons for believing that capital punishment provokes violence and other calamity; that it has a "brutalizing effect". For example, if persons are to be dissuaded from killing by fear of capital punishment, then why have executions been banned from public view since the late 1930s? Why are executions not televised? The first chapter noted that executions were hidden from public view to avoid the rowdiness and violence that frequently accompanied them; the same is said of televised executions.[56] Similarly, if capital punishment is an effective deterrent, then why are prison inmates not allowed to view executions? Executions are almost always scheduled for late at night when most inmates are asleep. The reason? To avoid violent reactions.[57] Professor Bowers remarks, "Our experience is that those who should benefit most react instead with anger, resentment, and hostility, if not overt violence, to the 'lesson' of an execution."[58]

The fourth counterargument—that because the homicide rate increased as the number of executions decreased from the mid–1960s through the 1970s, there must be a general deterrent effect—is also suspect. It underscores the need for rigorous scientific inquiry into conclusions based on common sense. Anthony Amsterdam states the problem with the counterargument succinctly:

> This is ridiculous [as evidence for general deterrence] when you consider that crime as a whole has increased during this period; that homicide rates have increased about *half* as much as the rates for all other FBI Index crimes; and that whatever factors are affecting the rise of most noncapital crimes (which *cannot* include cessation of executions) almost certainly affect the homicide–rate rise also (emphasis in original).[59]

Professor Bowers further notes, "[C]ompared with yearly changes in the national homicide rate from 1962 on, states with reduced executions tended to have reduced homicide rates and those with increased executions tended to have increased homicide rates."[60]

The fifth and related counterargument is that the death penalty's deterrent effect has been reduced to nothing in recent years (and thus does not show up in the research) because it has not been imposed often or quickly enough to have the desired effect. Such critics claim that a return to the "good old days" of more frequent and swifter executions would produce deterrence.[61] Evidence from the good old days, however, belies that hope.

During the 1930s, for example, there were a total of 1,676 executions in the United States.[62] That represents 167 executions per year, 14 executions per month, and the most executions in any single decade of the twentieth century. The most executions in any single year since 1930, the first year records were kept by the U.S. government, were the 199 recorded in 1935.[63] Furthermore, although data on the celerity of executions are not available for this period, data on celerity for 1951–1960 show that the average time between death sentence and execution was 14.4 months (the range was from 4.6 to 46.1 months); the average for 1996 was 125 months.[64] If capital punishment had a deterrent effect, and the frequency and celerity of executions were important, then one might expect a relatively low murder rate for the decade. The evidence shows, though, that homicide rates were higher in the 1930s than in the 1940s, 1950s, and early–to–mid–1960s—decades that had fewer executions.[65] Historical evidence provides no reason to believe that increasing the frequency and celerity of executions would dramatically increase the death penalty's deterrent effect.[66]

Assumptions and Problems with Deterrence Theory

According to Professor Bowers, "Deterrence theory assumes that potential offenders exercise rational judgment in deciding whether to kill and that they are predictably sensitive to the actual range of variation in certainty and severity of legal punishment for murder at the time of the decision to act."[67] Additional assumptions of deterrence theory are that potential killers "know what constitutes a capital murder," "that they view death as less acceptable than the other punishments imposed for capital murder," and "that the deterrence message is not neutralized by other confounding or contrary messages conveyed by capital punishment."[68] "From what we know about murder," Bowers surmises, "there is reason to doubt these assumptions."[69]

Most murderers, especially capital murderers, probably do not rationally calculate the consequences of their actions before they engage in them. Many murderers who end up on death row killed someone during the course of an armed robbery. Many never intended to kill but did so because of unexpected circumstances. Any who may have calculated the consequences of their actions before engaging in their crimes probably did not consider that the punishment might be death. And even if would-be killers knew that execution was the possible penalty for their actions, it likely would not deter them anyway. As Professor Bowers notes, "Police statistics reported to the Federal Bureau of Investigation and execution records from the National Bureau of Prisons indicate that only a small fraction of criminal homicides have resulted in executions—no more than two percent per year since 1930."[70] The chance of being executed for criminal homicide is very remote.

A problem is that the objects of deterrence theory—rational human beings—frequently do not calculate the consequences of their actions. The point is moot, however, because most people, whether they calculate consequence or not, do not kill. Without dismissing the tragedy of even a single murder victim, according to data from the Federal Bureau of Investigation, in recent years there have been only about 25,000 murders and nonnegligent manslaughters committed annually in the United States. Precise figures are not available, but it is estimated that only 10 to 25 percent of them, or about 2,500 to 6,250, are capital crimes and thus death-eligible.[71] In a well-armed country of more than 250 million people, one might expect many more murders. The point is that most people do not kill, and the reasons they do not kill generally do not include fear of the death penalty.

Those killers who do take into account the possible consequences of their actions commit crimes that usually are impossible for the police to detect.[72] When they are caught, the chances of their being convicted are small and their chances of being executed even less.[73] As noted earlier, 90 percent of all killers are not eligible for the death penalty. Consider the prototypical rational killer, the professional "hit person," who would be the most likely candidate for execution. According to a study by Sarah Dike, "during 1919-1968, there were 1,004 gangland murders in Chicago, 23 convictions, 4 sentences to life imprisonment, and no death sentences imposed."[74]

Critics of the death penalty point out that even if the penalty deterred some would-be killers, it does not logically follow, nor does available evidence support, that capital punishment is a more effective deterrent to capital crimes than is an alternative, noncapital punishment.[75]

The Counterdeterrent or Brutalizing Effect

Most of the replications of Ehrlich's research not only show no deterrent effect for the death penalty, but many of them actually found a counterdeterrent or brutalizing effect. In other words, the death penalty may actually cause murders rather than deter them! The idea that executions can provoke murders is an old one,[76] and for years, psychiatrists have provided anecdotal evidence of such an effect. One variant of this phenomenon is called the "suicide–murder syndrome," which is illustrated by the case of Pamela Watkins. Watkins was "a babysitter in San Jose who had made several unsuccessful suicide attempts and was frightened to try again. She finally strangled two children so that the state of California would execute her."[77] Gary Gilmore was probably another example of this syndrome. Another variant of this phenomenon has been termed the "executioner syndrome."[78] Those afflicted with the problem believe their killing performs a public service by eliminating a problem. Still another variant stems from the pathological desire to die by execution.[79] Finally, from what is known about capital murderers, it is likely that some of them kill to gain the attention and notoriety that being executed might bring: Their executions provide them a stage that would not be available to them under different circumstances.

Among those who believe most strongly in the death penalty's counterdeterrent or brutalizing effect are Professor Bowers and Professor Glenn L. Pierce, of the Center for Applied Social Research at Northeastern University. They attempted to replicate Ehrlich's research, and discovered that Ehrlich's finding of a deterrent effect for the death penalty appeared only "if the period of analysis is extended beyond 1965 to include years when executions had dwindled to one or two or had actually ceased, and only if logarithmic values of the variables are used, giving disproportionate weight to these recent years in the regression analysis."[80] When the analysis is limited to the period 1935 to1963, however, a period when executions actually took place, their research revealed:

- that execution risk tends to make a positive contribution to the homicide rate as measured by the FBI . . . and by the Census Bureau . . .

- that the number of executions imposed (a better index of possible brutalizing effects) makes a stronger and more consistent positive contribution to the FBI homicide rate . . . ; and

- that the evident brutalizing effects become even stronger and more statistically significant with the more reliable census measure of willful
  homicide.[81]

Later, in an analysis of the 692 executions and all of the homicides in New York state between 1906 and 1963, Bowers and Pierce found that each execution "adds rough-ly three more to the number of homicides in the next nine months of the year after the execution."[82]

Professor Bowers provides the following explanation for his findings:

> The lesson of the execution . . . may be to devalue life by the example of
> human sacrifice. Executions demonstrate that it is correct and appropriate
> to kill those who have gravely offended us. The fact that such killings are to
> be performed only by duly appointed officials on duly convicted offenders is
> a detail that may get obscured by the message that such offenders deserve to
> die. If the typical murderer is someone who feels that he has been betrayed,
> dishonored, or disgraced by another person—and we suggest that such feel-
> ings are far more characteristic of those who commit murder than is a ratio-
> nal evaluation of costs and benefits—then it is not hard to imagine that the
> example executions provide may inspire a potential murderer to kill the per-
> son who has greatly offended him. In effect, the message of the execution
> may be lethal vengeance, not deterrence."[83]

Bowers maintains that the brutalization effect requires a different type of identi-fication process than does the deterrent effect. If executions are to achieve deter-rence, would-be killers must identify with criminals who are executed. If they do not, deterrence cannot work. If executions brutalize, on the other hand, would-be killers must identify their victims with executed criminals and themselves with state–sanctioned executioners. Bowers describes the process:

> The potential murderer will not identify personally with the criminal who is
> executed, but will instead identify someone who has greatly offended him—
> someone he hates, fears, or both—with the executed criminal. We might call
> this the psychology of "villain identification." By associating the person who
> has wronged him with the victim of an execution, he sees that death is what
> his despised offender deserves. Indeed, he himself may identify with the
> state as executioner and thus justify and reinforce his desire for lethal
> vengeance.[84]

Bowers adds that capital punishment may provoke homicides in other ways, such as through the psychology of suggestion or imitation.[85] To that, Professor Van den Haag counters, "It is possible that all displays of violence, criminal or punitive, influ-ence people to engage in unlawful imitations. This seems one good reason not to have public executions. But it does not argue against executions."[86] Van den Haag seems to be implying that only the viewing of executions is suggestive, but knowl-edge of them is not. For Van den Haag, media representations of executions must be inconsequential, yet there is considerable evidence that the media influences many types of behavior, including criminal behavior.[87] Consequently, if displays of or knowledge of violence do influence people to engage in unlawful imitations, as Professor Van den Haag concedes in part, then it seems reasonable to conclude that executions, as a form of violence, could provoke some people to commit violent acts. If Professor Van den Haag is correct, then the imitation of violence may help account for the relatively high violent crime rate in the United States.

Murder versus Capital Punishment

Beyond the imitation of violence, some people equate capital punishment with murder. Beccaria wrote, "It seems to me absurd that the laws, which are an expression of the public will, which detest and punish homicide, should themselves commit it, and that to deter citizens from murder, they order a public one."[88] Professor Van den Haag's reply is that capital punishment is not murder:

> Legally imposed punishments . . . although often physically identical to the crimes punished, are not crimes or their moral equivalent. The difference between crimes and lawful acts is not physical, but legal . . . [Finally,] whether a lawful punishment gives an "example of barbarity" depends on how the moral difference between crime and punishment is perceived. To suggest that its physical quality, ipso facto, morally disqualifies the punishment, is to assume what is to be shown.[89]

On the other hand, Anthony Amsterdam writes that "the advocates of capital punishment can and do accentuate their arguments with descriptions of the awful physical details of such hideous murders as that of poor Sharon Tate," who was brutally killed by members of the infamous Manson family.[90] He argues that there are two main problems with justifying capital punishment by citing the heinousness of murders:

> First, the murders being described are not murders that are being done by us, or in our name, or with our approval; and our power to stop them is exceedingly limited even under the most exaggerated suppositions of deterrence. . . . Every execution, on the other hand, is done by our paid servants, in our collective name, and we can stop them all. Please do not be bamboozled into thinking that people who are against executions are in favor of murders. If we had the individual or the collective power to stop murders, we would stop them all—and for the same basic reason that we want to stop executions. Murders and executions are both ugly, vicious things, because they destroy the same sacred and mysterious gift of life which we do not understand and can never restore. Second, please remember therefore that descriptions of murders are relevant to the subject of capital punishment only on the theory that two wrongs make a right, or that killing murderers can assuage their victims' sufferings or bring them back to life, or that capital punishment is the best deterrent to murder. The first two propositions are absurd, and [for the third] the evidence is overwhelmingly against it.[91]

Albert Camus, the French philosopher, once wrote that an execution

> is not simply death. It is just as different. . . from the privation of life as a
> concentration camp is from prison. . . . It adds to death a rule, a public pre-
> meditation known to the future victim, an organization . . . which is itself a
> source of moral sufferings more terrible than death . . . [Capital punishment]
> is . . . the most premeditated of murders, to which no criminal's deed, how-
> ever calculated . . . can be compared. . . . For there to be an equivalency,
> the death penalty would have to punish a criminal who had warned his vic-
> tim of the date at which he would inflict a horrible death on him and who,
> from that moment onward, had confined him at his mercy for months. Such
> a monster is not encountered in private life.[92]

Whether or not capital punishment is the same as murder, or—as Amsterdam and Camus argue—worse, is an ethical issue that likely defies a definitive answer. Yet, it seems a critical issue to resolve because how one stands on the issue probably determines, to a large extent, one's position on capital punishment in general.

Conclusion

Researchers for more than a half century have conducted dozens of studies investigating the intuitively appealing belief in the death penalty's deterrent effect. With the exception of a handful of thoroughly discredited analyses, no evidence exists of the hypothesized effect. There is even some evidence of a counterdeterrent or brutalizing effect. Perhaps capital punishment both deters *and* brutalizes, producing the absence of a discernible deterrent effect by canceling each other out. In the final analysis, none of this may matter if results of the recent opinion poll are to be believed: Only 13 percent of death penalty proponents polled selected deterrence as a reason for their position.

The irony is that although capital punishment has virtually no effect on crime, capital or otherwise, it continues to be a favored political "silver bullet"—a simplistic solution to the crime problem used by aspiring politicians and law enforcement officials.[93] A problem is that, as long as politicians and law enforcement officials can gain political currency by perpetuating the belief in the death penalty's deterrent effect, attention will be diverted from more constructive and (it is hoped) more effective approaches to the prevention and control of violent behavior.[94] This may be yet another way that capital punishment contributes to an increase in violent crime rather than the expected decrease.

Discussion Questions

1. Is the death penalty a greater general deterrent to capital crime than an alternative noncapital punishment such as life imprisonment without opportunity of parole?

2. Is the death penalty a general deterrent to noncapital crimes?

3. Regarding the first two questions, does it matter?

4. Is the death penalty the most severe penalty?

5. Does the death penalty provide an added measure of protection for police officers?

6. Does the death penalty provide an added measure of protection for correctional officers?

7. Why have executions been banned from public view since the late 1930s?

8. Why are executions not televised?

9. Why are prison inmates not allowed to view executions?

10. In what ways, if any, could the general deterrent power of capital punishment be increased?

11. Does the death penalty have a counterdeterrent or "brutalizing" effect? (Does the death penalty cause capital crimes?)

12. Is capital punishment murder?

Notes

[1] Available evidence indicates that capital punishment does not deter noncapital felonies; specifically, murder and nonnegligent manslaughter, rape, assault, robbery, burglary, grand larceny, or vehicle theft, see Bailey, 1991.

[2] Ellsworth and Ross, 1983:121, fn. 15.

[3] See, for example, Bohm, Clark, and Aveni, 1991; Gallup Report, 1985; Kohlberg and Elfenbein, 1975.

[4] Ellsworth and Ross, op. cit., p. 149.

[5] Gallup and Newport, 1991; also see Longmire, 1996.

[6] Van den Haag, 1982:326.

[7] Ibid., p. 327.

[8] Ibid.

[9] O.J. Simpson's criminal trial jury was accused of jury nullification when they acquitted him.

[10] Beccaria, 1975:48-49.

[11] Stephan and Snell, 1996:10, Table 11.

[12] Beccaria, op. cit., p. 45.

[13] Ibid., p. 50.

[14] See, for example, Peterson and Bailey, 1998; Paternoster, 1991:Chap. 7; Zimring and Hawkins, 1986:Appendix; Conrad in Van den Haag and Conrad, 1983:133-4; Waldo, 1981; Glaser, 1979.

[15] Specifically, statistical significance refers to the unlikelihood that relationships observed in a sample, that is, a subset of a larger group, can be attributed to sampling error alone. Sampling error refers to the difference between the measure of a population (the larger group) and the measure of a sample (the subset of the larger group).

[16] See Peterson and Bailey, op. cit.; Paternoster, op. cit., Chap. 7; Zimring and Hawkins, op. cit., Appendix; Zeisel, 1982.

[17] Sellin, 1967:135-38. Sellin also conducted a year-by-year comparative analysis of contiguous states from 1920 to 1955, see Sellin, 1959.

[18] Also see Bye, 1919; Sutherland, 1925; Vold, 1932; 1952; Schuessler, 1952; Reckless, 1969. For examples of a similar type of analysis using data for the 1973-1984 and 1980-1995 periods, see Peterson and Bailey, 1988; 1998. These authors found no deterrent effect for capital punishment either.

[19] Sellin, 1959, op. cit.; 1967, op. cit., pp. 138-54.

[20] Sellin, 1967, op. cit., p. 138.

[21] Sellin, op. cit., p. 55; 1967, op. cit., p. 146.

[22] Sellin, 1967, op. cit., pp. 152-53. For multivariate analyses that found the same nondeterrent results, see Bailey and Peterson, 1987; 1994.

[23] Sellin, 1967, op. cit., pp. 154-60.

[24] Wolfson,1982:159-73.

[25] Based on the results of a 1950 survey by the International Penal and Penitentiary Commission, Sellin (1959:70) also notes that "countries without the death penalty reported no more serious disciplinary problems [in prisons] than the countries which had retained the penalty."

[26] See, for example, Baldus and Cole, 1975.

[27] See Bedau, 1982:123, Table 4-2-2.

[28] See, for example, Bye, op. cit.; Schuessler, op. cit.; Sellin, 1959, op. cit.; Reckless, op. cit.; Cochran et al., 1994.

[29] Archer et al., 1983; also see Sellin, 1959, op. cit., pp. 38-50 for cross-national comparisons.

[30] See, for example, Sellin, 1959, op. cit.; King, 1978; Bailey, 1990; Peterson and Bailey, 1991.

[31] See, for example, Dann, 1935; Savitz, 1958; Phillips, 1980; McFarland, 1983; Stack, 1987. Both Dann (1935) and Savitz (1958) overlooked seasonal variations in homicides, see Bowers, 1988:66. For a detailed critique of Phillips (1980), see Bowers, 1988:72-79. McFarland (1983) attributed the short-term decline in homicides following Gary Gilmore's execution in Utah, which was confined to only certain parts of the United States, to the abnormally severe winter conditions in those parts of the country. Bailey and Peterson (1989) replicated Stack's research, correcting some of Stack's coding errors, and failed to find a statistically significant relationship between execution publicity and homicide rates.

[32] See Bowers, op. cit.

[33] See Ehrlich, 1975.

[34] Ibid., p. 414.

[35] Zimring and Hawkins, op. cit., p. 175.

[36] Bowers, 1984:281, fn. 13.

[37] Peterson and Bailey, 1998, op. cit.; Haney and Logan, 1994:87-90. Some of the Supreme Court justices apparently are ignoring the bulk of the evidence showing that capital punishment has no marginal deterrent effect, see Haney and Logan, op. cit., p. 89, and the review of studies below.

[38] Wolpin (1978) reported that each execution may deter four murders; Layson (1985), about 18; Ehrlich (1977), 20-24; Yunker (1976), 156; and Cloninger (1977), 560.

[39] See, for example, Peterson and Bailey, 1998, op. cit.; Paternoster, op. cit., Chap. 7; Zimring and Hawkins, op. cit., pp. 175-181; Bowers, 1988, op. cit.; 1984, op. cit., pp. 280-282, 332-333; Andersen, 1983:35; Zeisel, 1982, op. cit.; Beyleveld, 1982; Klein, Forst, and Filatov, 1982; Barnett, 1981; Waldo, op. cit.; Friedman, 1979; Forst, 1977; Passell and Taylor, 1977; Bowers and Pierce, 1975. For Ehrlich's reply to Beyleveld's critique, see Ehrlich, 1982.

[40] See Zimring and Hawkins, op. cit., pp. 179-181.

[41] Klein, Forst, and Filatov, op. cit.

[42] Ibid., p. 158.

[43] Cited in Zimring and Hawkins, op. cit., p. 180.

[44] Ibid.

[45] Committee on the Judiciary, United States Senate, 1982:312.

[46] See, for example, King, 1982, who recognizes that other factors were also involved.

[47] Committee on the Judiciary, U.S. Senate, op. cit.

[48] Ibid.

[49] Bowers, 1984, op. cit., p. 190; also see Zimring and Hawkins, op. cit., Appendix.

[50] Petersilia, 1990:1.

[51] "Death Penalty Fails to Deter," 1997. In 1975, the Massachusetts Supreme Judicial Court reviewed the deterrence literature, including Ehrlich's study, and concluded that "there is simply no convincing evidence that the death penalty is a deterrent superior to lesser punishments" (*Commonwealth v. O'Neal*, 339 N. E. 2d 676, 1975 at 252).

[52] Committee on the Judiciary, U.S. Senate, op. cit.

[53] Ibid.

[54] Ibid.

[55] Amsterdam, 1982:357.

[56] Bowers, 1988, op. cit., p. 49.

[57] Ibid.

[58] Ibid.

[59] Amsterdam, op. cit., p. 356; also see Bowers, 1984, op. cit., p. 333.

[60] Bowers, ibid.; for a cross-national perspective, see Archer et al., op. cit.

[61] Cited in Peterson and Bailey, 1998, op. cit.

[62] See Schneider and Smykla, 1991:6, Table 1.1; Zimring and Hawkins, op. cit., p. 30, Table 2.2.

[63] Bedau, op. cit., p. 25, Table 1-3.

[64] Peterson and Bailey, 1998, op. cit., p. 177; Snell, 1997:12, Table 12.

[65] See Zahn, 1989:219, Figure 10.1.

[66] However, Peterson and Bailey warn that "because the celerity question has received so little attention, we are not able to conclude, 'with confidence', that prompt executions are/are not effective in preventing murder," see Peterson and Bailey, 1998, op. cit., p. 174.

[67] Bowers, 1984, op. cit., p. 272.

[68] Bowers, 1988, op. cit., p. 50. Peterson and Bailey write that "deterrence theory rests upon the premise that individuals weigh the costs and rewards associated with alternative sanctions, and choose behaviors that yield the greatest gain at the least cost. Thus, crime occurs when illegal actions are perceived either as more profitable (rewarding) or less costly (painful) than conventional alternatives. . . . [M]urder is discouraged because the threat of one's own death presumably outweighs the rewards gained from killing another", see Peterson and Bailey, 1998, op. cit., p. 158; also see Sellin, 1959, op. cit., p. 20.

[69] Bowers, 1984, op. cit.

[70] Ibid., pp. 272-3.

[71] Baldus et al., 1990:22; Andersen, op. cit., p. 32.

[72] Van den Haag and Conrad, op. cit., p.84.

[73] As Henry Schwarzschild, former director of the ACLU's Capital Punishment Project, observes: "the deterrent value [of capital punishment] (which very likely does not exist at all in any case) is reduced to invisibility by the overwhelming likelihood that one will not be caught, or not be prosecuted, or not be tried on a capital charge, or not be convicted, or not be sentenced to death, or have the conviction or sentence reversed on appeal, or have one's sentence commuted," see Schwarzschild, 1982:366.

[74] Cited in Van den Haag and Conrad, op. cit., p. 92.

[75] See, for example, Professor John Conrad: "Punishment certainly deters some potential offenders, but we must not rely on increasing severity to make a corresponding decrease in the number of crimes committed. If we cannot do more to reduce the economic and social causes of crime, we must increase the risks of apprehension by the police. With crime clearance rates as low as they are, it is idle to suppose that dramatic increases in the severity of punishment will seriously affect the incidence of any type of crime," see Van den Haag and Conrad, op. cit., p. 103.

[76] See Bowers, 1984, op. cit., pp. 273-274; 1988, op. cit., pp. 57-61; Sellin, 1959, op. cit., pp. 65-69.

[77] Amsterdam, op. cit., p. 357; also see Bedau, op. cit., p. 98; Sellin, ibid. Another recent example of the suicide-murder syndrome is the case of Daniel Colwell, who, in October 1998, was sentenced to die in Georgia's electric chair. Colwell confessed that, unable to kill himself, he shot two strangers (Mitchell and Judith Bell) in a parking lot so that the state would help him commit suicide. Diagnosed as a paranoid schizophrenic, Colwell had been released from a mental health program just two days before he committed the 1996 murders, see "Georgia Killer Is Granted His Wish to be Executed," 1998. Sellin remarks that such cases once must have been relatively frequent "because Denmark, by an ordinance of December 18, 1767, deliberately abandoned the death penalty in cases where 'melancholy and other dismal persons (committed murder) for the exclusive purpose of losing their lives'," see Sellin, ibid., p. 67. In some cases, the motivation for such actions was religious, explains Sellin: "by murdering another person and thereby being sentenced to death, one might still attain salvation whereas if one were to take one's own life, one would be plunged into eternal damnation," see Sellin, ibid.

[78] See Bedau, ibid.

[79] See Sellin, op. cit., p. 65.

[80] Bowers, 1984, op. cit., p. 333.

[81] Ibid.

[82] Bowers and Pierce, 1980:481; also see Bailey, 1984a; Cochran et al., 1994, who found a brutalization effect for killings involving strangers. For the most sophisticated analysis to date to find a brutalization effect involving different types of murders, see Bailey, 1998.

[83] Bowers, 1984, op. cit., p. 274.

[84] Ibid.

[85] Ibid., p. 275.

[86] Van den Haag, op. cit., p. 328.

[87] For a review of the literature on the subject, see Surette, 1992:Chap. 5.

[88] Beccaria, op. cit., p. 50.

[89] Van den Haag, op. cit., pp. 327-28.

[90] Amsterdam, op. cit., p. 348.

[91] Ibid., pp. 348-49.

[92] Cited in Amsterdam, op. cit., pp 347-48.

[93] Philosopher Ernest Van den Haag claims that, beyond deterrence, capital punishment, or at least the threat of capital punishment, has some technical advantages that should not be overlooked:

> By threatening it, prosecutors may persuade accomplices to testify against murderers, or persuade the murderers themselves to plead guilty in exchange for a life sentence. Also, in a hostage situation police can promise the criminal that the prosecution will not ask for the death penalty if he releases his hostages. Without the death penalty the criminal can threaten to kill his victims, while police can only threaten incarceration.

See Van den Haag, 1998:155.

[94] Bowers, op. cit., p. 164.

CHAPTER 6

Incapacitation
and Costs of
Capital Punishment

Incapacitation and Capital Punishment

Incapacitation refers to preventing convicted murderers (or other capital offenders) from killing (or committing other crimes) again by executing them. Though it is arguably the most defensible of all rationales in support of the death penalty, only 19 percent of recent supporters of capital punishment chose incapacitation—"keeps them from killing again"—as a reason for their support. Incapacitation was the second most important reason cited, far behind retribution at 50 percent.[1]

Are Executions Necessary? Death penalty opponents concede that capital punishment permanently removes a threat to society, but they question whether such a drastic measure is necessary. They argue that if an alternative penalty, such as life imprisonment without possibility of parole, accomplishes the same purpose, it would be preferable because of the other costs associated with the death penalty (e.g., a possible brutalizing effect, execution of innocent persons, etc.).

A key question, then, is whether the death penalty is necessary to protect society from the possible future actions of those who have already committed capital crimes. For proponents of the penalty, the answer to the question is a resounding yes. They argue that "some criminals are incorrigibly anti-social and will remain potentially dangerous to society for the rest of their lives."[2] They add that "mere imprisonment offers these people the possibility of escape or, in some cases, release on parole through error or oversight."[3]

Errors, Oversights, and Other Mistakes. It is ironic and perhaps somewhat hypocritical that parole authorities are distrusted because of decision errors they have made.[4] A similar distrust is not generally voiced about prosecutors who decide whom to charge with capital crimes, or with judges and juries who decide whether defendants charged with capital crimes are guilty and should be executed. Mistakes made by any of those decisionmakers can and have caused the deaths of innocent people. Attorney Anthony Amsterdam asks the pertinent question and supplies a thoughtful answer:

Are we really going to kill a human being because we do not trust other people—the people whom we have chosen to serve on our own parole boards—to make a proper judgment in . . . [a] case at some future time? We trust this same parole board to make far more numerous, difficult, and dangerous decisions: hardly a week passes when they do not consider the cases of armed robbers, for example, although armed robbers are much, much more likely statistically to commit future murders than any murderer is to repeat his crime. But if we really do distrust the public agencies of law—if we fear that they may make mistakes—then surely that is a powerful argument 'against' capital punishment. Courts which hand out death sentences because they predict that a man will still be criminally dangerous 7 or 25 years in the future cannot conceivably make fewer mistakes than parole boards who release a prisoner after 7 or 25 years of close observation in prison have convinced them that he is reformed and no longer dangerous.[5]

As for mistakes made by courts in capital cases, remember that "as a result of automatic appellate reviews, direct and discretionary appeals, collateral post-conviction proceedings in state and federal courts, and occasional gubernatorial commutations, nearly 100 death row inmates have their sentences vacated each year."[6] That represents a third to a half of the 200 to 300 death sentences imposed each year.

Why Not Execute All Capital Offenders? To ensure that no convicted capital offender killed again, all convicted capital offenders would have to be executed. There are several problems with such a strategy. First, as will be described in detail in the next chapter, innocent people, wrongfully convicted of capital crimes, have been executed. If all convicted capital offenders were executed to prevent any one of them from killing again, it would be impossible to rectify the injustices done to the innocent people executed, their families and friends, and to a society that considered such acts immoral. At least 400 Americans have been wrongly convicted of crimes punishable by death in this century,[7] and all of them would have died if this strategy were implemented.

To prevent such miscarriages of justice and still retain the death penalty it is necessary to identify convicted capital offenders who are innocent and spare them from death. This is no easy task because nearly all convicted capital offenders claim they are innocent, even though only a small percentage of them really are. Generally, it is only after considerable effort that proof of innocence is ever discovered, and rarely is such effort expended on death row inmates. For those family members and friends who would like to try, the financial and psychological resources necessary for such an endeavor are often not available.

LWOP as an Alternative. An alternative to capital punishment, and one that eliminates entirely the possibility of executing an innocent person, is true life imprisonment without possibility of parole (LWOP). Proponents of capital punishment object to this alternative, claiming that "even if they [convicted capital offenders] are successfully imprisoned for life, prison itself is an environment presenting dangers to guards, inmates and others."[8] They argue that LWOP inmates, without the threat of the death penalty, would have nothing to lose if they killed in prison.

Available evidence suggests, however, that the threat posed by inmates serving life sentences is probably more imagined than real. Wardens and superintendents of correctional institutions in the United States have long held that "lifers are generally . . . among the best behaved prisoners,"[9] and Amsterdam relates that "Warden Lawes of Sing Sing [Prison] and Governor Wallace of Alabama, among others, regularly employed murder convicts as house servants because they were among the very safest of prisoners."[10] It is important to emphasize that this evidence may not apply to LWOP inmates because they have no hope of release (this is why Professor Sellin advises against LWOP sentences) nor to capital murderers—yet a recent study found that capital murderers sentenced to LWOP were no greater threat to other prisoners or correctional staff than death-sentenced inmates or other murderers sentenced to terms of imprisonment.[11]

> *A* recent study found that capital murderers sentenced to life imprisonment without opportunity of parole (LWOP) were no greater threat to other prisoners or correctional staff than death-sentenced inmates or other murderers sentenced to terms of imprisonment.

The fact is that LWOP inmates do have something to lose if they kill or commit other infractions in prison. They have numerous privileges, which they could lose for violations. Among those privileges are visits from family and friends, access to mail and the telephone, being able to buy items from the commissary, being able to take educational and vocational classes, being able to participate in recreational activities, etc. They also can be removed from the general prison population and placed in isolation cells. Correctional authorities attest to the effectiveness that the threat of lost privileges has in controlling LWOP inmates: "[E]xperience with LWOP inmates in the Alabama penal system has shown that they commit about one-half as many infractions as other inmates."[12] LWOP inmates behave in prison because it is the only life they have. They become "institutionalized to the routines and limits of prison life."[13]

Death penalty opponents claim that historically only a small number of imprisoned capital offenders have killed other inmates and prison personnel. Inmates not sentenced to death, they contend, commit most prison killings. The available evidence suggests that such a contention is only partially true (depending on what offenses are considered capital and what is considered a small number).

For example, Sellin examined fatal and nonfatal prison assaults that occurred in 1965,[14] reporting that 603 victims were assaulted in the 37 jurisdictions that responded to his survey. Sixty-one of the assault victims died—8 staff members and 53 inmates. There were 59 killers, and 34 percent of them were serving time for capital offenses (11 for murder, 6 for robbery, 1 for assault, 1 for rape, and 1 for kidnapping). At the time, all of the listed offenses were death-eligible in at least some jurisdictions; today, only aggravated murder is. If the crimes that currently are not death-eligible are excluded, the largest group of killers was inmates convicted of robbery, accounting for 32 percent of the total. The second largest group of killers, accounting for 27 percent of the total, was inmates convicted of murder (only 18 percent were convicted of capital murder). Therefore, even if convicted murderers do not account for the largest number of prison killings, at least in 1965 they did account for more than one in four of them (or about one in five if only capital murderers are included).

The problem with this knowledge, observes Sellin, is that it does not help in the prediction of which convicted murderers will kill in prison and which ones will not. Evidence shows that at least 90 percent of convicted capital offenders probably will not kill again. But to prevent all prison killings by convicted capital offenders, it would be necessary to execute all of them (before they could kill), even though that strategy would not have prevented nearly three out of every four of the prison killings in 1965.

Another problem with LWOP as an alternative to capital punishment is that it is unnecessary for most convicted capital offenders who will not kill again, even if they are released from prison. Based on the 1953 Report of the Royal Commission on Capital Punishment, Appendix 15, for foreign countries; a study of parolees from Pennsylvania from 1914 to 1952; and a study of parolees from California from 1945 to1954, Sellin stated, "It is generally agreed that those who are allowed to return to the community after serving a term of years for a capital crime, behave themselves better than do other criminals similarly released."[15] He elsewhere noted, "The conclusion seems inescapable that the murderer who is not executed but instead sentenced to life imprisonment is not nearly so great a danger to the prison community, nor to the outside world when he is paroled or pardoned, as are many other classes of prisoners, who are regularly released after serving much shorter periods of imprisonment."[16]

Other data support Sellin's conclusion. For example, Bedau reports that of 2,646 murderers released in 12 states between 1900 and 1977, only 88 (approximately 3 percent) were reincarcerated after conviction for a subsequent felony and only 16 (approximately .6 percent) were reincarcerated after conviction for committing a subsequent criminal homicide.[17] He also used data from the National Council on Crime and Delinquency's Uniform Parole Reports to show that, between 1965 and 1975, 11,404 inmates originally convicted of "willful homicide" were released from prison nationwide. One year after release, only 170 (approximately 1.5 percent) were reincarcerated after conviction for the commission of a subsequent felony and only 34 (approximately .3 percent) after conviction for the commission of a subsequent criminal homicide.[18]

Admittedly, there are problems with those data. A problem with the figures from the National Council on Crime and Delinquency is that they only cover one year after release—certainly too short a time to draw any definitive conclusions about the future risks of released murderers (the amount of time on release in the first study cited above was not mentioned). A more recent study with a longer follow-up period discovered that 8 (4.9 percent) of 164 paroled Georgia murderers committed subsequent murders within 91 months of release.[19] A second problem is that the data includes both capital and noncapital murderers. Without separating the two groups, it is impossible to know whether one group is a greater risk than the other of committing subsequent homicides. A third problem is that the data includes only those recidivists who were caught and convicted. The actual number of released capital offenders who kill again, though probably very small, is unknown.

The *Furman*–Commuted Inmates. The first and second problems just discussed can be meaningfully addressed, thanks to a natural experiment created by the Supreme Court in 1972. The *Furman* decision resulted in all death row inmates in the United States at that time having their sentences automatically commuted to life imprisonment *with* opportunity for parole. Some of those death row inmates have since been paroled. An examination of their post–release criminal behaviors can provide a relatively good measure of the risks posed by capital offenders who, but for the luck of *Furman*, might have been executed. Because each of the studies described below defines recidivism as reconviction or reincarceration, they share, with the previous data, the problem of not showing the proportion of subsequent killers who are not reconvicted or reincarcerated. Death penalty opponents assume the number is very small.

The 26 states that responded to a 1987 survey by the National Clearinghouse on Prisons and Jails reported 457 living *Furman*-commuted inmates, of whom 185 (40.6 percent) were paroled.[20] Eight parolees died during the 14-year period and are excluded from the following analysis, reducing the percentage of *Furman*-commuted inmates paroled to 38.7 percent. Only 35 (19.7 percent) of the paroled inmates recidivated (were reincarcerated). Of those who did recidivate, 3 (8.6 percent) had committed murder, and 8 (23 percent) had committed a violent crime (3 murders, 3 robberies, 1 rape, and 1 kidnapping). The largest number of parolees was returned to prison for parole violations (12 or 34.3 percent). Other parolees were reimprisoned for burglary (6 or 17.1 percent), drug offenses (5 or 14.2 percent), and other property offenses (4 or 11.4 percent). Also worthy of note is that 29 (16.4 percent) of the 177 paroled *Furman*-commuted inmates successfully completed their parole terms and regained (in applicable states) their civil rights.

Another study examined the postrelease behavior of 28 *Furman*-commuted inmates in Texas over the 14-year period of 1973 to 1986.[21] Only 7 (25 percent) of the 28 recidivated. The average time they spent in the community was 4.1 years. One of the parolees (3.6 percent) committed a murder; 4 of them (14 percent) committed felonies (1 murder, 1 rape, 2 burglaries); and 3 of them (11 percent) were reincarcerated for technical parole violations. The one recidivist murderer killed his girlfriend and then committed suicide within 12 months of his release from prison.

A third study focused on the experiences of the 23 *Furman*-commuted death row inmates in Kentucky, of whom 17 were paroled.[22] The average follow-up period was 42 months. None of the parolees was rearrested for a murder; only 2 (12 percent) were rearrested for violent crimes (robberies); and only 4 (24 percent) for any new crime (2 for robbery, 1 for burglary, and 1 for drug possession). In all, 35 percent of the parolees were rearrested, 29 percent were reconvicted and reimprisoned, and 6 percent were put in jail. One of the parolees (6 percent) obtained his final release from parole supervision and 11 (65 percent) have been placed on inactive supervision.

Conclusion. Three arguments for the execution of all capital offenders are: (1) execution is the only way to guarantee they won't kill again, (2) life imprisonment provides opportunity for escape, parole, or additional murders, and (3) LWOP is costly.

The data just presented show that murderers, including capital murderers, do sometimes kill again even after having been imprisoned for many years, but the data also reveal that the number of such repeat killers is very small. A somewhat larger percentage of paroled death row inmates commit other offenses. However, most individuals are returned to prison for parole violations rather than for committing new crimes. Most convicted capital offenders will not kill again, even if they are released from prison, and a large majority of them will not be arrested for any new crimes.

> ■ *D*ata show that murderers, including capital murderers, sometimes kill again even after having been imprisoned for many years. They also reveal that the number of such killers is very small.

For those who claim that life imprisonment provides the opportunity for escape or parole through error or oversight, or that life prisoners are a threat to other inmates and correctional personnel, Anthony Amsterdam responds, "You cannot tell me or believe that a society which is capable of putting a man on the moon is incapable of putting a man in prison, keeping him there, and keeping him from killing while he is there."[23]

Some people oppose LWOP because they believe it would be too costly; they assume that the death penalty is cheaper than LWOP. If they have in mind only the costs of the eventual execution, they are right, but if they consider the entire process of capital punishment, including trials, appeals, and executions, then they are wrong. The financial costs of capital punishment are the subject of the next section.

The Costs of Capital Punishment versus Life Imprisonment[24]

One of the most common myths about capital punishment is that it is cheaper than alternative punishments such as life imprisonment without opportunity for parole. Political science professor John Culver claims that "the execution of an individual in his or her 30s is less expensive than maintaining that person in prison for 30 or more years until a natural death occurs."[25] Surveys show that approximately 70 percent of all respondents and about 80 percent of death penalty proponents (60 percent of opponents) hold this belief.[26] Perhaps more importantly, 13 percent of supporters of capital punishment in a recent Gallup poll selected as a reason for their support that it is too "costly to keep them in prison."[27]

The principal purpose of this section is to compare the costs of capital punishment with the costs of alternative punishments. Implicit in the analysis are comparisons of three types: (1) capital punishment versus an alternative punishment applied after a successful plea bargain, (2) capital punishment versus an alternative punishment imposed after a trial only, and (3) capital punishment versus an alternative punishment imposed after a trial and post-conviction review. Assuming the same alternative punishment, the comparisons are listed in descending order from largest to smallest cost differential. The first comparison reveals the largest cost differential because the costs of the alternative punishment do not include trial or post–conviction review expenses, all of which are invariably incurred in capital cases (unless post–conviction proceedings are waived). Also briefly discussed are past practices and their costs (which may help explain why some people believe in the myth), financial and other ramifications of recent efforts to streamline the process, "start–up" costs for jurisdictions contemplating reinstatement of the death penalty, and some of the consequences if capital punishment were to be replaced with LWOP in the future.

Costs of Capital Punishment under Pre–*Furman* Statutes. Prior to the *Furman* decision in 1972, the costs of capital punishment were not an issue. The death penalty was not an expensive punishment relative to LWOP because capital cases were disposed of quickly, no extraordinary procedures were followed, reversals were relatively rare, and the costs associated with executions alone were minimal. Regarding the relatively quick disposal of capital cases, data from 1956 to1960 show that the average time between death sentence and execution was 14.4 months; however, by year–end 1996, the average had risen to 125 months.[28] A primary reason for the 768 percent increase in time between conviction and execution in capital cases is the super due process now required by the Supreme Court's "death is different" doctrine.[29] Super due process, as noted previously, refers to the unique procedural safeguards afforded people charged with capital crimes. Those safeguards apply primarily to the trial and post–conviction stages of the process.

Costs of Capital Punishment under Post–*Furman* Statutes. Although the actual death–causing procedure may be relatively inexpensive, the process of getting to that point is quite costly under post–*Furman* statutes. The Supreme Court requires that defendants charged with capital crimes be provided with super due process, and super due process is expensive: The average cost per execution in the United States (that is, the entire process) ranges from $2 million to $3 million.[30] Extraordinary cases can cost much

> *The* average cost per execution in the United States (that is, the entire process) ranges from $2 million to $3 million. Extraordinary cases can cost much more. The state of Florida, for example, reportedly spent $10 million to execute serial murderer Ted Bundy.

more. The state of Florida, for example, reportedly spent $10 million to execute serial murderer Ted Bundy.[31]

If the average annual cost of imprisonment in the United States is about $20,000 per inmate,[32] and an inmate sentenced to LWOP lives 50 years,[33] then the cost of that LWOP sentence is roughly $1 million (assuming the LWOP sentence was the result of a successful plea bargain), making capital punishment, on average, two to three times more expensive than LWOP imposed as a result of plea bargaining. If the LWOP sentence is imposed after a trial and includes other post–conviction proceedings, then the difference will be much smaller. Nevertheless, the costs of a death sentence will probably always be more expensive than the costs of an LWOP sentence because super due process is required only in capital cases.[34] In North Carolina, for example, the cost differential between a capital case culminating in an execution and a non-capital case resulting in a 20-year sentence has been estimated to be between $163,000 and more than $216,000.[35]

Why is super due process so expensive? That question is answered in the next sections. It must be emphasized that many of the costs reported are estimates, that there can be great variation in the costs of specific services among different jurisdictions, that cost estimates are not available for every part of the process, and that not every cost or part of the process occurs in every case. Some costs can be duplicated when retrials or resentencings follow the vacation of a conviction or capital sentence on appeal or during the post-conviction review process. It should also be remembered that whenever a capital trial does not result in a death sentence and execution, the added costs associated with the death penalty process have been incurred without any "return" on the state's investment of resources.

The following analysis is divided into five general stages of the capital punishment process: (1) pretrial, (2) trial, (3) posttrial, (4) imprisonment, and (5) execution.

The Pretrial Stage. The costs of capital punishment begin to mount soon after a potentially capital crime (in most cases, an aggravated murder) has been reported to the police. The investigation of potentially capital crimes tends to be more rigorous than the investigation of other felonies. When the crime may be a capital offense, forensic experts examine the crime scene more carefully, and this greater attention and time result in an added but unknown cost.[36]

Investigation of the case frequently continues through trial and can last several years.[37] The investigation of potentially capital crimes has been estimated to take three to five times longer than for other felonies, primarily because the prosecution as well as the defense must prepare for both stages of the bifurcated trial—the guilt and penalty phases.[38] Because defense counsel can present any relevant mitigating evidence during the penalty phase of a capital trial (see *Lockett v. Ohio*, 1978), a thorough investigation of possible mitigators is time-consuming and expensive. Investigators working for the state of North Carolina were paid $22.16 per hour in 1991–92.[39] Experienced private investigators, who frequently are hired by the defense, are paid between $75 and $200 an hour.[40]

Once a suspect has been identified and arrested, a bond hearing is held. The costs of those processes probably do not differ greatly for potentially capital crimes and other serious felonies, but estimates of the costs have not been reported. If bond is denied, however, and the suspect is incarcerated—which is nearly always more likely with potentially capital crimes—then additional costs will be incurred as a result of the tighter security that will be provided through the entire process.[41] There are no estimates for those extra security costs, either.

If the prosecutor believes that there is evidence to convict the suspect of the crime, and the crime is an aggravated murder (or other capital offense), then the prosecutor will seek an indictment for capital murder in jurisdictions that employ grand juries.[42] In those jurisdictions that do not use grand juries, formal charges are filed through an information. The costs of each capital indictment are believed to be "enormous" (though no dollar figure has been cited) because each indictment must be prepared, even though only about 20 percent of them will reach trial.[43]

The most expensive part of the pretrial process frequently involves the motions filed in death penalty cases. Defense counsel has both a professional and an ethical obligation to represent his or her client's interests by filing nonfrivolous motions which, at a minimum, create and preserve the defendant's record for appeal.[44] Extensive amounts of time can be devoted to researching and writing pretrial motions. The prosecution must respond to the motions as well as prepare and file its own. In North Carolina, at least 34 different motions have been made in recent capital litigation, not to mention 11 more motions made during the penalty phase of the trial.[45] Those motions are in addition to the more standard ones that are frequently filed by both sides in other felony cases.[46] Typical motions filed in capital cases involve voir dire, jury composition, death qualification process challenges, change of venue, and challenges to the death penalty's constitutionality in general and to the state's death penalty statute in particular.[47] It is estimated that two to six times more motions are

> *The most expensive part of the pretrial process frequently involves the motions filed in death penalty cases. Defense counsel has both a professional and an ethical obligation to represent his or her client's interests by filing nonfrivolous motions which, at a minimum, create and preserve the defendant's record for appeal. It is estimated that two to six times more motions are filed in death penalty cases than in other felony cases.*

filed in death penalty cases than in other felony cases.[48] Between five and seven motions are typically filed in noncapital cases in New York.[49] In a single North Carolina capital case in 1991, the cost of pretrial motions was $115,247.[50]

A big part of the expense of motions is the cost of experts who are paid for their research/consulting and for their testimony at trial. Experts are employed by both the defense and the prosecution. Among the experts used in capital cases are: (1) psychiatrists, who are paid $100 to $150 an hour or $500 to $1,000 a day;[51] (2) medical examiners, who are paid $700 to $1,000 a day;[52] (3) polygraph experts, who are paid $200 to $300 a day for courtroom testimony and $150 to $250 per examination;[53] (4) experts on eyewitness identification, who are paid about $100 an hour or about $500 a day for courtroom testimony;[54] and (5) forensic scientists, juristic psychologists, and criminologists, who (in 1996) were paid a maximum of about $130 an hour in Florida (Orange County) unless special circumstances existed.[55] Defense expert witnesses alone can easily cost more than $40,000 in capital cases.[56]

The Trial Stage. Approximately 90 percent of criminal cases never reach trial, but instead are resolved through plea bargaining. Capital cases are an exception; they are rarely plea bargained.[57] Because "death is different," death penalty cases go to trial 10 times more often than do other felony cases.[58]

The most striking difference between a capital trial and trials for other serious felonies is that capital trials are bifurcated, that is, divided into two separate stages: a guilt phase and a penalty phase. In bifurcated trials, all of the expenses of the guilt phase can possibly be duplicated in the penalty phase.[59] An average capital trial in California in 1983 was about 3.5 times or 30 days longer than an average noncapital murder trial, which required approximately 12 days.[60] The average death penalty trial in Texas in 1992 lasted 14 weeks and cost $265,640.[61] The average death penalty trial in North Carolina in 1991–92 lasted 14.6 days and cost $84,099,[62] with the range being a low of $24,777 and a high of $179,736.[63] By contrast, the average noncapital murder trial in North Carolina lasted 3.8 days and cost $16,697,[64] with a range of $7,766 to $30,952.[65]

The guilt phase of the bifurcated capital trial in North Carolina was considerably more expensive than the penalty phase. The costs of the guilt phase ranged from $9,802 to $137,500; the average guilt phase cost $52,290 and lasted 10.6 days.[66] The guilt phase, in other words, accounted for about 62 percent of the costs and 73 percent of the time spent on the entire trial. The cost of a capital trial's guilt phase in North Carolina may be atypical, however. Paternoster claims that the penalty phase, and not the guilt phase, is "the single greatest cost inflator of a capital trial."[67] He explains that in most capital trials, the prosecutor's overwhelming evidence makes the defendant's guilt obvious, so there is little to contest. Consequently, defense counsel focuses on saving his or her client's life in the penalty phase of the trial. To aid the effort, counsel is allowed to present mitigating evidence on his or her client's behalf, which requires a considerable, but unknown amount of time.

Among the specific costs of the guilt phase of a capital trial are voir dire, attorney hours, expert testimony, witnesses, and court costs. Most of those expenses involve payments for time expended on the case. It is estimated that voir dire during the selection of the jury takes five times longer in capital cases than in other felony cases[68] and may increase the cost of the capital trial by nearly $90,000 (in 1985).[69] Jury selection in capital cases typically takes six weeks to complete.[70] The average cost of empaneling a jury in capital cases in Texas in 1992 was $17,220.[71] A survey of 20 California capital murder trials conducted in the early 1980s found that jury selection was the most expensive part of a capital trial.[72]

A major reason voir dire in capital cases is so costly is that many death penalty jurisdictions require that jurors not only be questioned individually, but that they also remain sequestered until the full jury is selected or until they are dismissed.[73] Many jurisdictions allow defendants to waive this requirement. Although data on the frequency of such waivers are not available, they are probably not requested very often. Other reasons that voir dire in capital cases takes longer and is more expensive are: (1) the increased number of peremptory challenges allowed in capital cases,[74] (2) the increased number of jurors who are likely to be dismissed for cause,[75] (3) the increased number of jurors who try to disqualify themselves,[76] and (4) in some jurisdictions, the need to select jurors for both the guilt and penalty phase of the trial.[77]

Many states require that capital defendants have two attorneys; no state requires two attorneys in noncapital cases.[78] Attorneys can spend from 300 to 1,000 hours on capital cases.[79] In North Carolina in 1991–92, for example, defense attorneys and prosecutors spent an average of 613 and 282 hours, respectively, on capital cases.[80] By contrast, they spent an average of 150 and 61 hours, respectively, on noncapital cases.[81]

Public defenders in North Carolina were paid an average of $68.31 an hour; assistant public defenders received an average of $48.34 an hour.[82] District attorneys, on the other hand, were paid an average of $83.10 an hour and assistant district attorneys received an average of $55.63 an hour.[83] Based on those hourly rates, the average cost of a public defender in North Carolina capital cases in 1991–92 was about $42,000 per case; the average cost of an assistant district attorney (assuming most capital cases are handled by ADAs) was about $16,000 per case (it would be about $23,000 if handled by a DA).[84]

The cost of defense counsel through sentencing in Maryland in 1982 was estimated to range from $50,000 to $75,000 per capital case.[85] In 1993, the Connecticut Public Defender's Office spent $138 to defend an average noncapital case (this included plea bargains) and approximately $200,000 to defend each death penalty case.[86] Private defense fees in a recent California capital trial involving three defendants cost the state $1.1 million.[87]

The hourly or daily rates of expert witnesses for in–court testimony were described previously and are not repeated here.

A larger number of witnesses are usually called in capital trials. Those witnesses must be interviewed, their testimony must be prepared, and they must be deposed by the other side. All of this requires considerable attorney time. Total costs for two defense attorneys, three prosecutors, investigators, and expert witnesses in capital cases in Texas in 1992 averaged $150,452 ($112,400 for the two defense attorneys, investigators, and expert witnesses and $38,052 for the three prosecutors).[88]

Court costs are estimated to be 3.5 times greater in capital cases than they are in other felony cases.[89] In North Carolina in 1991–92, superior court judges were paid an average of $631 a day; court reporters, an average of $191 a day; deputy court clerks, $146 a day; and bailiffs, $125 a day.[90] Two bailiffs were generally assigned to each capital trial.[91] In Texas in 1992, the average cost per judge in a capital case was $23,968.[92] Courtroom space in North Carolina was estimated to cost $174 a day.[93] In sum, the total per day cost of a capital trial in a North Carolina Superior Court in 1991–92 was estimated to be $1,416; the cost of a capital trial per day in California in 1983 was approximately $2,186, not including extra security or transcript costs.[94]

As mentioned earlier, all of the expenses of the guilt phase could be duplicated in the penalty phase. The penalty phase will require, at a minimum, additional expenditures for attorney time, expert testimony, witnesses, and court costs.[95] Some jurisdictions require separate juries for the penalty phase of a capital trial, in which case the costs of voir dire also could be duplicated.

The Posttrial Stage. The posttrial stage generally is the most expensive part of the entire process.[96] Automatic appeal of conviction and/or death sentence to the state supreme court is required in nearly all jurisdictions with capital punishment statutes.[97] If the appellant wins, the costs of the original trial, or at least part of those costs, could be replicated at the retrial or resentencing.[98]

It is estimated that a typical capital appeal requires from 500 to 2,000 hours of attorney time, not including travel, photocopying, etc.[99] In North Carolina in

> *The* posttrial stage generally is the most expensive part of the entire capital punishment process.

1991–92, appellate defenders received an average of $61.89 an hour; assistant appellate defenders were paid an average of $43.80 an hour.[100] Appointed appellate defense attorneys in California received an average of $60 per hour in 1985.[101] North Carolina Supreme Court justices were paid an average of $96.92 an hour, while their law clerks received an average of $28.02 an hour.[102] The average cost of a North Carolina Supreme Court justice for a capital appeal was estimated to be $1,887; the average cost of a court clerk was $2,083.[103] The average cost of the North Carolina attorney general for a capital appeal was estimated to be $5,261.[104]

Many states also provide proportionality review, although the Supreme Court does not require it (see *Pulley v. Harris,* 1984). Proportionality review is a process whereby state appellate courts compare the sentence in the case being reviewed with sentences imposed in similar cases in the state.[105] Its purpose is to identify disparities in sentencing. To perform proportionality review, data must be gathered and analyzed, and a report must be written. The costs of proportionality review have not been estimated.

Besides the automatic appellate review, capital defendants may contest their conviction and/or sentence through both state and federal post-conviction proceedings. Including the automatic appeal, there are at least nine or ten possible levels of review following the guilt and penalty phase of a capital trial.[106] The average cost of the state post-conviction process for capital cases in Texas in 1992 was $94,240,[107] the biggest expense being for attorney time. The U.S. Constitution does not require the appointment of attorneys for indigent capital defendants beyond the automatic appeal, that is, for state post-conviction collateral review (see *Murray v. Giarratano,* 1989), but many jurisdictions provide them anyway.[108] It has been estimated that attorneys spend an average of 700 to 1,000 hours on state post-conviction proceedings in capital cases.[109] A 1986 American Bar Association survey found that lawyers spent an average of 963 hours on state post-conviction appeals.[110] Specific cost averages in Texas were as follows:

1.   defense costs = $15,000,

2.   prosecution costs = $29,000,

3.   cost of reproducing the trial record[111] = $20,000, and

4.   court of criminal appeals (three-day estimate) = $30,240.[112]

The cost of state post-conviction proceedings in two North Carolina cases was considerably higher—$293,393 and $216,387 per case—although that may be due to the inclusion of stages such as clemency/commutation proceedings not included in the Texas costs.[113] Specific costs in the more expensive North Carolina case included the following (years in which expenses were incurred are in parentheses):

1. state motion for appropriate relief = $29,957 (1985-87),

2. petition for certiorari to North Carolina Supreme Court = $6,188 (1987-88),

3. state motion hearing = $2,057 (1988),

4. motion for stay of execution in North Carolina Supreme Court = $833 (1989),

5. motions in North Carolina Supreme Court = $3,642 (1990),

6. motions in North Carolina Superior Court = $115,247 (1991), and

7. clemency/commutation proceedings = $84,888 (1991-92).[114]

Federal post-conviction proceedings for Texas capital appellants averaged six years and cost about $1.7 million per appellant.[115] Unlike the situation for state post-conviction proceedings, the federal government requires legal representation for capital defendants pursuing federal habeas corpus appeals.[116] The federal courts have (or had) three options in meeting this statutory requirement.[117] First, they may appoint attorneys from the private bar. Those attorneys submit vouchers for payment to the Administrative Office of the United States Courts which allocates funds according to provisions in the Criminal Justice Act (1994).[118] Although the Act does not prescribe any limitation on the amount that can be paid for services, in *In re Berger* (1991), the Court limited appointed counsel representing capital defendants before the Supreme Court to $5,000 in fees. A second option is to appoint attorneys employed by federal public defender organizations which are funded through grants made available by the Judicial Conference of the United States.[119] A problem with these first two options is that neither one guarantees the appointment of attorneys with expertise in capital jurisprudence.[120]

The third and best option (for capital defendants) is (or was) the appointment of attorneys employed by Post-Conviction Defender Organizations (PCDOs), which were originally called Death Penalty Resource Centers. Those agencies were created by Congress in 1988 and deal only with capital cases and related post-conviction issues. They employ full-time, salaried attorneys, investigators, and support staff, and, in the mid-1990s, operated in 20 of the 38 death penalty states.[121] The Judicial Conference funds PCDOs through grants that are contingent upon the receipt of state funding for any state court work PCDOs do. In fiscal year 1994, the 20 PCDOs received nearly $20 million for their work on capital cases.[122]

Because of the success of PCDO attorneys in getting convictions and death sentences overturned, the agencies have come under fire from death penalty proponents. It appears, moreover, that critics of the PCDOs have won the day. On January 6, 1996, President Clinton signed into law HR-1358 (Pub. L. No. 104-91, 110 Stat. 7). The law provided a budget of approximately $262 million for the Federal Judiciary's Defender Services but stipulated that none of the money was to be spent on

PCDOs after April 1, 1996—to allow for an orderly end to the program.[123] After the 1996 fiscal year ended on September 30, no further federal funding of the PCDOs was to be provided.[124]

With the demise of PCDOs, the federal courts will be left with only the first two options of providing attorneys for capital defendants pursuing federal habeas corpus relief. The debate in Congress suggested that the abolition of PCDOs would save the government about $20 million annually,[125] but the Chief Judge of the U.S. Court of Appeals for the Eighth Circuit, Richard Arnold, disagrees. He predicts "that elimination of the PCDOs will significantly increase delays in handling an ever-increasing death penalty caseload by creating an insufficient pool of qualified and experienced attorneys to handle the petitions."[126] He estimates that "the cost of representing death row inmates would rise from the current expenditure of $21.2 million to 'between $37 million and $51.1 million' with the elimination of the PCDOs."[127]

It has been estimated that attorneys in capital cases spend an average of 700 to more than 1,000 hours on federal post-conviction proceedings.[128] The 1986 American Bar Association survey found that lawyers spent an average of 1,037 hours on federal post-conviction litigation.[129] In Texas, defense attorneys received an average of $92,300 for their federal post-conviction work in capital cases, while it cost the Texas attorney general's office an average of $19,600 per capital case challenged on federal habeas corpus.[130] The remainder of the estimated $1.7 million per federal post-conviction capital case went for court costs and outlays.[131]

Cost estimates of federal post-conviction proceedings for North Carolina capital prisoners included the following (years on which estimates are based are in parentheses):

1. certiorari petition to the U.S. Supreme Court = $7,885 (1984),

2. motion for stay of execution in the federal district court = $757 (1989),

3. federal district court habeas proceedings = $17,383 (1989-90), and

4. federal appellate proceedings = $24,556 (1990-92).[132]

Imprisonment. Under current practices, convicted capital offenders serve a long prison term on death row (now averaging more than 10 years), in addition to being sentenced to death.[133] Put somewhat differently, because of super due process protections, capital offenders typically serve 22 percent of what otherwise might be a 50-year-LWOP sentence before they are executed.

It almost certainly is more expensive to house inmates on death row than to confine them with the general population in a maximum-security prison.[134] Reasons are added security precautions, which include single cell confinement. The available evidence, however, suggests that the difference in the annual costs of confinement is not great—approximately $1,000 to $2,000 per inmate.[135] An additional and unique cost of confinement for death row inmates involves the death watch—the period just before the execution, generally 24 hours, when the condemned inmate is watched by the guards who will also take part in the execution process.[136] The extra costs of the death watch have not been estimated.

Execution. Executions themselves are fairly inexpensive, regardless of the method employed. The electricity needed for an electrocution costs about 31 cents; the sodium cyanide pellets used in executions by lethal gas are about $250; and the chemicals needed for a lethal injection cost anywhere from $71.50 to $700.[137] The prices of the bullets and rope used in shooting and hanging

> *U*nder current practices, convicted capital offenders serve a long prison term on death row (now averaging more than 10 years), in addition to being sentenced to death. Put somewhat differently, because of super due process protections, capital offenders typically serve 22 percent of what otherwise might be a 50-year-LWOP sentence before they are executed.

executions have not been reported, but must be minimal. The costs of the execution apparatuses also vary considerably and are not very expensive when averaged over a large number of executions. An electrocution system is about $35,000; the cost of a gallows, about $85,000; a gas chamber is around $200,000; and a lethal injection system is around $30,000. These costs do not include payments to the "execution technicians," which may range from $150 to $500 per execution.[138]

One last cost of capital punishment involves disposal of the body—a potential cost for any inmate who dies in prison. If the family of the executed offender does not make final arrangements, which typically is the case, burial or cremation is left to the state. This final cost has not been estimated, but it is unlikely to be very expensive.

Streamlining the Appellate and Post–Conviction Process. Proponents of capital punishment argue that the costs of the penalty could be reduced significantly if the appellate and post-conviction process were streamlined. They contend that most of the legal challenges filed by death row inmates or their attorneys are without merit—that they are nothing more than desperate attempts to keep the inmate alive. The evidence presented in Chapter 2, however, shows that many of the habeas corpus petitions filed by death row inmates or their attorneys do have merit. Nevertheless, it is true that, until recently, it was possible for death row inmates to employ the dual system of collateral review numerous times, but this is no longer the case. The Supreme Court began placing restrictions on the federal review process in state capital cases in the 1980s.[139]

In addition, as explained in Chapter 3, the passage of the Antiterrorism and Effective Death Penalty Act of 1996 (and similar measures by state legislatures) has made access to both the federal and state courts during the post-conviction process more difficult. However, while the recent restrictions on federal habeas corpus in capital cases may reduce costs at the federal level, they may not reduce costs overall. Costs likely will be shifted to the states and counties where post-conviction motions in state courts will be litigated more extensively.[140]

"Start–Up" Costs. Another cost of capital punishment is the substantial start-up expense incurred when a jurisdiction decides to reinstate the death penalty. Those expenses are of three types: (1) building and facility costs, (2) judicial and attorney training costs, and (3) equipment costs.[141] Because the costs of execution equipment were described previously, only the first two types of start-up costs are examined here.

Building and facility costs vary greatly, but jurisdictions can expect to spend hundreds of thousands and, in some cases, millions of dollars to construct death rows and execution chambers. For example, in 1993, the Wisconsin Department of Corrections estimated that "a new twelve-unit death row, including a lethal injection death chamber" would cost $1.4 million to construct.[142] An estimated $144,600 would have to be spent on one-time start-up overhead costs, and about $500,000 annually for security personnel.[143]

When New York reinstated the death penalty in 1995, the legislature appropriated a little more than $1 million for start-up costs: $389,000 for a 12-cell death row, $190,000 to convert an old correctional hospital into a three-cell death row for women, and $475,000 for a death chamber, injection room, and three holding cells.[144] Florida spent $9.5 million in 1992 to build a new 336-unit death row,[145] and in 1996 the federal government spent $500,000 to build a lethal injection chamber at the new federal death row in Terre Haute, Indiana.[146]

Because "death is different," special training is needed for judges and attorneys involved in death penalty cases. A few jurisdictions require such training. When the New York legislature reinstated captial punishment in 1995, it appropriated about $3.5 million for a new agency for training capital defense attorneys, and another $2 million for the training of capital prosecutors.[147] Kansas reinstated the death penalty in 1994, then budgeted $1.4 million for a death penalty defense agency.[148] In 1995, the Wisconsin legislature contemplated the reenactment of capital punishment and considered spending $60,000 to $70,000 to bring in national experts for a one-time seminar to train 50 to100 lawyers.[149] It also estimated that attorney and judicial training costs for the first two years after reenactment would be about $400,000 and then $200,000 annually, thereafter.[150] In short, attorney and judicial training in capital jurisprudence involves both substantial start-up costs and ongoing expenses to keep both lawyers and judges abreast of changes in capital punishment law.

The LWOP Alternative. LWOP is the only alternative to capital punishment in 16 death penalty jurisdictions in the United States; in 12 jurisdictions, the alternative to capital punishment is either LWOP or a lesser punishment, usually life imprisonment with parole eligibility.[151] The preceding discussion shows that it is less costly to sentence capital offenders to LWOP than it is to sentence them to death—in some cases, as much as two to three times less costly on average.

The greatest savings occur when LWOP sentences are imposed following a guilty plea (but see note 57). In such cases, the substantial costs of the bifurcated trial, the automatic appeal, and post-conviction processes are eliminated.

Even if LWOP sentences were imposed after trial (and post-conviction review), they would still be cheaper than capital punishment because the Supreme Court has ruled that LWOP sentences do not require the super due process procedures necessary when the penalty is death.[152] Thus, the replacement of death sentences with LWOP sentences would reduce financial expenditures considerably.

Critics fear that such a strategy would have the undesirable effect of exacerbating the current prison–overcrowding crisis, but this has not been a problem for states with LWOP statutes. For example, fewer than two percent of Alabama and Kentucky prison inmates are serving LWOP sentences.[153] If all death sentences were changed to LWOP, the 200 to 300 offenders sentenced to death each year, together

*L*WOP is the only alternative to capital punishment in 16 death penalty jurisdictions in the United States; in 12 jurisdictions, the alternative to capital punishment is either LWOP or a lesser punishment, usually life imprisonment with parole eligibility. The Supreme Court has ruled that LWOP sentences do not require the super due process procedures necessary when the penalty is death.

with the approximately 3,000 current death row inmates, would hardly be noticed among the more than one million inmates now confined in American prisons (but see note 32 regarding the added costs of elderly inmates).

In sum, death sentences could be replaced with LWOP at considerable cost savings to the taxpayer, with negligible impact on the current prison overcrowding crisis. LWOP sentences would also allow for the correction of miscarriages of justice when they were discovered and would eliminate any brutalizing effect of capital punishment—to name just a few benefits. At this writing, legislation is pending in North Carolina that would allow prosecutors to offer capital defendants the chance to plead guilty and accept an LWOP sentence. Prosecutors currently do not have that option. If the legislation is enacted, it would theoretically save the state millions of dollars by eliminating the costs of a capital trial and appellate and post–conviction review. Whether such a strategy is desirable for other reasons is another matter.

Conclusion. The evidence clearly shows that capital punishment systems in the United States are always more expensive than punishment systems without capital punishment because super due process is required in the former but not in the latter. If the ultimate penal sanction is supported because of the belief that it is cheaper than noncapital punishments, then this chapter establishes why such a belief is mistaken. Thus, a fair question in the capital punishment debate is whether the death penalty is worth the extra cost.

Discussion Questions

1. Is the death penalty necessary to adequately protect society from the possible future actions of those who have already committed capital crimes?

2. Is the death penalty necessary to protect prison guards and other inmates?

3. Why not execute all capital offenders?

4. Should capital punishment be replaced with LWOP?

5. Which costs more: capital punishment or LWOP? How much more?

6. In a society with limited resources, is capital punishment worth the costs?

7. Why is "super due process" so expensive?

8. Could and should the costs of capital punishment be significantly reduced? (If answered in the affirmative, how?)

9. Should the cost of capital punishment matter?

Notes

[1] See Gallup and Newport, 1991.
[2] Committee on the Judiciary, 1982:315; also see Van den Haag, 1982.
[3] Ibid.
[4] California has sentenced inmates to LWOP for more than 25 years, and not one inmate with such a sentence has ever been released from prison, see Dieter, 1993:13.
[5] Amsterdam, 1982:354.
[6] Haas and Inciardi, 1988:12.
[7] Radelet et al., 1992.
[8] Committee on the Judiciary, op. cit.; also see Van den Haag, op. cit.
[9] Sellin, 1959:72.
[10] Amsterdam, op. cit.
[11] Sorensen and Wrinkle, 1996.
[12] Paternoster, 1991:279.
[13] Ibid.
[14] Sellin, 1967:154-60.
[15] Ibid., p. 76.
[16] Sellin, 1959, op. cit., pp. 77-8.
[17] Bedau, 1982:176, Table 4-5-1.
[18] Ibid., p. 177, Table 4-5-2.
[19] Heilbrun et al., 1978.
[20] Vito et al., 1991.
[21] Marquart and Sorensen, 1988.
[22] Vito and Wilson, 1988.
[23] Amsterdam, op. cit.
[24] A version of this section appeared as "The Economic Costs of Capital Punishment: Past, Present, and Future," pp. 437-58 in Acker et al., 1998. It is reprinted with permission of the publisher.
[25] Culver, 1985:574.
[26] Ellsworth and Ross, 1983:142, Table 6; Bohm et al., 1991:371, Table 1.
[27] Gallup and Newport, op. cit.; but see Longmire, 1996, for the finding that cost effectiveness does not greatly affect death penalty attitudes.
[28] Peterson and Bailey, 1998; Snell, 1997:12, Table 12.
[29] On "super due process," see Radin, 1980.

[30] See New York State Defenders Association 1982; Garey, 1985; Spangenberg and Walsh, 1989; Hoppe, 1992; Dieter, 1992; Cook and Slawson, 1993.

[31] Muwakkil, 1989:6.

[32] See Bohm and Haley, 1997:326. The annual cost of confining an inmate on death row generally is somewhat greater than the annual cost of housing an LWOP inmate among the general population of a maximum security prison, see Brooks and Erickson, 1996:883. Also, the $20,000 average annual cost of imprisonment does not include additional expenses that may be incurred because of the medical problems of elderly inmates. The amount of such costs is unknown. However, any added medical costs should be offset somewhat by the reduced security level needed for elderly inmates.

[33] Because of the conditions of prison life, such as violence, HIV and other diseases, poor diets, and poor health conditions, it has been estimated that an inmate sentenced to LWOP will live an average of 31 years in prison, see Brooks and Erickson, op. cit. At year-end 1995, the median age of a death row inmate at time of arrest was 27 (the median age of death row inmates was 35), see Snell, 1996:8, Table 7.

[34] Paternoster, op. cit.; also see *Harmelin v. Michigan,* 1991.

[35] Cook and Slawson, op. cit., pp. 97-8.

[36] Spangenberg and Walsh, op. cit.; New York State Defenders Association, op. cit.

[37] Spangenberg and Walsh, op. cit., p. 49; Garey, op. cit., p. 1252.

[38] Spangenberg and Walsh, ibid.; Garey 1985, ibid.; Brooks and Erickson, op. cit., p. 893.

[39] Cook and Slawson, op. cit., p. 44, Table 5.3.

[40] Spangenberg and Walsh, op. cit.

[41] Spangenberg and Walsh, ibid., p. 48; Brooks and Erickson, op. cit., p. 901.

[42] Grand juries are involved in felony prosecutions in about half the states and in the federal system, see Bohm and Haley, op. cit., p. 261.

[43] Spangenberg and Walsh, op. cit., p. 49.

[44] Garey, op. cit., p. 1251, n. 134.

[45] Cook and Slawson, op. cit., p. 28-9, n. 47.

[46] Ibid., p. 30, n. 47.

[47] Garey, op. cit., pp. 1249-1250; Cook and Slawson, op. cit., pp. 28-9, n. 47.

[48] Garey, op. cit., p. 1248; Spangenberg and Walsh, op. cit., p. 50.

[49] New York State Defenders Association, op. cit., p. 12.

[50] Cook and Slawson, op. cit., p. 81, Table 7.6.

[51] Spangenberg and Walsh, op. cit.; Garey, op. cit., p. 1253.

[52] Ibid.

[53] Ibid.

[54] Ibid.

[55] Author's own experience.

[56] Brooks and Erickson, op. cit., p. 895.

[57] In some cases, the threat of the death penalty may encourage guilty pleas, thus providing substantial cost savings in comparison to capital cases that go to trial. However, the death penalty is not often used in that way, see Brooks and Erickson, op. cit., pp. 890-891. In some jurisdictions, such as North Carolina, district attorneys are prohibited by statute to plea bargain in first-degree murder cases, see Cook and Slawson, op. cit., p. 2. If capital punishment were replaced with LWOP, on the other hand, it is unlikely that defendants would plead guilty to LWOP (what would they have to lose if they went to trial?). Consequently, in jurisdictions that provide for both capital punishment and LWOP sentences, the availability of capital punishment, as at least a threat, may sometimes reduce costs.

[58] Spangenberg and Walsh, op. cit.; Garey, op. cit., p. 1247, n. 114.

[59] Spangenberg and Walsh, op. cit., p. 52; Brooks and Erickson, op. cit., p. 897.

[60] Garey, op. cit., p. 1258 and p. 1258, n. 175.

[61] Hoppe, op. cit.

[62] Cook and Slawson, op. cit., pp 59 and 61, Tables 6.2 and 6.3.

[63] Ibid., p. 59, Table 6.2.

[64] Ibid., pp. 59 and 61, Tables 6.2 and 6.3.

[65] Ibid., p. 59, Table 6.2.

[66] Ibid., pp. 59 and 61, Tables 6.2 and 6.3.

[67] Paternoster, op. cit., p. 198; also see Garey, op. cit., p. 1259.

[68] Spangenberg and Walsh, op. cit.; Garey, op. cit., p. 1257.

[69] Garey, ibid.

[70] Brooks and Erickson, op. cit., p. 896, n. 134.

[71] Hoppe, op. cit.

[72] Kaplan, 1983:571.

[73] Spangenberg and Walsh, op. cit., p. 51; Garey, op. cit., p. 1255.

[74] Spangenberg and Walsh, ibid., p. 52; Garey, ibid., p. 1256.

[75] Garey, ibid.

[76] Ibid., p. 1257, n. 173.

[77] Spangenberg and Walsh, op. cit.; Garey, ibid.; Brooks and Erickson, op. cit., p. 897.

[78] Spangenberg and Walsh, op. cit., p. 54; Cook and Slawson, op. cit., p. 15.

[79] Spangenberg and Walsh, ibid., p. 53.

[80] Cook and Slawson, op. cit., p. 61, Table 6.3.

[81] Ibid.

[82] Ibid., p. 44, Table 5.3.

[83] Ibid.

[84] Although the hourly costs of district attorneys, public defenders, judges, etc. are usually "fixed" (because they receive salaries) and would be the same whether the case was capital or noncapital, the costs of those participants in the process are provided for two reasons. First is to allow the reader to gauge the costs of a capital case (or any case) that goes to trial (and is further reviewed) in comparison to the costs of a capital case that is plea bargained to LWOP. Second is to help in the estimation of some of the "hidden costs" of capital punishment. When district attorneys spend much of their time trying capital cases, when court time is consumed with lengthy death trials, and when appellate courts spend so much of their time reviewing death penalty appeals, other, noncapital cases are affected. For example, other serious cases receive less attention than they would otherwise, or cases that ordinarily would be tried are plea bargained, simply because there is not enough time to do otherwise.

[85] Garey, op. cit., p. 1258.

[86] Brooks and Erickson, op. cit., p. 892.

[87] Ibid., p. 894.

[88] Hoppe, op. cit.

[89] Spangenberg and Walsh, op. cit.; Garey, op. cit.

[90] Cook and Slawson, op. cit., p. 46, Table 5.4.

[91] Ibid., p. 45.

[92] Hoppe, op. cit.

[93] Cook and Slawson, op. cit., p. 46.

[94] Ibid.; Garey, op. cit., p. 1255. See note 84, supra.

[95] Spangenberg and Walsh, op. cit., p. 52.

[96] Paternoster, op. cit., p. 212.

[97] Spangenberg and Walsh, op. cit. At year-end 1996, Arkansas and the federal government were the only exceptions. In South Carolina, the defendant, if deemed competent, may waive right of sentence review. Idaho, Indiana, Oklahoma, and Tennessee require only review of the sentence. Review of conviction in Idaho has to be filed through appeal or forfeited. Review of conviction can be waived in Indiana and Kentucky, see Snell, 1997:3.

[98] Spangenberg and Walsh, op. cit., p. 53; Brooks and Erickson, op. cit., pp. 897-98.

[99] Spangenberg and Walsh, ibid., pp. 52-53; Garey, op. cit., p. 1263; Paternoster, op. cit., p. 205.

[100] Cook and Slawson, op. cit., p. 48, Table 5.6.

[101] Garey, op. cit.

[102] Cook and Slawson, op. cit., p. 47, Table 5.5.

[103] Ibid., p. 79, Table 7.5.

[104] Ibid. See note 84, supra.

[105] See, for example, Paternoster, op. cit., pp. 81-82.

[106] Freedman, 1997; Garey, op. cit. See Chapter 2, note on the appellate process in capital cases.

[107] Hoppe, op. cit.

[108] Spangenberg and Walsh, op. cit., p. 54.

[109] Ibid., p. 55, for both state and federal post-conviction proceedings.

[110] Paternoster, op. cit., p. 205.

[111] In 1981, it was estimated that the typical trial record in a capital case in California was 4,000 pages or more, while the opening brief averaged about 200 pages, see Garey, op. cit., p. 1263, n. 217.

[112] Hoppe, op. cit.

[113] Cook and Slawson, op. cit., pp. 81-82, Tables 7.6 and 7.7.

[114] Ibid., p. 81, Table 7.6.

[115] Hoppe, op. cit.

[116] 21 U.S.C. S 848 (q)(4), 1994; also see Howard, 1996.

[117] See Howard, ibid., p. 903.

[118] 18 U.S.C. S 3006A, 1994.

[119] 18 U.S.C. S 3006A(g)(2)(A), 1994; 28 U.S.C. S 605, 1994.

[120] Howard, op. cit.

[121] Ibid., p. 904.

[122] Ibid.

[123] Ibid., p. 914

[124] Ibid.

[125] Ibid., p. 915.

[126] Ibid.

[127] Ibid.

[128] Spangenberg and Walsh, op. cit., p. 55, for both state and federal post-conviction proceedings.

[129] Paternoster, op. cit.

[130] Hoppe, op. cit.

[131] Ibid.

[132] Cook and Slawson, op. cit., p. 81, Table 7.6.

[133] Some death row inmates have served more than 20 years awaiting execution. For a description of the "living hell" that death row inmates experience, see Johnson, 1990; 1989.

[134] See Spangenberg and Walsh, op. cit., p. 56.

[135] See Brooks and Erickson, op. cit., p. 883.

[136] See Johnson, 1990, op. cit., Chap. 6.

[137] Denno, 1994:655.

[138] Ibid. Denno notes that before 1990, states were increasingly buying "execution trailers" costing $100,000. The trailers included "a lethal-injection machine, a steel holding cell for the prisoner, and additional areas for witnesses, the chaplain, prison employees, and medical personnel," see ibid.

[139] See, for example, *Barefoot v. Estelle*, 1983; *Saffle v. Parks*, 1990; *Clemons v. Mississippi*, 1990.

[140] Brooks and Erickson, op. cit., pp. 900 and 902.

[141] See ibid.

[142] Ibid., p. 886.

[143] Ibid.

[144] Ibid., p. 886, n. 62.

[145] Ibid., p. 886.

[146] Ibid., pp. 886-887.

[147] Ibid., p. 887.

[148] Ibid., p. 892.

[149] Ibid., p. 887.

[150] Ibid.

[151] Acker and Lanier, 1995:55. Nine nondeath penalty jurisdictions also have LWOP statutes, see Dieter, 1993:11, Table 4.

[152] *Harmelin v. Michigan,* 1991; Paternoster, op. cit., p. 279.

[153] Paternoster, ibid., p. 280.

CHAPTER 7

Miscarriages of
Justice and
the Death Penalty

When assessing the administration of capital punishment, it is helpful to distinguish between how the death penalty might be administered ideally, and the way it is administered in practice. To support the death penalty is to support actual practice and not some unobtainable ideal. It is noteworthy, in this regard, that much of the Supreme Court's workload during the last 20 years has been devoted to refining capital punishment procedures—to making the process work "right." The record of that effort clearly shows that the death penalty in the United States remains very much a work in progress.

One of the enduring problems with capital punishment is that it "not merely kills people, it also kills some of them in error, and these are errors which we can never correct."[1] This irrevocability of capital punishment is one reason why "death is different" and why it requires "super due process."

Ironically, super due process sometimes creates a false sense of security. Some people believe that the chances of a miscarriage of justice in the administration of the death penalty (such as a wrongful arrest, a wrongful charge or indictment, a wrongful conviction, a wrongful sentence, or a wrongful execution) have been reduced to a mere possibility, and probably do not occur in any case. The Committee on the Judiciary wrote: "The Court's decision with respect to the rights of the individual . . . have all but reduced the danger of error in these [capital] cases to that of a mere theoretical possibility. Indeed, the Committee is aware of no case where an innocent man has been put to death."[2] But miscarriages of justice are still a possibility because human beings are fallible. Had the committee examined the evidence, which at the time was anecdotal but, in many cases, persuasive, it could have drawn a different conclusion. For example, M. Watt Espy, Jr., the capital punishment historian who has confirmed over 19,000 legal executions in the United States since 1608, estimates that approximately five percent, or 950, of those executed were innocent.[3]

Definitions of Innocence

To determine whether any innocent people have been victims of miscarriages of justice in capital cases, it is necessary to settle on a definition of "innocence." There are several possibilities.[4] Probably the most conservative definition is one that includes only those cases in which a government official admitted error. A problem is that in the twentieth century, no government official in the United States has ever admitted to being involved in the execution of an innocent person. That does not mean that none has occurred.

The next most conservative definition of innocence includes only officially exonerated defendants who either were completely uninvolved in the capital crime for which they were convicted or were convicted of a capital crime that did not occur. Examples of the latter category are defendants who were convicted of capital rape (when rape was a capital crime) even though sexual relations were consensual, or defendants convicted of capital murder even though the alleged victim was alive.[5] This was the definition of innocence employed by Professors Bedau and Radelet (1987) in their research (which is discussed later) and the definition used in this chapter (unless indicated otherwise).

> *In the twentieth century, no government official in the United States has ever admitted to being involved in the execution of an innocent person.*

A more liberal definition of innocence might include capital defendants whose cases are dismissed or who are found not guilty at retrial. A problem with that definition is that such defendants may be legally innocent but factually guilty. Other definitions might include defendants convicted of capital crimes even though those crimes were accidental, committed in self–defense, or the product of mental illness. In none of those examples should the crime have been considered capital in the first place, even though in some cases it was. In short, a more liberal definition of innocence produces a larger number of such people, while a more conservative definition produces a smaller number.

It should also be noted that the best evidence of miscarriages of justice in capital cases are those convicted capital offenders who have been freed prior to their executions. The reason is that once a person has been executed, there is usually little interest in pursuing his or her claim of innocence. Critics may complain that such "freed" individuals should not count because they were not executed, and, furthermore, they show that the system works. However, it should be remembered that, in each case, the freed individual was the victim of a miscarriage of justice (many of them spent years on death row despite their innocence) and in all likelihood would have been executed if not for sheer luck.

Miscarriages of Justice in Pre–*Gregg* (1976) Capital Cases

Some of the allegedly innocent people executed under pre–*Gregg* (1976) statutes have become a part of American folklore. Among the most famous are the Scottsboro Boys in Alabama, Bruno Hauptmann, the alleged abductor and killer of the Lindbergh baby, in New Jersey, and Julius and Ethel Rosenberg, who were convicted in New

York of selling atomic bomb secrets to the Soviet Union. There is lingering doubt about each of those cases, but no definitive proof of their innocence—or guilt. Most cases do not receive such publicity and attention.

Typical Cases and Indemnity. More typical are the cases of Freddie Lee Pitts and Wilbert Lee, two black men who, in 1975, were finally pardoned by the Florida Cabinet.[6] Pitts and Lee had been tried and sentenced to death twice. They spent 12 years apiece on death row for a murder that somebody else committed. Not until 1997, however, after years of failed efforts, did Pitts and Lee receive a few hundred thousand dollars each as compensation from the state of Florida for its mistakes. That they received any compensation at all is unusual.

Rarely do victims of miscarriages of justice in capital cases receive indemnity from the state that wrongfully convicted them. Another fortunate exception is Bobby Joe Leaster who, in 1992, finally received a check for $75,000. The money was the first installment of the $1 million annuity the state of Massachusetts will pay him for wrongly imprisoning him for 15 years for a murder he did not commit.[7] Leaster was arrested in 1970 for the killing of a variety store owner during a holdup. After reading a newspaper article about Leaster, an eyewitness to the crime told police he knew the killer, and the killer was not Leaster. Leaster was released from prison in 1986 after prosecutors declined to pursue a retrial. Because of the state's fiscal problems, it took several attempts before Massachusett's legislators approved the indemnification measure.

Bedau's Research. One of the first scholars to publish a study of miscarriages of justice in capital cases in the United States (in 1964) was Professor Hugo Adam Bedau.[8] Bedau reported:

> 74 cases between 1893 and 1962 involving criminal homicide, and thus the possibility of a death sentence, in which the evidence suggested that the following major errors had occurred: In each of the 74 cases an innocent person was arrested and indicted; in 71, the innocent person was convicted and sentenced; in 30 (including 11 in states with no death penalty), there was a sentence to prison for life; in 31 cases, there was a sentence to death; in *eight an innocent person was executed* (emphasis in the original).[9]

Bedau has since added 50 "new" cases to the 74 above. The new cases cover 1930 to 1980.

Bedau and Radelet's Research. The most recent and ambitious attempt to document miscarriages of justice in capital cases is the joint effort by Professor Bedau and Professor Michael L. Radelet.[10] They have catalogued 416 cases involving 496 defendants who were convicted of capital or potentially capital crimes in this century, in many cases sentenced to death, and who were later found to be innocent.[11] The 416 cases represent those found through the summer of 1991, when the research was formally concluded. Among the innocent people wrongfully convicted were 23 people who were executed (about 5 percent of the total) and another 22 people who were reprieved within 72 hours of execution.

Of the 496 people wrongfully convicted, 84 percent were convicted prior to 1976 and the implementation of super due process. All but one of the wrongful executions (96 percent) occurred before 1976. One should not infer from those percentages that super due process has significantly reduced miscarriages of justice in capital cases, however. The "prior-to-1976 data" are for seven and one-half decades, while the "1976-and-after data" are for only about one and one-half decades. The average number of people wrongfully convicted of capital crimes in the first six decades of this century is 59 per decade. The number of wrongful convictions for the 1980s is also 59.[12] During the first seven and one-half decades of this century, there was an average of six wrongful convictions in capital cases discovered each year. That was about the same number of discovered wrongful convictions per year during the 1980s with super due process. The yearly average is based on the number of wrongful convictions discovered by Bedau and Radelet, which, according to them, may represent only the "tip of the iceberg."

> *The* most recent and ambitious attempt to document miscarriages of justice in capital cases in the United States is the joint effort by Professors Hugo Adam Bedau and Michael L. Radelet. They have catalogued 416 cases involving nearly 500 defendants who were convicted of capital or potentially capital crimes in this century, in many cases sentenced to death, and who were later found to be innocent. Among the innocent people wrongfully convicted were 23 people who were wrongfully executed.

Miscarriages of Justice in Post–*Gregg* (1976) Capital Cases: Despite Super Due Process

Bedau and Radelet's research reveals that 16 percent of the wrongful convictions in capital cases and one of the 23 wrongful executions occurred between 1976 and the summer of 1991—after the reimposition of the death penalty and super due process and the conclusion of their research. Between 1976 and 1979, 21 wrongful convictions were discovered (an average of seven per year); during the 1980s, 59 wrongful convictions were discovered (almost six per year); and in 1990, only one wrongful conviction was found. Under post-*Gregg* statutes and super due process, there has been an average of six or seven discovered wrongful convictions (excluding the one in 1990) in capital cases per year. That average is about the same as the one for the prior period.

Again, it must be remembered that the averages are based only on those wrongful convictions that have been discovered. It does not appear that super due process protections have made much of a difference in the incidence of wrongful convictions in capital cases.[13] The evidence shows that despite super due process safeguards, miscarriages of justice in capital cases continue. Following are a few recent examples that have received some publicity.

Recent Examples from News Accounts. Wayne Williams, the so-called Atlanta child murderer, was arrested on June 21, 1981 and later convicted of killing two ex-felons (27 and 21 years old). He was sentenced to two life terms.[14] Police also linked Williams to 21 of 27 child murders, and those cases were then closed. Meanwhile, the unsolved murders of young blacks continued for three more years, until 1984. Police refused to say how many murders occurred following Williams's arrest, but the Fulton County medical examiner's log listed at least 23 that seemed to fit the pattern. Many people feel that Williams was a scapegoat.

In 1984, Larry Hicks of Gary, Indiana, won his freedom two weeks before his scheduled execution. Apparently an innocent bystander, Hicks had been convicted of murder on the testimony of one person in a trial that lasted only a day and a half.[15]

Also in 1984, Earl Charles was nearly executed in Georgia for a double murder. He was freed after proving that he was in Florida at the time.[16]

Randall Dale Adams was released from a Texas prison in 1989 after serving more than 12 years following his 1977 conviction for the murder of a Dallas police officer.[17] Adams, the subject of an award-winning documentary, *The Thin Blue Line*, once came within three days of execution, despite steadfastly maintaining his innocence. In the documentary, the state's key witness against Adams, David Harris, all but confessed to the shooting for which Adams was convicted. The Texas Court of Criminal Appeals set aside Adams's conviction and noted that prosecutors had suppressed evidence and that witnesses had given perjured testimony in the case.

Also in 1989, Timothy Hennis walked away from a New Hanover County, North Carolina, courthouse a free man after serving 844 days on death row at Central Prison in Raleigh.[18] Hennis was convicted of three murders in July, 1986. He was granted a new trial when the North Carolina Supreme Court ruled that the state's use of victim photographs may have inflamed the jury. The jury acquitted him at his second trial.

Leonel Torres Herrera was executed in Texas on May 12, 1993, for the murder of two police officers.[19] Prior to his execution, the Supreme Court rejected evidence (sworn statements) that his then-dead brother had committed the crimes. The Court ruled that Herrera and others like him are not entitled to federal hearings on belated evidence of innocence unless they meet an undefined "extraordinarily high" level of proof. The Court opined that relief in cases such as Herrera's should be sought through executive clemency.

In June, 1993, Anson Avery Maynard's death sentence was commuted to life in prison by North Carolina Governor Jim Martin.[20] Maynard had been convicted of the 1981 killing of his thief-partner, Steven Henry. It was believed that Henry had made a deal to testify against Maynard and that Maynard had killed Henry to keep him silent. Maynard was convicted on the testimony of a man who swore he had witnessed the killing. No physical evidence tied Maynard to the crime. As Maynard awaited his execution, the wife of the man who had testified against him admitted she had lied during her part of the trial in order to protect her husband—who may have been Henry's killer in a drug deal gone bad. Several alibi witnesses then came forward, including a truck driver who corroborated Maynard's claim that he had hitchhiked a ride after his car broke down far from where the crime was committed.

In 1993, a Baltimore County, Maryland, circuit judge overturned Kirk Bloodsworth's conviction for the rape and murder of a nine-year-old girl and ordered him freed from prison.[21] Bloodsworth had served nine years in prison, part of it on death row, despite his continued claim of innocence. His conviction was overturned after DNA testing of the semen on the girl's underpants indicated that someone else had committed the crime. Bloodsworth had been convicted on the testimony of three eyewitnesses who stated that they saw the defendant with the girl shortly before she disappeared. Bloodsworth insisted that he had never met the girl.

Jesse Dwayne Jacobs was executed in Texas on January 4, 1995. Two days prior to the execution, the Supreme Court denied his request for a stay of execution, even though the state of Texas conceded that he did not kill the victim of the kidnapping and murder for which he was convicted in 1987.[22] Jacobs originally confessed to the crime, but later recanted and told authorities that his sister, Bobbie Hogan, had committed the murder. He said that he confessed to the murder because he preferred death to spending the rest of his life in prison. Seven months after Jacobs was convicted of capital murder, his sister was tried and convicted of the same crime. During the sister's trial, the prosecutor, who had also prosecuted Jacobs, told the jury that the sister had pulled the trigger and that Jacobs did not even know that she had a gun. Jacobs was called to testify at his sister's trial and claimed that he was outside when the killing took place in an abandoned house. The Supreme Court has held (in *Enmund v. Florida*, 1982) that the Eighth Amendment prohibits the execution of a person who participated in a crime that led to murder when that person did not actually kill or intend for a killing to occur.

Wrongful Executions under Post–*Gregg* (1976) Statutes. Documenting cases of innocent persons executed is an extraordinarily difficult task. Once an alleged murderer is dead, it is almost impossible to right the record, so a degree of uncertainty nearly always characterizes such cases. Of particular interest are wrongful executions that have taken place under post–*Gregg* (1976) statutes and super due process. Bedau and Radelet report one (as of the summer of 1991): James Adams, a black man, convicted of first-degree murder in 1974 and executed in Florida in 1984. Following is Bedau and Radelet's description of the facts of the case, as taken from their catalogue of defendants:

> Witnesses located Adams' car at the time of the crime at the home of the victim, a white rancher. Some of the victim's jewelry was found in the car trunk. Adams maintained his innocence, claiming that he had loaned the car to his girlfriend. A witness identified Adams as driving the car away from the victim's home shortly after the crime. This witness, however, was driving a large truck in the direction opposite to that of Adams' car, and probably could not have had a good look at the driver. It was later discovered that this witness was angry with Adams for allegedly dating his wife. A second witness heard a voice inside the victim's home at the time of the crime and saw someone fleeing. He stated this voice was a woman's; the day after the crime he stated that the fleeing person was positively not Adams. More importantly, a hair sample found clutched in the victim's hand, which in all likelihood had come from the assailant, did not match Adams' hair. Much of this

exculpatory information was not discovered until the case was examined by a skilled investigator a month before Adams' execution. Governor Graham, however, refused to grant even a short stay so that these questions could be resolved.[23]

Bedau and Radelet also cite the case of Edward Earl Johnson who was executed in Mississippi on May 20, 1987. Although they describe why they doubt his guilt, they did not include him in their catalogue apparently because his case did not meet their conservative definition of innocence.

Besides Leonel Torres Herrera and Jesse Dwayne Jacobs, who were both executed in Texas in 1993 and 1995, respectively (both cases were described previously but were not included in Bedau and Radelet's catalogue of cases because their executions occurred after the summer of 1991 when Bedau and Radelet's research was formally concluded), another post–*Gregg* (1976) execution involved Robert Sullivan, who was convicted in 1973 and executed in Florida in 1983. Enough questions were raised about Sullivan's guilt that Pope John Paul II made a personal plea to Florida Governor Graham to halt the execution. Other people executed after 1976 and the implementation of super due process, despite evidence of their innocence, include (state and date of execution in parentheses): Girvies L. Davis (Illinois, 1995), Roger Keith Coleman (Virginia, 1992), Willie Jaspar Darden (Florida, 1988), Robert Nelson Drew (Texas, 1994), Roy Stewart (Florida, 1994), Barry Fairchild (Arkansas, 1995), and Larry Griffin (Missouri, 1995).[24]

As many as a dozen people (and likely more) may have been executed in error in the United States since 1976 and the implementation of super due process. That represents nearly three percent of all executions through April 1, 1998. How could those wrongful executions (and wrongful convictions) occur, especially within the context of super due process? That question is addressed next.

> *A*s many as a dozen people (and likely more) may have been executed in error in the United States since 1976 and the implementation of super due process. That represents nearly three percent of all executions through April 1, 1998.

Why Wrongful Convictions Occur in Capital Cases: Errors Prior to Trial

As law professor Samuel Gross surmises, "The basic cause for the comparatively large number of errors in capital cases is a natural and laudable human impulse: We want murderers to be caught and punished."[25] Many of the errors that contribute to wrongful convictions in capital cases frequently occur long before the case goes to trial. Some of the sources of those errors are discussed in the following sections.

Shoddy Investigation by the Police. Many wrongful convictions in capital cases are a product of shoddy investigation by the police, who sometimes identify the wrong person as the criminal. When a capital crime is committed, there is usually great pressure on the police to solve it. When the police are unable to do so within a reasonable amount of time, they sometimes cut corners and jump to conclusions. They (or others who aid them) may even go so far as to manufacture evidence against a suspect. For example, in 1993, the West Virginia Supreme Court of Appeals ruled as invalid hundreds of blood tests that West Virginia prosecutors had used over a 10-year period to link defendants to crime scenes.[26] The state police serologist in every case had lied about, made up, or manipulated evidence to win convictions. There was also evidence that the serologist's supervisors may have ignored or concealed complaints of his misconduct. At least 134 prisoners may be entitled to new trials because of the falsified testimony that put them in prison. These errors were discovered; how many such errors go undetected cannot be known.

Eyewitness Misidentification and Perjury by Prosecution Witnesses. Eyewitness misidentification is the most important contributing factor to wrongful convictions in noncapital cases.[27] It is probably less common in capital cases, but it still was the second most important factor, accounting for 16 percent of the errors in the capital cases discovered by Bedau and Radelet.

In noncapital cases, the crime victim is often able to identify the offender; in capital cases, that is not possible. Consequently, in capital cases, the police frequently must rely on evidence from other people, such as accomplices, jailhouse snitches, other disreputable characters, and even the defendant himself or herself. Some offenders implicate innocent people to divert suspicion from themselves. Other people, who may or may not have had a role in the crime, perjure themselves for money or for other favors from criminal justice officials, such as the dropping of charges in another unrelated case. It should come as no surprise, then, that perjury by prosecution witnesses is the foremost cause of wrongful convictions in capital cases. Bedau and Radelet identified witness perjury as a factor in 35 percent of the wrongful convictions that they discovered.

> *P*erjury by prosecution witnesses is the foremost cause of wrongful convictions in capital cases.

False Confessions. The third most common cause of errors in capital cases is false confessions, which accounted for 14 percent of the errors in the cases discovered by Bedau and Radelet.[28] Police officers in the United States have powerful techniques for extracting confessions:

> They confuse and disorient the suspect, they lie about physical evidence, about witnesses, about statements by other suspects; they pretend that they already have their case sealed and are only giving the suspect a chance to explain his side of the story; they pretend to understand, to sympathize, to excuse; they play on the suspect's fears, his biases, his loyalty to family and friends, his religion; they exhaust the suspect and wear him down; in some cases, they use violence, even torture.[29]

By using such coercive and manipulative methods, the police are often successful in getting guilty defendants to confess. Sometimes, however, they get innocent people to confess, too.

Guilty Pleas by Innocent Defendants. Another source of error in capital cases is guilty pleas by innocent defendants. Because of their fear of being executed, some innocent people charged with capital crimes plead guilty to lesser, noncapital offenses. Radelet and his colleagues list 16 cases of innocent people in this century who pled guilty to noncapital murder to avoid the possibility of execution.[30]

Failure of Prosecutors to Dismiss the Charges Against Ostensibly Innocent Defendants. Still another source of error in capital cases is the failure of prosecutors to dismiss the charges against ostensibly innocent defendants. Prosecutors may be reluctant to dismiss charges even when the case is a weak one, especially when there is public clamor for a conviction. Much of this has to do with ego. For example, a sign seen in the Dallas County, Texas, prosecutor's office reads: "Convicting the guilty is easy. It's the innocent that keep us working late."[31] The problem is that not only are some weak cases tried, but, as the quotation suggests, in some cases innocent defendants are convicted.

> *A* sign seen in the Dallas County, Texas prosecutor's office reads: "Convicting the guilty is easy. It's the innocent that keep us working late."

Why Wrongful Convictions Occur in Capital Cases: Errors at Trial

Professor Gross claims that despite some of the problems just cited, the capital trial "plays a comparatively minor role in the production of errors in capital cases."[32] Gross says the reason is that capital defendants usually have superior (as compared to other felony defendants) defense counsel:

> Capital defendants . . . may be better represented than other criminal defendants. The attorneys who are appointed to represent them may be more experienced and skillful, and their defenders may have more resources at their disposal. Other things being equal, higher quality representation will decrease the likelihood of conviction, and may operate as a check on errors and misconduct that drive some innocent capital defendants to trial and to conviction.[33]

The evidence, however, suggests that Gross may be wrong on this point.

The Quality of Legal Representation in Capital Cases. Professor Bedau relates that "experienced criminal trial attorneys . . . say that 'no really capable defense lawyer should ever lose a capital case.'"[34] Most capital defendants, though, are not represented by capable defense attorneys, but by those who are inexperienced, overworked, understaffed, less resourceful, less independent, and who frequently lose capital cases.[35]

A good example is the case of John Spinkelink, the third person executed in the United States under post-*Gregg* (1976) statutes and the first person during that period executed against his will. Spinkelink's last appeal was based on a Sixth Amendment claim of counsel ineffectiveness. According to Ramsey Clark, former attorney general of the United States:

> John Spinkelink's trial attorneys were court-appointed. They lacked sufficient resources to prepare and conduct the defense. One publicly stated that the case was beyond his competence. One was absent during part of the jury selection to be with his wife in childbirth. He had not sought a delay in the proceeding or permission of the court to be absent. Spinkelink's lawyers also failed to challenge the composition of the grand and petit juries. Both were later found to underrepresent blacks, women and young people— groups considered by most experienced attorneys to be favorable to the defense in capital cases. The lawyers failed to ask that Spinkelink be tried separately from his co-defendant who was acquitted. Severance was authorized under Florida law and would seem strategically important. Counsel failed to challenge excessive security measures in the courtroom, which are generally thought to be prejudicial to a defendant. . . . They [the prosecution] had (wrongly) informed the jury in their closing argument that the judge could not impose a more severe sentence than the jury recommended. This may have encouraged the jury to ask for a maximum sentence, leaving the judge the full range of punishment alternatives. Counsel failed to obtain a transcript of questions asked prospective jurors, which was necessary in determining if they were constitutionally selected. The Florida Supreme Court ruled that all objections had been waived. With their client facing death, counsel did not request oral argument on appeal in the Supreme Court of Florida.[36]

Spinkelink's experience is not uncommon. A Texas study by the governor's judicial council found that three-quarters of murderers with court-appointed attorneys were sentenced to death, while only about a third of those represented by private lawyers were so sentenced.[37]

A 1990 *National Law Journal* study found that many poor defendants sentenced to death (and nearly all capital defendants are poor) had lawyers who had never handled a capital trial before, lacked training in life-or-death cases, made little effort to present evidence in support of a life sentence, or had been reprimanded, disciplined, or subsequently disbarred.

A 1990 *National Law Journal* study shows that criminal defendants in six states of the South—Alabama, Florida, Georgia, Louisiana, Mississippi, and Texas—often wind up on death row after being represented by inexperienced, unskilled, or unprepared court-appointed lawyers.[38] The study found that many poor defendants sentenced to death (and nearly all capital defendants are poor) had lawyers who had never handled a capital trial before, lacked training in life–or–death cases, made little effort to present evidence in support of a life sentence, or had been reprimanded, disciplined, or subsequently disbarred. Consider the following examples from the study:

- Nine years after John Young was condemned to death in Georgia in 1976, his disbarred lawyer, Charles Marchman Jr., admitted that his drug use, the breakup of his marriage, the discovery of his homosexuality, and other factors prevented him from defending Young adequately.

- James Copeland, on Louisiana's death row, had a lawyer at his second trial who confessed that he never read the first trial's transcript and did little to uncover evidence for life imprisonment.

- Texas lawyer Jon Wood unsuccessfully defended Jesus Romero against the death penalty with 29 words, among them: "You've got that man's life in your hands. You can take it or not. That's all I have to say."

Even an attorney who sleeps through the trial is not necessarily considered ineffective, as is seen in the following description of a capital case in Houston, Texas:

Seated beside his client—a convicted capital murderer—defense attorney John Benn spent much of Thursday afternoon's trial in apparent deep sleep. His mouth kept falling open and his head lolled back on his shoulders, and then he awakened just long enough to catch himself and sit upright. Then it happened again. And again. And again.

Every time he opened his eyes, a different prosecution witness was on the stand describing another aspect of the Nov. 19, 1991, arrest of George McFarland in the robbery-killing of grocer Kenneth Kwan.

When state District Judge Doug Shaver finally called a recess, Benn was asked if he truly had fallen asleep during a capital murder trial. "It's boring," the 72-year old longtime Houston lawyer explained.[39]

Attorney Benn's performance did "not offend the right to counsel guaranteed by the United States Constitution, the trial judge explained, because, '[t]he Constitution doesn't say the lawyer has to be awake.'"[40] Agreeing with the trial judge's assessment was the Texas Court of Criminal Appeals, which rejected McFarland's claim of ineffective assistance of counsel.[41]

Benn is not the only Texas attorney who has fallen asleep during a capital trial. Houston attorney Joe Frank Cannon also has that reputation. He continually dozed off while defending Calvin Burdine, and the Texas Court of Criminal Appeals again held that "a sleeping attorney was sufficient 'counsel' under the Constitution."[42] Another one of Cannon's death penalty clients, Carl Johnson, eventually appealed to the United States Court of Appeals for the Fifth Circuit. That court ruled that Johnson was not denied the effective assistance of counsel "notwithstanding the sleeping lawyer."[43]

The *National Law Journal* study discovered a general failure of the states (except Florida) to provide effective assistance of counsel to capital defendants. Among the problems were the following:

- Florida, Texas, and Mississippi have no statewide standards for appointing defense lawyers;

- Georgia has standards that are unenforced;

- Louisiana's requirement of five years of law practice allows civil lawyers to be appointed to murder cases; and

- Alabama's requirement of five years of criminal law experience "means nothing in rural areas" where felony trials are rare.

In addition, and contrary to what Gross reports, defense counsel in capital cases rarely has the resources necessary to mount an effective defense. According to a 1982 study, court-appointed attorneys in Florida had a $3,500 cap on the payment for defense services in capital cases.[44] In the 1990s, attorneys in Alabama were being paid only $20 an hour for out-of-court time in capital cases, with a limit of $2,000 per case; Mississippi was limiting payment to $1,000 a case.[45] Professor Bowers explains:

> Dollar-wise [an appointed attorney] peaks out before going to trial, meaning the trial is his gift to the defendant—it's free—that's his practice he's cutting into. . . . The cap makes hungry, inexperienced guys take cases but attorneys who can command fees can't afford to.[46]

Some jurisdictions have attempted to provide more adequate resources in capital cases, but in none could the provision of those resources be considered generous. Most provide woefully inadequate resources. (See Chapter 6 for the costs of capital punishment.)

Even if the necessary financial resources *were* provided, that would not compensate entirely for deficient intellectual resources. Defense attorneys, however, are not entirely to blame for this problem. Capital jurisprudence is a highly specialized area of the criminal law, and most attorneys have not received instruction in it.[47] Consequently, even when they are conscientious, they may make numerous mistakes.

Defense attorneys who lack experience in capital cases are often stymied at the penalty phase of the bifurcated trial. Many attorneys have experience pleading their client's innocence (the focus of the guilt phase), but only those lawyers who have tried several capital cases are experienced in making an affirmative case for their client's life in the penalty phase. As attorney Margot Garey relates:

> Many defense attorneys fail to make the transition and do not adequately prepare or effectively present the defendant's penalty phase trial. For example, a defense attorney may structure a guilt trial strategy that is inconsistent with the penalty phase theory. This situation may negate any effective defense at

the penalty proceeding since a consistent trial strategy increases the defendant's believability and credibility. Should a guilty verdict be rendered in the guilt phase, it is imperative that the jury believe the defendant's mitigating circumstances proffered in the penalty phase. Therefore, the defense attorney cannot plan the theory of the guilt phase trial independent of the penalty phase. She must develop and structure a defense theory that will include the penalty phase. Because the preparation required for structuring a bifurcated proceeding is categorically different from that required for a noncapital trial, defense counsel who may be very competent in complex noncapital criminal trials may, without training, be ineffective in capital trials.[48]

In sum, whether it is the result of a lack of training, experience, or heart, most capital defendants receive what appears to be ineffective legal representation. An interesting question is what constitutes effective legal counsel. To what type of defense should capital defendants be entitled? That question is addressed in the next section.

What Constitutes Effective Assistance of Counsel? Not only do capital defendants have a Sixth Amendment right to counsel, they also have the right to the "effective assistance of counsel."[49] It was not until 1984, however, that the United States Supreme Court provided any guidelines for determining when counsel is ineffective. The case was *Strickland v. Washington* (466 U.S. 668).

Strickland's claim of ineffective assistance of counsel was denied, but the Court did create a two-pronged test for determining when counsel is ineffective at either the guilt or penalty phase of a bifurcated capital trial. First, the defendant must show (and the burden of proof is on the defendant) that his or her attorney's performance was deficient based on "prevailing professional norms." If the Court agrees with the defendant on this first claim, then the defendant must also show that his or her attorney's deficient performance contributed to the adverse outcome of the case. Professor Paternoster observes, "This part of the test requires that a court reviewing an attorney's performance for effectiveness must, with hindsight, determine if the outcome of the trial would have been different had counsel not been incompetent."[50]

The Court's holding in *Strickland* seems to suggest that it is unnecessary for defense lawyers in capital cases to be effective; it is only necessary for them not to be ineffective.[51] As the evidence presented previously shows, the standard is not very high.

The Illusive Hope of Clemency

Clemency generally provides the final opportunity to consider whether a death sentence should be imposed.[52] All 50 states, the federal government, and the military have provisions for granting clemency. They allow the governor of a state or the president of the United States, when federal or military law is violated, to exercise leniency or mercy. Many states have specialized administrative boards or panels authorized to assist the governor in making the clemency decision. In a few states, the governor is not authorized to grant clemency unless an administrative body has first recommended it. Three types of clemency relevant to capital punishment are reprieve, commutation, and pardon.

Reprieve is the most common type of clemency employed in capital cases and the most limited. A reprieve temporarily postpones an execution. It is typically used to allow a death row inmate the opportunity to complete a pending appeal or to give the governor a last-minute chance to review questions about the inmate's guilt.

Commutation involves the substitution of a lesser punishment for the one imposed by the court. A sentence of life imprisonment (with or without the opportunity for parole) is the sentence most likely to be substituted for a death sentence. Sometimes commutations are contingent on certain conditions, such as the inmate waiving his or her right to a new trial or agreeing not to profit from the sale of an account of his or her crime. From January 1, 1973, to April 1, 1998, only 76 pardons were granted to condemned inmates, including those by the governor of Texas who was required to do so because of favorable court decisions.[53]

A pardon is the most expansive type of clemency. With a pardon, the prisoner's crime is erased and his or her punishment is terminated. A pardoned individual is freed entirely from the criminal justice system and is treated legally as if he or she had never been charged or convicted of a crime. Pardons are rarely granted to people convicted of capital crimes.

Chief Justice Rehnquist considers executive clemency the "fail safe" of the criminal justice system.[54] It is the last, best chance of rectifying miscarriages of justice. Unfortunately for those who would rely on clemency to correct errors made earlier in the process, recent experience contradicts the promise. Few death sentences have been commuted under post-*Furman* statutes because of increased media attention devoted to capital clemency deliberations and the realization by governors that a decision to commute a death sentence is likely to lead to political suicide. This is a change from the past. Prior to 1970, governors in death penalty states "routinely commuted up to a third of the death sentences that they reviewed," but since then only about one death sentence a year (in the entire country) has been commuted.[55]

> *P*rior to 1970, governors in death penalty states "routinely commuted up to a third of the death sentences that they reviewed," but since then only about one death sentence a year (in the entire country) has been commuted.

Conclusion

Contrary to the beliefs of some death penalty proponents, miscarriages of justice in capital cases, including wrongful executions, do occur and, unfortunately, they happen with some regularity and frequency. Moreover, the evidence suggests that super due process requirements have not had the desired effect of significantly reducing those mistakes. Professor Gross maintains that:

The basic conclusion is simple. The steady stream of errors that we see in cases in which defendants are sentenced to death is a predictable consequence of our system of investigating and prosecuting capital murder. . . . But what about what happens after trial? Everybody knows that direct and collateral review are more painstaking for capital cases than for any others. Isn't it likely that all these mistakes are caught and corrected somewhere in that exacting process? The answer, I'm afraid, is No. At best, we could do an imperfect job of catching errors after they occur, and in many cases we don't really try. As a result, most miscarriages of justice in capital cases never come to light.[56]

Some death penalty proponents argue that even if some innocent persons are executed, those mistakes, though regrettable, are justified nonetheless by the protection executions provide society.[57] Those who make the argument clearly believe that executions (whether of the guilty or the innocent) have a general deterrent effect. As shown in detail in Chapter 5, however, there is no credible evidence to support such a belief.

Finally, some death penalty proponents generalize the preceding argument and maintain that (unspecified) advantages of capital punishment morally justify miscarriages of justice in capital cases. Professor Van den Haag writes:

> Most human activities—medicine, manufacturing, automobile and air traffic, sports, not to speak of wars and revolutions—cause the death of innocent bystanders. Nevertheless, if the advantages sufficiently outweigh the disadvantages, human activities, including those of the penal system with all its punishments, are morally justified.[58]

A recent Gallup poll found that if people were convinced that 1 percent of those sentenced to death were innocent, then 74 percent of those interviewed would still favor the death penalty for a person convicted of murder (77 percent favored the death penalty in general).[59]

One must wonder whether there is a threshold level for miscarriages of justice at which people who favor the death penalty in general would oppose it.[60] If other, less final punishments can achieve the same purposes as capital punishment—and can do so without the liabilities associated with capital punishment, such as miscarriages of justice—then, morally, the alternative punishments should be preferred.

Discussion Questions

1. Have innocent people been wrongly convicted and executed under post-*Furman* statutes?

2. Should the state be required to indemnify innocent people wrongly convicted of capital crimes when they have spent years in prison?

3. Should the state be required to indemnify the families of innocent people who have been executed?

4. How can wrongful convictions and executions occur, especially within the context of "super due process"?

5. To what type of defense should capital defendants be entitled?

6. Should attorneys who represent capital defendants be required to possess any special qualifications or training? What should the special qualifications or training be?

7. Should we trust capital defendants' lives to juries?

8. If not juries, who should make the decision of whether a convicted capital defendant should live or die?

9. What constitutes effective assistance of counsel?

10. Do you agree with the Court's decision in *Strickland v. Washington* regarding what constitutes ineffective assistance of counsel?

11. Is the possibility of executing innocent people reason enough to abolish the death penalty?

12. How can the human sacrifice of innocent persons (any persons?) be morally justified in the last decade of the twentieth century?

Notes

[1] Amsterdam, 1982:349.

[2] Committee on the Judiciary, 1982:317.

[3] Personal communication between Espy and the author.

[4] The following discussion is from Radelet and Bedau, 1998.

[5] In 20 of the 350 cases (6 percent) of wrongful convictions in capital cases catalogued by Bedau and Radelet (1987), no crime actually occurred, though a defendant was convicted of a capital offense.

[6] See Amsterdam, op. cit.

[7] See *The Charlotte [NC] Observer*, November 13, 1992.

[8] But also see Sellin, 1959:63-5; Bye, 1919:80-1.

[9] Bedau, 1982:234.

[10] Bedau and Radelet, op. cit.; also see Radelet et al., 1992.

[11] Most of the information in this chapter about the Bedau and Radelet research is from Radelet et al., 1992, op. cit. Note also that although Radelet et al. report 416 cases, the author's count of cases in their Inventory of Cases revealed only 375.

[12] The specific number for each decade is as follows: 1900s = 30; 1910s = 93 (This total is misleading because one case had 51 defendants. The "crime"—a race riot between blacks and whites—occurred in Arkansas in 1919. All 51 of the defendants were black; no whites were charged with crimes. Excluding those 51 defendants in the 1910s, the average for the six decades was 51 and not 59.); 1920s = 64; 1930s = 69; 1940s = 41; 1950s = 31; and 1960s = 27. Between 1970 and 1976, before the reimposition of the death penalty and super due process, there were 60 wrongful convictions in capital cases.

[13] Theoretically, one might assume that super due process protections would reduce the number of wrongful convictions in capital cases. On the other hand, one might reasonably argue that miscarriages of justice might be easier to detect and, therefore, more numerous the more recently they occur because of the "fresher trail" that is left.

[14] See *The Anniston [AL] Star*, September 9, 1984.

[15] *U.S. News and World Report*, December 17, 1984, p. 45.

[16] Ibid.

[17] See *The Anniston [AL] Star*, March 22 and 24, 1989.

[18] *The Charlotte [NC] Observer*, September 5, 1989.

[19] See *The Charlotte [NC] Observer*, January 26, 1993.

[20] See *The Charlotte [NC] Observer*, June 27, 1993.

[21] See *The Charlotte [NC] Observer*, June 29, 1993.

[22] See *The Charlotte [NC] Observer*, January 3, 1995.

[23] Bedau and Radelet, op. cit., p. 91.

[24] Lehner, 1996.

[25] Gross, 1996:499-500. Unless indicated otherwise, most of the information in this section is from Gross, 1996, who based his analysis on data from Bedau and Radelet, op. cit., and Radelet et al., 1992, op. cit.

[26] See *The Charlotte [NC] Observer*, November 12, 1993, p. 8A.

[27] Huff et al., 1986.

[28] On the other hand, the discovery of most miscarriages of justice in capital cases is the result of a confession by the real criminal.

[29] Gross, op. cit., p. 485.

[30] Radelet et al., 1992, op. cit.

[31] Lehner, op. cit.

[32] Gross, op. cit., pp. 492-93.

[33] Ibid., p. 496.

[34] Bedau, op. cit., pp. 189-90.

[35] Bedau, ibid., p. 190; Bowers, 1984:339.

[36] Quoted in Bowers, ibid., pp. 352-53.

[37] Andersen, 1983:39.

[38] Coyle et al., 1990; also see Mello and Perkins, 1998:268. Those six states account for approximately 60 percent of all post-*Gregg* executions.

[39] Cited in Bright, 1998:130; also see Mello and Perkins, ibid., p. 271.

[40] Bright, ibid.

[41] Ibid.

[42] Ibid., pp. 130-31.

[43] Ibid.

[44] Bowers, op. cit., p. 351.

[45] Bright, 1997:11.

[46] Bowers, op. cit.

[47] To help remedy that problem, some states, such as Florida, have created capital punishment defense agencies. The attorneys who work in the agencies handle only capital punishment cases, and, thus, are able to develop expertise. A problem is that most of the agencies are understaffed and underfunded, and, consequently, have only the resources to handle appeals.

[48] Garey, 1985:1240-41; also see Wollan, 1989, regarding the complexities of capital jurisprudence.

[49] See *McMann v. Richardson*, 397 U.S. 759, 771, note 14, 1970.

[50] Paternoster, 1991:88.

[51] See Paternoster, ibid., p. 89; also see Mello and Perkins, op. cit.

[52] Unless indicated otherwise, material in this section is from Kobil, 1998.

[53] *Death Row, U.S.A.,* 1998.

[54] Cited in *Herrera v. Collins*, 1993:415.

[55] See Baldus and Woodworth, 1998:388-9 for the pre-1970's figure; also see Dieter, 1996:26.

[56] Gross, op. cit., p. 497.

[57] See, for example, the Committee on the Judiciary, op. cit.

[58] Van den Haag, 1982:325.

[59] Gallup, 1995.

[60] See Longmire, 1996, for the finding that evidence of the execution of innocent persons is one of the most effective ways of changing the opinions of death penalty supporters to opponents.

CHAPTER 8

Arbitrariness and Discrimination in the Administration of the Death Penalty

In its *Furman* decision, two of the major problems the Supreme Court found with existing death penalty statutes were that they did not prevent the death penalty from being imposed arbitrarily and in a discriminatory fashion. Professors Nakell and Hardy provide relevant definitions of the two key terms:

- Arbitrariness involves the question of whether discretion permits the death penalty to be applied randomly, capriciously, irregularly, or disproportionately among the qualified defendants without any evident regard for the legal criteria designed to determine the selection. Arbitrariness is random.[1]

- Discrimination involves the question of whether discretion permits the death penalty to be deliberately directed disproportionately against certain qualified defendants, not because of the nature of their crimes, but because they belong to a particular class or group, determined by such considerations as race, sex, nationality, religion, or wealth. Discrimination is deliberate.[2]

Recall from the discussion in Chapter 2 that the Supreme Court approved, on faith, the new guided discretion statutes enacted in the wake of *Furman*. The Court assumed, without any evidence, that the new statutes and other procedural reforms would rid the death penalty's administration of the problems cited in *Furman*, including arbitrariness and discrimination. The purpose of this chapter is to examine the evidence amassed since the Court's 1976 decision and to determine whether the Court's faith was justified.

Arbitrariness in the Administration of the Death Penalty under Post-*Furman* Statutes

As evidence of arbitrary application of the death penalty under post-*Furman* statutes, critics point to the small percentage of all death-eligible offenders who are executed and to the patterns in which the death penalty has been applied across jurisdictions and over time. Sources of that arbitrariness have been identified as: (1) post-*Furman* statutes that justify arbitrariness, (2) jurors' misunderstanding or underestimating their sentencing obligations, (3) rule changes by the Supreme Court, (4) problems in determining murderous intent, (5) the availability and use of plea bargaining, and (6) the appellate courts.

Few Death–Eligible Offenders are Executed. Only one to two percent of all death-eligible offenders have been executed from 1930 to the present. Thus, not only is the vast majority of capital offenders able to escape execution, but there is no meaningful way to distinguish between the eligible offenders who were executed and those who were not. Even during the peak of executions in the United States in the 1930s, only 20 percent of all death-eligible offenders were executed.

> *O*nly one to two percent of all death-eligible offenders have been executed from 1930 to the present.

The situation has not changed much under post-*Furman* statutes. Professor Bowers found that:

> of the first 607 sentences imposed on convicted murderers under Georgia's post-*Furman* capital statute—not counting guilty pleas resulting in life sentences—113 were death sentences. . . . That is to say, more than 80 percent of the death-eligible murderers in Georgia—the vast majority—were given life sentences. And Georgia is among the states most likely to impose death sentences; in most other states the percentage of death-eligible murderers receiving death sentences will be even less.[3]

Application of the Death Penalty Across Jurisdictions and Over Time. Arbitrariness is evident in the way the death penalty has been applied across jurisdictions and over time. As attorney Amsterdam, who has defended dozens of capital offenders, describes:

> [T]here is a haphazard, crazy-quilt character about the administration of capital punishment that every knowledgeable lawyer or observer can describe but none can rationally explain. Some juries are hanging juries, some counties are hanging counties, some years are hanging years; and men live or die depending on these flukes. However atrocious the crime may have been for which a particular defendant is sentenced to die, 'experienced wardens know many prisoners serving life or less whose crimes were equally, or more atrocious.'[4]

Consider, for example, the distribution of executions among death penalty juris-dictions. Although 40 jurisdictions in the United States (which includes 38 states, the U.S. government, and the U.S. military) have death penalty statutes, only 29 states have executed at least one person under their post-*Furman* statutes.[5] Neither the government nor the military has executed anyone under their post-*Furman* statutes at this writing, and more than 60 percent of the executing states have executed fewer than 10 people since executions resumed in 1977.[6] That represents about one death sentence per 200 criminal homicides, or 20 death-eligible offenders.[7] Professor Bow-ers contends, "Capital punishment appears to be not an integral part of the criminal justice process in these states, but an occasional product of chance—an unpre-dictable occurrence."[8]

Only eight of the 29 states account for almost 80 percent of the 451 people executed under post-*Furman* statutes as of April 1, 1998; three states (Texas, Vir-ginia, and Florida) can lay claim to about 54 percent of the total; and one state (Tex-as) has executed one-third.[9] Still, even Texas executes only a small percentage of its death-eligible offenders.

> *O*nly eight of the 29 states that have executed at least one person under their post-*Furman* statutes account for almost 80 percent of the 451 people executed under post-*Furman* statutes as of April 1, 1998; three states (Texas, Virginia, and Florida) can lay claim to about 54 percent of the total; and one state (Texas) has executed one-third.

Regional variation in executions also suggests arbitrariness in application. His-torically, capital punishment has been employed mostly in the South. Sixty percent of the approximately 4,000 persons legally executed under state authority in the United States between 1930 and 1980 were in the South. The distribution by region is as follows:

South	2,307 (60 percent)
Northeast	602 (16 percent)
West	511 (13 percent)
North Central	403 (11 percent)
Total	3,823

During the period, 3.75 times more capital offenders were executed in the South than in any other region of the United States.[10] More than 75 percent of executions under post-*Furman* statutes have occurred in the South.[11]

There is also regional variation within states. For example, in Florida and Geor-gia, the probability of receiving a death sentence for felony homicide (death-eligible murder) by judicial circuit or county varied greatly.[12] In Florida, a capital offender was more than four times more likely to be sentenced to death for a felony homicide in the panhandle area of the state than in either the northern or southern regions of the state, and more than twice as likely to be sentenced to death in the panhandle than in the central region of the state. Similarly, in Georgia, a capital offender was nearly nine times more likely to be sentenced to death in either the central or southwest regions than in Fulton County (Atlanta), more than four times more likely to be sentenced to death in either the central or southwest regions of Georgia than in the northern region, and twice as likely to be sentenced to death in the northern region than in Fulton County.

These data do not necessarily indicate arbitrariness if it can be shown that a similar proportion of death-eligible murders are committed in the South or in a particular region of a state. However, in 1996, only 43 percent of [all] homicides occurred in the South[13]—a smaller percentage than might be predicted, given that 75 percent of executions occur in the South. But the 43 percent is for all homicides and not just death-eligible homicides, and data separating the two categories are not available. Thus, it is still possible, though improbable, that a much larger proportion of murders are death-eligible in the South than in other regions of the country.

Data of regional variation within states suggest that greater numbers of death-eligible homicides do not increase the overall probability of a death sentence, as one might expect. Rather, the data show that the odds of being sentenced to death are either greater in regions with fewer death-eligible homicides or not related to the number of death-eligible homicides at all; it may be that where capital murders are few, those that are committed receive harsher punishment.

In Florida, for example, other regions had between 4.5 and nearly 9 times more homicides than the panhandle, yet in the panhandle, the probability of a death sentence was two to four times greater than in other regions of the state. That finding was the exception, however. The overall probability of a death sentence in the central region of Florida was at least twice as great as the probability in either the north or south regions, even though the number of death-eligible homicides in the central region (172) was more than the 140 in the north region and less than the 270 in the south region. In Georgia, the central and southwest regions were nearly nine times more likely than Fulton County to impose a death sentence, yet the 154 death-eligible homicides in Fulton County were greater than the 103 in the southwest region and fewer than the 162 in the central region. These combined data show that the application of the death penalty under post-*Furman* statutes, in the words of the Court in its *Furman* decision, has been "rare," "uncommon," and "freakish."

Post–*Furman* Statutes Justify Arbitrariness. Professor Bowers suggests that the post-*Furman* statutes may have an effect different from the one intended by the Court. Rather than reducing or eliminating arbitrary and discriminatory application, the new statutes may facilitate both problems, especially in states such as Texas. He further explains, "Perhaps explicitly enumerated aggravating circumstances do not serve to guide sentencing discretion as much as they become means of justifying arbitrary or discriminatory sentencing practices in places where social or political influences favor such practices."[14]

Jurors' Misunderstanding or Underestimating their Sentencing Obligations. Another troublesome problem with post-*Furman* statutes—a problem that also contributes to arbitrary application—is the failure of many jurors to understand their statutory sentencing obligations. Research shows that jurors commonly misapprehend judges' capital-sentencing instructions, especially those pertaining to mitigating circumstances.[15] Particularly troublesome is evidence from the Capital Jury Project indicating that nearly 75 percent of jurors "acknowledge that sentencing instructions did not guide their decision-making on punishment but served instead as an after-the-fact façade for a decision made prior to hearing the instructions."[16]

Many jurors also underestimate their sentencing responsibilities, seeming to believe that they are only to follow a prescribed formula in determining a sentence in capital cases. For them, it is "the law" or "legal instructions" that ultimately determines whether a capital defendant lives or dies. Other jurors assume that the sentence they impose is only preliminary and nonbinding since it will be reviewed and corrected, if necessary, by an appellate court.[17] In *Caldwell v. Mississippi* (1985), the Supreme Court opined that for jurors to believe that "the responsibility for any ultimate determination of death will rest with others" is an "intolerable danger." Such thinking on the part of capital jurors may lead to arbitrarily imposed death sentences.

Rule Changes by the Supreme Court. Arbitrariness is also inevitable whenever the Supreme Court changes the rules by which the penalty is imposed. This is especially true when those changes have a retroactive effect (that is, when they are applied to earlier cases). An example is the Court's 1968 *Witherspoon* decision, which held as unconstitutional the practice of excluding people from capital juries simply because they generally opposed capital punishment. This ruling resulted in dozens of death row inmates having their death sentences set aside because of constitutional errors in jury selection. *Witherspoon* was welcome news to those inmates who received new trials, but the decision did nothing for the dozens who had been executed even though their trials were infected with identical errors.[18]

Similarly, the Court's 1977 *Coker* decision declared capital punishment for rape of an adult unconstitutional. *Coker* did nothing for the 455 men (405 of whom were black) who had been executed for rape in the United States since 1930.[19] Had they been tried under the *Coker* standard, they would have met a different fate. There are numerous other such examples of changes in death penalty laws where the laws are held to be retroactive. The point is that whether or not an inmate is executed depends, in part, on chance—that is, whether his or her execution date came before or after a crucial Supreme Court decision.

Problems in Determining Murderous Intent. Another source of arbitrariness in the application of capital punishment involves the charge for which a defendant is prosecuted. Generally, whether a defendant is charged with first- or second-degree murder or capital or noncapital murder depends on such considerations as whether or not the defendant acted with "premeditation" or "criminal intent."[20] Determining what a person intended to do before he or she acted is a difficult, if not impossible, task. Former Supreme Court Justice Benjamin Cardoza underscored this dilemma when he wrote "that [he] did not understand the concept of premeditation after several decades of studying and trying to apply it as a judge,"[21] yet whether or not a defendant is tried for his or her life depends on just such a determination.

Availability and Use of Plea Bargaining. A related source of arbitrariness involves whether or not a capital suspect is allowed to plea bargain to a noncapital offense. The plea bargain option creates a particular dilemma for the capital suspect who is innocent (or at least innocent of a capital offense). If the suspect pleads guilty to a noncapital offense and, thus, escapes the death penalty, he or she will still have to serve a prison sentence (in all likelihood), perhaps for a crime that he or she did not commit. On the other hand, if the innocent suspect (or suspect who did not commit a capital crime) elects to be tried for the capital charge, he or she risks the chance of being found guilty and executed. This scenario is more than hypothetical. Julian Bond recounts that "on the date of his death [May 25, 1979], [John] Spinkelink could have already been paroled if he had plea bargained and accepted the uncontested second-degree murder conviction offered him by the state [of Florida]."[22]

> *J*ulian Bond recounts that "on the date of his death [May 25, 1979], [John] Spinkelink could have already been paroled if he had plea bargained and accepted the uncontested second-degree murder conviction offered him by the state [of Florida]."

The Appellate Courts. Approximately 30 to 40 percent of death sentences imposed under post-*Furman* statutes have been found legally faulty. Many people may believe that appellate review detects and corrects arbitrary and discriminatory application of capital punishment, and, in some cases, it does—at a considerable burden in time and other resources to the appellate courts. Sometimes, though, appellate review becomes another independent source of arbitrariness. The description of John Spinkelink's final appeal to the Eleventh U.S. Circuit Court illustrates how this occurs.[23] Professor Bowers summarizes the lesson to be learned from Spinkelink's experience (as well as an unanticipated consequence):

> The final appeal of Spinkelink . . . reveals arbitrariness at the highest levels of legal authority. Federal judges are not exempt from or immune to personal, social, or situational influences; they are subject to the same pressures and temptations as everyone else who handles capital cases. . . . It is a seductive illusion to believe that the highest courts can intercept arbitrariness wherever it occurs in the handling of capital cases.
>
> Indeed, [for some] the assumption that the federal appellate process can serve as a fail-safe mechanism against arbitrariness and discrimination now sustains the institution of capital punishment in America. But the truth . . . is that the federal courts themselves are an independent source or conduit of such arbitrariness.[24]

Conclusion. Perhaps it is impossible to completely eliminate arbitrary application of the death penalty because of human involvement in the process. Perhaps the Supreme Court, in *Gregg*, was naive to believe that the new guided-discretion statutes and other procedural reforms would eliminate arbitrary imposition of the death penalty. Either way, faced with evidence from the post-*Gregg* experience, the

Court would seem to have two alternatives. First, it could decide that some arbitrariness in the death penalty's application is tolerable (which may be its current unofficial and implicit position, anyway). However, if it were to officially recognize the arbitrariness, then it probably would have to determine how much arbitrariness it will allow. That task might lead down a slippery slope to the second alternative—the abolition of capital punishment. The Court might conclude that arbitrary application of capital punishment is inevitable (intolerable though it may be) as long as the penalty is administered.

Discrimination in the Administration of the Death Penalty under Post–*Furman* Statutes

Only a select few of all murderers eligible for execution are ever actually executed. Consideration of the unique characteristics of those executed, the laws under which they are prosecuted, and the behavior of defense attorneys, prosecutors, and jurors reveals objectionable forms of discrimination. Before turning to evidence of discrimination, however, it is important to distinguish between disparity and discrimination.

Disparity versus Discrimination. Disparity refers to numerical differences based on some characteristic, such as race. There has been a pattern of racial disparity in the imposition of the death penalty in the United States because the penalty has been imposed on blacks disproportionately to their numbers in the population.[25] The Supreme Court holds that as long as racial or other disparities can be justified by relevant legal factors (e.g., that blacks commit a disproportionate number of capital crimes), there is nothing inherently problematical with those disparities in the administration of capital punishment. For the most part, the Court considers it legally irrelevant that disparities may be either wholly or partially products of factors antecedent to the criminal act (e.g., growing up in a racist or psychologically impoverished environment).[26]

Discrimination is a violation of the equal protection clause of the Fourteenth Amendment and of special restrictions on the use of capital punishment under the Eighth Amendment. Discrimination is evident to the Court when the death penalty is intentionally or purposefully imposed on persons because of some characteristic, such as race, and not because of or in addition to legitimate sentencing considerations. Proving intentional discrimination in specific cases is an extremely difficult task.

Discrimination Based on Social Class and the Definition of Murder. The FBI's Uniform Crime Report shows that approximately 25,000 murders and nonnegligent manslaughters are committed each year. About 20 percent (or 5,000) of them are death–eligible. A problem with the murders reported by the FBI is that they represent only a fraction of the people killed intentionally or negligently each year and an even smaller fraction of potentially death-eligible murders. Conservative estimates indicate that each year in the United States at least 10,000 lives are lost because of unnecessary surgeries, 20,000 to errors in prescribing drugs, 20,000 to doctors spreading diseases in hospitals, 100,000 to industrial disease, 200,000 to environmentally caused cancer, and an unknown number to lethal industrial products.[27]

While the proximate decisionmakers and perpetrators in most of those deaths are not death–eligible, because their actions or inactions are neither intentional nor criminally negligent, a small but significant fraction are. Yet, few of them are defined legally as murderers, especially death–eligible murderers. One reason is that few of the offenders are readily identifiable because their decisions are hidden by the complexities of the workplace environment or by the corporate chain of command. Another more cynical reason is that, by virtue of their class position, the perpetrators of these "white-collar crimes," no matter how malicious and heinous their actions, simply are not considered appropriate candidates for capital punishment in the United States. Justice Douglas wrote in his *Furman* decision, "One searches our chronicles in vain for the execution of any member of the affluent strata of this society."[28]

> *In his Furman decision, Justice Douglas wrote, "One searches our chronicles in vain for the execution of any member of the affluent strata of this society."*

The point, however, is not to argue for the death penalty for such offenses and offenders, but to show that an unacceptable form of discrimination is created by the way death–eligible murders are defined.[29] If death–eligible murder also included those actions and inactions just listed that are particularly reprehensible, then the distribution of persons convicted of death–eligible murder would be more evenly divided among social classes.[30]

Discrimination by Gender. The death penalty is rarely inflicted on women, even though women commit roughly one in five of all criminal homicides.[31] (The percentage of women who commit death–eligible homicides is unknown.) Approximately 19,000 people have been legally executed in the United States since 1608, and about 2 percent of those have been women. Most of them (nearly 90 percent) were executed prior to 1866.[32] Between 1930 and 1980, approximately 4,000 persons were executed by civil authority in the United States—32, or about .8 percent, were women.[33]

It has been estimated that under current death penalty laws if women and men were treated equally, and that no factor other than offense was considered, women would receive between 4 and 6 percent of all death sentences.[34] Under post-*Furman* statutes, however, women have received about 2 percent of all death sentences—5 or 6 death sentences a year—113 between 1973 and June 30, 1996.[35] The reason for the difference is that from arrest through execution, women are filtered from the process. Women account for about:

- 8 percent of murder arrests,

- 2 percent of death sentences imposed at trial,

- 1.3 percent of persons on death row, and

- .7 percent of persons executed under post-*Furman* statutes (451 executions as of April 1, 1998).[36]

Only three women have been executed under post-*Furman* statutes as of this writing. Fourteen years separated the first execution from the recent two. The women executed were Velma Barfield, who was executed in North Carolina on October 2, 1984; Karla Faye Tucker, who was executed in Texas on February 3, 1998; and Judy Buenoano, who was executed in Florida on March 30, 1998.

More than 95 percent of the post-*Furman* women sentenced to death but no longer on death rows had their death sentences reversed.[37] Only Barfield, Tucker, and Buenoano have been executed. As of April 1, 1998, 43 women occupied death rows—about 1.3 percent of the total.[38]

Law professor Victor Streib observes that the women who have been executed, both historically and in modern times, share certain distinctive characteristics:

> The executed females tended to be very poor, uneducated, and of the lowest social class in the community. Their victims tended to be white and of particularly protected classes, either children or socially prominent adults. Comparatively few executed females committed their crimes with a co-defendant, so they could not claim they were under the domination of another. Most of the executed females manifested an attitude of violence, either from past behavior or present acts, that countered any presumption of nonviolence. Finally, and perhaps most fatally for them, they committed shockingly "unladylike" behavior, allowing the sentencing judges and juries to put aside any image of them as "the gentler sex" and to treat them as "crazed monsters" deserving of nothing more than extermination.[39]

Professor Streib is among the scholars who believe gender discrimination is evident in the application of the death penalty.[40] He identifies two principal sources of this discrimination: (1) the conscious or subconscious attitudes of key actors in the criminal justice process, and (2) death penalty laws, themselves.[41] Streib contends that the aggravating and mitigating circumstances enumerated in death penalty laws bias the application of the death penalty in favor of women. For example, among aggravating factors that generally advantage women over men charged with capital crimes are those that pertain to: (1) previous criminal record (women are less likely than men to have one), (2) premeditation (homicides by women tend to be unplanned and sudden acts), and (3) felony–murders (women are rarely involved in them).[42] Mitigating factors that tend to advantage women involve: (1) committing a capital crime while under extreme mental or emotional disturbance (female murderers are perceived to be more emotionally disturbed than male murderers), and (2) acting under the substantial domination of another person (when both women and men are involved in a capital crime, the man is generally considered the principal actor).[43]

As for the key actors in the criminal justice process, judges (who are predominately male) admit that, in general, they tend to be more lenient toward female offenders. They also tend to believe that women are better candidates for rehabilitation than are men. Jurors also tend to be more lenient toward female offenders, particularly in cases of serious crimes.[44]

Professor Streib describes an ethical dilemma with the practice of reserving execution almost entirely for men:

> Making women ineligible for the death penalty, as Russia has done expressly and as the United States has done in practice, seems harder to defend. This practice, while explainable in some of its dimensions, seems at bottom to be unvarnished gender bias—a queasiness among criminal justice officials for putting a woman to death. One need not be a supporter of the death penalty to observe that if men are eligible for it then women should be also. Otherwise, women are lumped in with children and the mentally retarded as not fully responsible human beings.[45]

In short, if women are to be accorded full dignity as human beings, and illegal discrimination is to be avoided, then, as Professor Streib contends, women either must be executed for their capital crimes, or no one should be executed for a capital crime.

Discrimination by Age. About 1.8 percent (approximately 346) of the approximately 19,000 people executed in the United States since 1608 have been juveniles, that is, individuals who committed their capital crimes prior to their 18th birthday. Like women, juveniles are filtered from the process. They account for about:

- 15 percent of murder arrests,

- 2.5 percent of death sentences imposed at trial,

- 2 percent of persons on death row, and

- 2 percent of persons executed under post-*Furman* statutes (451 executions as of April 1, 1998).[46]

Only nine juveniles—all of whom were 17 years old at the time they committed their crimes—have been executed under post-*Furman* statutes: (1) Charles Rumbaugh in Texas on September 11, 1985, (2) James Terry Roach in South Carolina on January 10, 1986, (3) Jay Pinkerton in Texas on May 15, 1986, (4) Dalton Prejean in Louisiana on May 18, 1990, (5) Johnny Garrett in Texas on February 11, 1992, (6) Curtis Paul Harris in Texas on July 1, 1993, (7) Frederick Lashley in Missouri on July 28, 1993, (8) Ruben Cantu in Texas on August 24, 1993, and (9) Christopher Burger in Georgia on December 7, 1993.[47] Since 1990, the United States is one of only five countries that have executed anyone under 18 years of age at the time of the crime; the others are Iran, Pakistan, Saudi Arabia, and Yemen.[48] The last executed juvenile in the United States who was younger than 17 at the time of his crime was 16-year-old Leonard Shockley, who was executed in Maryland on April 10, 1959.[49]

The typical juvenile currently on death row is a 17-year-old African-American or Hispanic male who killed, after robbing or raping, a white adult female.[50] Five of the nine juveniles executed under post-*Furman* statutes, however, were white, three were black, and one was Hispanic.[51] As of this writing and since 1973, jurisdictions in the United States have imposed death sentences on 143 offenders under the age of 18 at the time of their crime,[52] but the chances of any juvenile currently on death row being executed are remote. The reversal rate for juveniles sentenced to death under post-*Furman* statutes is about 90 percent.[53]

Whether or not juveniles should be subjected to capital punishment has been a controversial issue. A recent Gallup poll revealed that 60 percent of Americans thought that when a teenager commits a murder and is found guilty by a jury, he (the survey item did not address female teenage killers) should get the death penalty (compared with 80 percent who favored the death penalty for adults), 30 percent opposed the death penalty for teenagers, and 10 percent had no opinion.[54] Seventy-two percent of those who favored the death penalty for adults also favored it for teenage killers.

When asked whether juveniles convicted of their first crime should be given the same punishment as adults convicted of their first crime, 50 percent of Americans believed juveniles should be treated the same as adults, 40 percent believed they should be treated less harshly, 9 percent responded that it depends, and 1 percent had no opinion. When asked whether juveniles convicted of their second or third crimes should be given the same punishment as adults convicted of their second or third crimes, 83 percent of Americans believed juveniles should be treated the same as adults, only 12 percent believed they should be treated less harshly, 4 percent thought it depends,

> *A* recent Gallup poll revealed that 60 percent of Americans thought that when a teenager commits a murder and is found guilty by a jury, he (the survey item did not address female teenage killers) should get the death penalty (compared with 80 percent who favored the death penalty for adults).

and 1 percent had no opinion. As for how juveniles who commit the same crimes as adults should be treated, 52 percent of Americans believed they should receive the same punishment, 31 percent believed that juveniles should be rehabilitated, 13 percent responded that it depends on the circumstances, 3 percent chose another sanction, and 1 percent had no opinion. One problem with alternatives to capital punishment is that Americans have little confidence in the rehabilitative programs available to juveniles. Only 25 percent of Americans believe that rehabilitation programs for juveniles are even moderately successful, but nearly half (48 percent) of the respondents also believed that the rehabilitation programs for juveniles had not been given the necessary money and support to be successful.

Among the reasons for not subjecting juveniles to capital punishment are the following:

- our society, as represented by our legislatures, prosecutors, judges, and juries, has rejected the juvenile death penalty;

- other nations, including many that share our Anglo–American heritage, have rejected the juvenile death penalty;

- the threat of the death penalty does not deter potential juvenile murderers because juveniles often do not consider the possible consequences prior to committing their murderous acts and because, even if they did consider these consequences, they would realize that very few juveniles actually receive the death penalty;

- juveniles are especially likely to be rehabilitated or reformed while in prison, thus rendering the juvenile death penalty especially inappropriate;

- the juvenile death penalty does not serve a legitimate retributive purpose, since juveniles are generally less mature and responsible than adults, and should therefore be viewed as less culpable than adults who commit the same crimes.[55]

An additional reason for treating juveniles differently than adults in the administration of justice is that juveniles are already treated legally differently than adults in other areas of life, such as driving, voting, gambling, marriage, and jury service.[56]

On the other hand, some of the reasons for subjecting juveniles to capital punishment are:

- the evidence of a societal consensus against the juvenile death penalty is nonexistent or at least too weak to justify a constitutional ban;

- the views of other nations are irrelevant to the proper interpretation of our Constitution, at least absent a consensus within our own society;

- the threat of the death penalty can deter potential juvenile murderers, or at least the judgments of legislatures and prosecutors to that effect deserve deference;

- the most heinous juvenile murderers, who are the only ones likely to receive the death penalty, are not good candidates for rehabilitation or reform;

- there are some juvenile murderers who are sufficiently mature and responsible to deserve the death penalty for their crimes, and thus the juvenile death penalty serves a legitimate retributive purpose.[57]

As for other areas of the law that distinguish between adults and juveniles, proponents of capital punishment for juvenile offenders stress that while juveniles may not vote conscientiously or drive safely, they do know that killing other human beings is wrong.[58]

Another reason for supporting the death penalty for at least some juvenile capital offenders, and what makes the current practice of excluding most death-eligible juveniles from the death penalty discriminatory, is that the designation of "juvenile" is arbitrary and only a proxy for more relevant characteristics. It was not until the sixteenth and seventeenth centuries that the young began to be viewed other than as miniature adults or property.[59] Before that time, juveniles as young as five or six were expected to assume the responsibilities of adults and, when they violated the law, were subjected to the same criminal sanctions as adults. Moreover, is there a significant difference on any relevant social characteristic between a 17 and 18 year old, other than what has been created by law? Is it really meaningful to consider a 17-year-old a juvenile and an 18-year-old an adult?

In considering whether a person deserves the death penalty from a retributive standpoint, law professor Joseph Hoffmann points out that age is largely irrelevant. It is used because it serves as an imperfect proxy for more relevant social characteristics. Whether a murderer, regardless of age, deserves the death penalty depends, not on age, argues Hoffmann, but on maturity, judgment, responsibility, and the capability to assess the possible consequences of his or her actions.[60] Some juveniles possess those characteristics in greater quantity than some adults, or in sufficient quantities to be death-eligible; some do not. The use of age as a basis for determining who is or is not death-eligible is therefore discriminatory.

Racial Discrimination. Post-*Furman* statutes also have failed to end racial discrimination in the imposition of the death penalty. In the past, discussions of racial discrimination have focused almost entirely on the race of those executed, and while race of offender is not the only form of racial discrimination, that issue is considered first.

Between 1930 and 1980, 3,862 prisoners were executed under civil authority in the United States: 1,754 (45 percent) were white and 2066 (53 percent) were black.[61] Blacks constituted around 10 percent of the population during that period. Among the 3,862 persons executed were 455 convicted of rape. Of those, 48 (11 percent) were white and 405 (89 percent) were black. Ninety-seven percent (443) were executed in the South.[62] Professors Wolfgang and Riedel reported in a 1975 study of 361 rape convictions from a sample of 25 Georgia counties from 1945-1965, "that the most important predictor of which among the 361 rapists would be sentenced to death was the racial combination of offender and victim. . . . [b]lack offenders who raped white victims . . . were significantly more likely to be sentenced to death in comparison to rapes involving all other racial combinations."[63]

The statistics on executions for the crime of rape indicate that the case for racial discrimination in the imposition of the death penalty is strongest for the South.[64] Recall that between 1930 and 1980, 60 percent of all executions in the United States occurred in the South. Of those executed, 28 percent were white and 72 percent were black.[65] Again, those figures do not necessarily indicate an undesirable form of racial discrimination if blacks committed a disproportionately greater number of death-eligible murders or rapes, but that was unlikely the case. From roughly 1973 through 1977, for example, 617 persons were arrested or suspected by police of death-eligible murder in Florida, 535 in Georgia, and 702 in Texas.[66] In Florida, 49 percent of the death-eligible murderers were black, in Georgia, 63 percent, and in Texas, 42 percent.[67] Racial distributions for rape were similar. Those figures suggest the unlikelihood that 89 percent of the death-eligible rapists and 72 percent of the death-eligible murderers in the South were black.

*A*ccording to an "evaluation synthesis" of 28 post-*Furman* studies prepared by the U.S. General Accounting Office, "more than half of the studies found that race of defendant influenced the likelihood of being charged with a capital crime or receiving the death penalty . . . [and in] more than three-fourths of the studies that identified a race-of-defendant effect . . . black defendants were more likely to receive the death penalty."[68] A 1994 study by the *Houston Post* found that in Harris County—which accounts for more post-*Furman* executions than any state other than Texas itself and more death sentences than most states—blacks were sentenced to death twice as often as whites.[69]

In some cases (cf., *Village of Arlington Heights v. Metropolitan Hous. Dev. Corp.*, 429 U.S. 252, 266, 1977), but, interestingly, not in capital cases (*McCleskey v. Kemp*, 481 U.S. 279, 1987, see the discussion in Chapter 2), the Supreme Court has allowed racially discriminatory intent to be inferred from "a clear pattern, unexplainable on grounds other than race." Criteria of proof are more restricted in capital cases, but short of public admission of racially discriminatory intent or other unlikely happenstance, it is not clear how such intent on the part of participants in the administration of capital punishment could be shown.[70] Even when overt racially offensive remarks are made in capital trials, racial discriminatory intent is not always inferred. For example, in a 1985 capital case in Florida, the trial judge referred to the family of a black defendant as "niggers." The Florida Supreme Court did not strongly reprimand the judge for his remark; the Court only reminded him that he must always maintain an "image of impartiality."[71] In Utah, two black men were sentenced to death by an all-white jury and executed, "even though jurors received a note which contained the words 'Hang the Nigger's' [sic] and a drawing of a figure hanging on a gallows."[72] According to attorney Stephen Bright, "No court, state or federal, even had a hearing on such questions as who wrote the note, what influence it had on the jurors, and how widely it was discussed by the jurors."[73] It may be that racially discriminatory outcomes are not generally the product of a conscious process and that participants in the administration of capital punishment do not "know" that their behavior is racially motivated.

Available evidence indicates that post-*Furman* statutes have not eliminated a second, less obvious form of racial discrimination: *victim-based racial discrimination*. Whether the death penalty is imposed continues to depend on the race of the victim. For example, between 1973 and 1977, under a post-*Furman* statute in Florida, the probability of a black person receiving the death penalty for the aggravated murder of a white was 32 percent (143 offenders; 46 persons sentenced to death). The probability of a white person receiving the death penalty for the aggravated murder of a white was 21.5 percent (303 offenders; 65 persons sentenced to death). The probability for a black who killed a black was 4 percent (160 offenders; 7 persons sentenced to death), and the probability for a white who killed a black was 0 percent (11 offenders; no persons sentenced to death).[74]

In other words, a black person convicted of an aggravated murder of a white in Florida between 1973 and 1977 was more than seven times more likely to receive a death sentence than was a black who killed a black. A white person convicted of an aggravated murder of a white was almost five times more likely to receive a death sentence than was a black who killed a black. A person convicted of aggravated murder of a white, whether the killer was a black or a white, was more likely to receive the death penalty than was a person of either race convicted of aggravated murder of a black. Moreover, a white person convicted of aggravated murder of a black almost never received a death sentence (the total of such cases for Florida, Georgia, and Texas was 54; in three (5.5 percent) there was a death sentence).[75] A similar pattern was found in Georgia,[76] Texas,[77] South Carolina,[78] North Carolina,[79] Louisiana,[80] Alabama,[81] Mississippi,[82] Tennessee,[83] Kentucky,[84] California,[85] Illinois,[86] Missouri,[87] Oklahoma,[88] Maryland,[89] Virginia,[90] and New Jersey.[91]

The evaluation synthesis of the General Accounting Office further reported that "in 82 percent of the studies, race of victim was found to influence the likelihood of being charged with capital murder or receiving the death penalty. . . . This finding was remarkably consistent across data sets, states, data collection methods, and analytic techniques."[92] The report also noted that "the race of victim influence was stronger for the earlier stages of the judicial process (e.g., prosecutorial decision to charge defendant with a capital offense, decision to proceed to trial rather than plea bargain) than in later stages."[93]

> The evaluation synthesis of the U.S. General Accounting Office reported that "in 82 percent of the studies, race of victim was found to influence the likelihood of being charged with capital murder or receiving the death penalty."

Law professor David Baldus and his colleagues found that in Georgia under its post-*Furman* statute "race-of-victim effects were particularly strong in the midrange of cases when prosecutors and juries have the greatest room for the exercise of discretion."[94] They estimate that the outcomes in more than one-third of the midrange (in aggravation) cases were determined by the race of the victim. At least in the aforementioned states, these findings suggest that the life of a black victim is valued less than the life of a white victim, regardless of the race of the offender.

More recent data do not indicate any change in the situation. As of April 1, 1998, defendant-victim racial combinations for post-*Furman* executions were as follows (based on 611 victims):[95]

Combination	Percent
white defendant/white victim	58.10
white defendant/black victim	1.31
white defendant/Asian victim	.33
white defendant/Latino(a) victim	1.31
black defendant/white victim	21.77
black defendant/black victim	10.80
black defendant/Asian victim	.49
black defendant/Latino(a) victim	.33
Latino defendant/white victim	2.29
Latino defendant/Latino(a) victim	1.64
Latino defendant/Asian victim	.16
Latino defendant/black victim	.16
Native American/white victim	.82
Asian defendant/Asian victim	.49

The data reveal that nearly 80 percent of the victims of those persons executed under post-*Furman* statutes have been white, and that only 12 percent have been black. Yet, 56 percent of defendants executed have been white, 37 percent have been black, 5 percent have been Latino(a), 1 percent have been Native American and .44 percent have been Asian.[96] Discrimination seems apparent because, historically, capital crimes have generally been intraracial.[97] For example, in 1996, 88 percent of murders and nonnegligent manslaughters were intraracial (84 percent involved whites and 92 percent involved blacks).[98] Still, uncertainty remains about whether the data show discrimination because only about 20 percent of murders and nonnegligent manslaughters are capital crimes.[99] It seems likely that the percentage of interracial murders may be somewhat greater for capital murders than it is for noncapital murders. In any event, two major implications of these data are: (1) "in places that currently treat black defendants more punitively than similarly situated non-black defendants, an evenhanded system would reduce the absolute number of black defendants sentenced to death . . . [and] the proportion of black defendants on death row", and (2) "if an evenhanded policy were applied to the black and white victim cases (at the current rate for either black or white victim cases), the 'proportion' of black defendants on death row would increase."[100]

Sources of Racial Disparity/Discrimination. Studies that have found post-*Furman* racial disparity/discrimination have located the source of it predominately in the discretionary actions of prosecutors and juries. (Evidence suggests that prosecutors and juries are also sources of arbitrariness in the death penalty's application.) Professor Baldus and his colleagues declare that "the exercise of prosecutorial discretion [in seeking a death sentence] is the principal source of the

> Studies that have found post-*Furman* racial disparity/discrimination have located the source of it predominately in the discretionary actions of prosecutors and juries.

race-of-victim disparities observed in the system."[101] In Georgia (and in other states) a capital sentencing hearing is a preliminary stage in the process that leads to a capital trial. Baldus and colleagues report that under Georgia's post-*Furman* statute, black defendants whose victims were white were advanced to a capital sentencing hearing by prosecutors at a rate nearly five times that of black defendants whose victims were black, and more than three times the rate of white defendants whose victims were black.[102] More recent research found that prosecutors have sought the death penalty in 70 percent of cases involving black defendants and white victims and in only 35 percent of the cases involving other racial combinations.[103]

In Florida, prosecutors have "upgraded" and "downgraded" potential capital cases under post-*Furman* statutes by alleging aggravating circumstances, charging defendants with an accompanying felony, ignoring evidence in police reports, and withholding an accompanying charge depending on the race of the offender and of the victim.[104] Professors Radelet and Pierce report that "cases in which blacks were accused of killing whites were the most likely to be upgraded and least likely to be downgraded."[105] Prosecutors have engaged in similar actions in South Carolina,[106] Kentucky,[107] and other states.[108]

Prosecutors also have reduced death-eligible white-defendant or black-victim cases to noncapital ones through plea bargaining, or they have foregone a penalty trial and thus waived the death penalty, even when a defendant had been convicted by a jury of a capital offense.[109] The evidence is quite clear that racial disparities continue to be produced through the exercise of prosecutorial discretion in capital or potentially capital cases.

These findings are truly ironic in light of the majority's response in *Gregg* that:

> Petitioner's argument that the prosecutor's decisions in plea bargaining or in declining to charge capital murder are standardless and will result in the wanton or freakish imposition of the death penalty condemned in *Furman*, is without merit, for the assumption cannot be made that prosecutors will be motivated in their charging decisions by factors other than the strength of their case and the likelihood that a jury would impose the death penalty if it convicts.[110]

Although perhaps not as critical as the prosecutor, juries also play a role in racial disparities produced under post-*Furman* statutes. Juries impose death sentences in only about one-half of all capital cases that go to trial.[111] Juries in capital cases are distinctively different from juries in any other type of case because they are death qualified (that is, death penalty opponents can be excluded from capital juries if they are opposed to the death penalty under any circumstances).[112] Capital juries generally are not representative of the community from which they are drawn (as is more likely the case of juries in noncapital cases).[113] In addition, research shows that "death-qualified jurors . . . are more conviction-prone, less concerned with due process, and they are more inclined to believe the prosecution than are excludable jurors."[114] Historically, blacks are the demographic group most likely to oppose the death penalty[115] and thus are the group most likely to be excluded from jury service in capital cases.

Even if blacks are not opposed to the death penalty categorically, they also can be underrepresented on capital juries by the prosecutor's (or, on rare occasions, the defense attorney's) exercise of peremptory challenges.[116] For example, if jurors express some opposition to the death penalty but not enough to exclude them for cause, they still can be eliminated through the prosecutor's peremptory challenge.

Recent evidence from two judicial circuits in Georgia show that, at least in Georgia under post-*Furman* statutes, blacks play only a small role in capital cases, except, of course, as defendants—a category in which they are overrepresented.[117] In the words of Georgia state senator Gary Parker, "The classic death penalty case in Georgia remains a black person prosecuted by a white district attorney before a white judge and an all-white jury for a crime against a prominent white person."[118]

> *I*n the words of Georgia state senator Gary Parker, "The classic death penalty case in Georgia remains a black person prosecuted by a white district attorney before a white judge and an all-white jury for a crime against a prominent white person."

Theories of Racial Discrimination in the Administration of the Death Penalty. There are several plausible theories of racial discrimination in the administration of the death penalty. The first and more obvious theory is that prosecutors, judges, jurors, and even defense attorneys intentionally discriminate against black defendants and victims because blacks are feared, disliked, or both. Such an explanation certainly is believable, given the history of race relations in the United States, particularly in the South.[119] Recent evidence shows that death penalty support by many whites continues to be associated with prejudice against blacks.[120]

A second theory is that many actors in the legal system today, even in the South, believe they are not racially prejudiced or are not conscious that they are. Yet racially discriminatory outcomes are produced through a sometimes unconscious psychological process of racial identification.[121] Professors Gross and Mauro describe the process of victim-based racial identification:

> We are more readily horrified by a death if we empathize or identify with the victim, or if we see the victim as similar to ourselves or to a friend or relative, than if the victim appears to us as a stranger. In a society that remains segregated socially if not legally, and in which the great majority of jurors are white, jurors are not likely to identify with black victims or to see them as family or friends. Thus jurors are more likely to be horrified by the killing of a white than of a black, and more likely to act against the killer of a white than the killer of a black. This reaction is not an expression of racial hostility but a natural product of the patterns of interracial relations in our society.[122]

Victim-based racial identification also may affect judges, prosecutors, and defense attorneys.[123] Thus, if victim-based racial identification affects all of the actors in the administration of capital punishment and, further, if nearly all of those actors are white, then it follows that racial discrimination against black defendants, particularly those who are the killers of whites, may be a real, albeit unintended outcome of the process.[124]

A third theory is that racial disparities are the result of institutional racism. Institutional racism occurs when members of a race are subordinated, disadvantaged, or overrepresented in negative outcomes through the normal functioning of social institutions, whether or not that subordination, disadvantage, or overrepresentation is consciously or deliberately intended.[125] It is possible that the racial disparities are not so much a product of overt racial animus as they are of the pragmatic goals of the courtroom participants. Consider two prosecutor examples. First, prosecutors may not underrepresent blacks in capital jury pools because of racial prejudice per se, but rather because of the belief that blacks are more likely than whites to oppose the death penalty and to acquit capital defendants if they are jurors. Because prosecutors are constrained by limited resources and highly motivated to win their trials, they increase their odds of winning by excluding as many blacks as possible.

From the mid-1960s through the mid-1970s, that was a reasonable strategy because, in those years, over 50 percent of blacks nationwide opposed the death penalty, but beginning in 1978 and continuing through the 1980s, less than a majority of blacks nationwide were opponents.[126] A 1988 Gallup poll shows that only 31 percent of blacks opposed the death penalty, the lowest level of opposition in over 50 years of Gallup polling.[127] Still, the 31 percent of blacks was more than twice the 14 percent of whites who opposed the penalty.[128]

The second example may not be the result of overt racial enmity but rather of a political consideration. Elected prosecutors may believe that their key constituencies want their limited resources expended on white victim cases and not on black ones. Prosecutors themselves may not be racially prejudiced (they would focus their efforts on the prosecution of any social group if it would win them votes), but they may bow to the racial prejudices of their voters. In sum, whether racial discrimination is the product of institutional racism or of intentional or purposeful action, its existence in the administration of capital punishment is odious and intolerable.

The Supreme Court has implicitly recognized the existence of institutional racism in some types of cases (e.g., housing, public accommodations, jury selection, and employment) and has held it to be impermissible. The Court has not been equally responsive to institutional racism in death penalty cases but, instead, requires proof of intentional or purposeful discrimination in individual cases. One reason for this was given by Justice Powell in the *McCleskey* decision:

> McCleskey's claim, taken to its logical conclusion, throws into serious question the principles that underlie our entire criminal justice system. . . . [I]f we accepted McCleskey's claim that racial bias has impermissibly tainted the capital sentencing decision, we could soon be faced with similar claims as to other types of penalty.[129]

Professors Baldus and Woodworth provide two additional reasons why the Court may have rejected the claim of racial discrimination in McCleskey's particular case. First, "as a convicted murderer, McCleskey did not enjoy the same status of an 'oppressed minority' as would a blameless claimant seeking equal access to housing, employment, or schools."[130] Second, "McCleskey's claim primarily pointed not to discrimination on the basis of his race (over which he had no control) but rather to discrimination on the basis of the victim's race. . . . [I]t was McCleskey [however] who 'chose' his victim, a fact that weakened the moral appeal of his claim."[131] Finally, Professor Hoffmann argues that in *McCleskey* the Court, in effect, conceded that comparative injustice (that is, discrimination) was inevitable in any sentencing scheme, but decided that "none of the available alternative approaches to capital sentencing would be more 'just' than the guided discretionary approach employed in Georgia."[132]

Another theory suggests that the continuing practice of racial discrimination in the administration of the death penalty is evidence that capital punishment serves other latent purposes. According to this theory, it serves (1) as an instrument of minority group oppression ("to keep blacks in the South in a position of subjugation and subservience"), (2) as an instrument of majority group protection ("to secure the integrity of the white community in the face of threats or perceived challenges from blacks"), and (3) as a repressive response ("to conditions of dislocation and turmoil in . . . time of economic hardship").[133] From this viewpoint, the death penalty as administered devalues the lives of blacks—particularly in the South—by using them as tools in a social (racial) and economic power struggle. Advocates of the theory contend that the death penalty in the United States is, at least in part, a race relations mechanism that controls blacks by extermination or, perhaps even more importantly, by threat of extermination.

Counterarguments to Claims of Racial Discrimination. Many proponents of capital punishment claim that there is no longer any racial discrimination in its administration. The more sophisticated among them concede that there may have been racial discrimination in the past, but that evidence under post-*Furman* statutes reveals racial disparities and not discrimination.[134] Another argument is that even if some post-*Furman* death sentences are a product of racial discrimination, society's interests in retribution, justice, and concern for crime victims and their families are more important, so that racial discrimination in the death penalty's application can be and should be ignored.[135] A related argument suggests that even if there is racial discrimination in the application of the death penalty, that in no way reduces either the blameworthiness of the guilty defendants who are sentenced to death for racial reasons or society's justification for executing them.[136] A final argument is that racial discrimination is inevitable and that it infects all social institutions, the death penalty being no exception. Hence, there is nothing that can be done about such racial discrimination short of abolishing the death penalty.[137] Proponents of capital punishment who make this argument clearly believe the merits of capital punishment outweigh any racial discrimination in its application.

Conclusion. The counterarguments of death penalty proponents, notwithstanding, the Supreme Court has not and likely cannot rid the imposition of the death penalty from repugnant forms of racial discrimination. Yet, in *Zant v. Stephens* (1983), *McCleskey v. Kemp* (1987), and other cases, it has clearly indicated that either defendant-based or victim-based racial discrimination in the administration of capital punishment, whether overt or covert, is constitutionally impermissible.[138] Even under post-*Furman* statutes, Professors Bowers and Pierce observe that:

> race is truly a pervasive influence on the criminal justice processing of potentially capital cases, one that is evident at every stage of the process . . . it is an influence that persists despite separate sentencing hearings, explicitly articulated sentencing guidelines, and automatic appellate review of all death sentences. . . .[139]

The same could also be said about social class, gender, and age discrimination.

Discussion Questions

1. What does it mean to say that the death penalty has been imposed in an arbitrary and discriminatory way?

2. Are arbitrariness and discrimination acceptable in the administration of capital punishment?

3. Has the death penalty been administered in an unacceptably arbitrary and discriminatory way?

4. Is the death penalty currently administered in an unacceptably arbitrary and discriminatory way?

5. If the answer to the former question is yes, what are the sources of arbitrariness and discrimination?

6. Is there a significant difference in any relevant social characteristic between a 17- and 18-year-old, other than what has been created by law?

7. Is it really meaningful to consider a 17-year-old a juvenile and an 18-year-old an adult?

8. Have post-*Furman* death penalty statutes and Court decisions had the effect desired by the Court's majority in *Furman*? Can death penalty statutes be made constitutionally acceptable?

Notes

[1] Nakell and Hardy, 1987:16.

[2] Ibid.

[3] Bowers, 1984:191.

[4] Amsterdam, 1982:351.

[5] *Death Row, U.S.A.*, 1998.

[6] Ibid.

[7] Adapted from Bowers, op. cit., p. 188.

[8] Ibid.

[9] *Death Row, U.S.A.*, 1998, op. cit.

[10] See Bedau, 1982:56-7.

[11] *Death Row, U.S.A.*, 1998, op. cit.

[12] Bowers, 1984, op. cit., p. 236, Table 7-5, from the effective dates of those states' respective post-*Furman* statutes through 1977.

[13] Federal Bureau of Investigation, 1997:14.

[14] Bowers, op. cit., p. 189.

[15] Sandys, 1998:304; Acker and Lanier, 1998:105; Bowers and Steiner, 1998:311, 321, 323; Haney, 1998:357-9; Frank and Applegate, 1998; Blankenship et al., 1997; Haney et al., 1994.

[16] Bowers and Steiner, ibid., p. 328; Bowers, 1995.

[17] Acker and Lanier, op. cit.; Bowers and Steiner, op. cit., pp. 320-1; Hoffmann, 1995.

[18] Amsterdam, op. cit., p. 350.

[19] Ibid.

[20] See ibid.

[21] Quoted in ibid.

[22] Quoted in Bedau, op. cit., p. 190.

[23] See Bowers, 1984, op. cit., pp. 368-70.

[24] Ibid., p. 372.

[25] Bedau, op. cit.; Bowers, 1984, op. cit.; Schneider and Smykla, 1991.

[26] But see, Haney, 1998, op. cit., for a discussion of the importance of antecedent factors in the penalty phase of capital trials.

[27] Reiman, 1998; Simon and Eitzen, 1996; Pepinsky and Jesilow, 1984.

[28] *Furman v. Georgia*, 1972, at 251-2.

[29] See Reiman, op. cit.; Tifft, 1982.

[30] See Marquart et al., 1994, for an examination of class effects on the death penalty in Texas.

[31] Bedau, op. cit., p. 187.

[32] Schneider and Smykla, op. cit., p. 6, Table 1.1.

[33] From data in Bedau, op. cit.

[34] Rapaport, 1993:147.

[35] Streib, 1998:202-205.

[36] Federal Bureau of Investigation, 1997, op. cit.; Streib, 1998, op. cit., p. 202; *Death Row, U.S.A.*, 1998, op. cit.

[37] Extrapolated from Strieb, 1998, op. cit., pp. 203-204.

[38] *Death Row, U.S.A.*, 1998, op. cit.

[39] Streib, 1993:144.

[40] See Marquart et al., 1994, op. cit., for an examination of gender effects on the death penalty in Texas. Also see Rapaport, 1993:151, who argues "that the undervaluation of the heinousness of domestic murder is the most serious form of gender discrimination."

[41] Streib, 1993, op. cit., p. 142.

[42] Ibid., pp. 142–43.

[43] Ibid., p. 143.

[44] Ibid.

[45] Streib, 1998, op. cit., p. 220; also see Rapaport, 1993, op. cit., p. 146.

[46] Federal Bureau of Investigation, 1997, op. cit.; Streib, 1998, op. cit., p. 206; *Death Row, U.S.A.*, 1998, op. cit.

[47] *Death Row, U.S.A.*, ibid.

[48] Bright, 1997:21.

[49] Streib, 1998, op. cit., p. 207.

[50] Streib, 1998, ibid., p. 211; 1989:41.

[51] *Death Row, U.S.A.*, 1998, op. cit.

[52] Bright, 1997, op. cit.

[53] Streib, 1998, op. cit., pp. 209–10.

[54] Moore, 1994.

[55] Hoffmann, 1993:117.

[56] Ibid.

[57] Ibid., pp. 117–18.

[58] Ibid., p. 118.

[59] See Bohm and Haley, 1997:435.

[60] Hoffmann, op. cit., pp. 118–19.

[61] See Bedau, op. cit., pp. 58–9.

[62] Ibid., pp. 58–61.

[63] Cited in Paternoster, 1991:127. As noted in Chapter 2, in *Coker v. Georgia* (433 U.S. 584, 1977), the Supreme Court effectively ended the possibility of a death penalty for rape of an adult woman where the victim is not killed.

[64] See Marquart et al., 1994, op. cit.; Kleck, 1981; Hagan, 1974.

[65] See Bedau, op. cit.

[66] See Bowers, 1984, op. cit., pp. 221–22 for methodology.

[67] Ibid., p. 230.

[68] U.S. General Accounting Office, 1990:6.

[69] Bright, 1997, op. cit., p. 4; also see Marquart et al., 1994, op. cit., for an examination of race effects on the death penalty in Texas.

[70] Lawrence, 1987:387, has argued that "the intent requirement is a centerpiece in an ideology of equal opportunity that legitimizes the continued existence of racially and economically discriminatory conditions and rationalizes the superordinate status of privileged whites."

[71] Radelet and Pierce, 1985:32.

[72] Bright, 1998:131.

[73] Ibid.

[74] Bowers, 1984, op. cit.; also cf. Baldus et al., 1986; Foley, 1987; Gross and Mauro, 1989, 1984; Radelet and Pierce, 1991, 1985; Radelet and Vandiver, 1983; Radelet, 1981; Zeisel, 1981; Arkin, 1980.

[75] Bowers, 1984, ibid.

[76] Baldus et al., 1990, 1986, op. cit.; 1983; Barnett, 1985; Bowers, 1984, ibid.; Gross and Mauro, 1984, op. cit.

[77] Baldus et al., 1986, ibid.; 1983; Bowers, 1984, ibid.; Ekland–Olsen, 1988.

[78] Paternoster, 1991, op. cit.; 1984; 1983; Paternoster and Kazyaka, 1988.

[79] Gross and Mauro, 1984, op. cit.; Nakell and Hardy, 1987, op. cit.; but see Paternoster, 1991, ibid.

[80] Smith, 1987.

[81] Baldus et al., 1986, op. cit.

[82] Baldus et al., 1986, ibid.; Gross and Mauro, 1989, op. cit.; 1984, op. cit.

[83] Baldus et al., 1986, ibid.

[84] Keil and Vito, 1995; Keil and Vito, 1990, 1989; Vito and Keil, 1988.

[85] Baldus et al., 1986, op. cit.

[86] Baldus et al., 1986, ibid.; Gross and Mauro, 1989, op. cit., 1984, op. cit.; Murphy, 1984.

[87] Baldus et al., 1986, ibid.

[88] Gross and Mauro, 1989, op. cit., 1984, op. cit.

[89] Baldus et al., 1986, op. cit.

[90] Baldus et al., 1986, ibid.

[91] Bienen et al., 1988.

[92] U.S. General Accounting Office, 1990, op. cit., p. 5.

[93] Ibid.

[94] Baldus et al., 1990, op. cit., p. 185.

[95] *Death Row, U.S.A.*, 1998, op. cit.

[96] Ibid., p. 7.

[97] See Zahn, 1989, for homicide trends during the twentieth century.

[98] Federal Bureau of Investigation, 1997, op. cit., p. 17, Table 2.8.

[99] Baldus and Woodworth claim that "in most death sentencing states only about 10 to 15 percent of defendants arrested for homicide have committed death-eligible crimes," see Baldus and Woodworth, 1998:395-96. Note that Baldus and Woodworth are referring to homicide arrests and not to murders and nonnegligent manslaughters committed.

[100] Baldus and Woodworth, ibid., p. 402.

[101] Baldus et al., 1990, op. cit., p. 403.

[102] Baldus et al., 1983.

[103] Bright, 1997, op. cit.

[104] Bowers, 1984, op. cit., pp. 340-41; Radelet, 1981, op. cit.; Radelet and Pierce, 1985, op. cit.

[105] Radelet and Pierce, 1985, ibid., p. 601.

[106] Jacoby and Paternoster, 1982; Paternoster, 1984, op. cit.; Paternoster and Kazyaka, 1988, op. cit.

[107] Vito and Keil, 1988, op. cit.

[108] Baldus et al., 1990, op. cit.; Gross and Mauro, 1989, op. cit.

[109] Baldus et al., ibid., p. 398.

[110] *Gregg v. Georgia*, 1976 at 157.

[111] Baldus et al., 1990, op. cit.

[112] See *Lockhart v. McCree*, 1986, and the discussion in Chapter 2.

[113] Sandys, 1998, op. cit., p. 291.

[114] Ibid., p. 305.

[115] Bohm, 1991.

[116] See Hans, 1988.

[117] Bohm, 1994.

[118] Parker, 1991:505.

[119] Although the prevalence of racial discrimination in the United States probably has declined over the last few decades, it has not disappeared. A 1979 study by the National Conference of Christians and Jews found that 74 percent of blacks felt that they were discriminated against in white collar jobs, 68 percent in blue collar jobs, and 58 percent in finding decent housing; only 39 percent of blacks believed that the government was committed to equality, see *Facts on File*, 1979. The National Opinion Research Center's 1988 General Social Survey shows that 25 percent of white respondents believed that there should be laws against interracial marriages, 37 percent would not attempt to change the rules of racially segregated social clubs so that blacks could join, 24 percent agreed (strongly (8 percent) or slightly (16 per-

cent)) that white people have a right to keep blacks out of their neighborhoods, 46 percent are living in racially segregated neighborhoods, and 44 percent of all respondents attended racially segregated churches, see Niemi, 1989.

[120] Barkan and Cohn, 1994.

[121] See, for example, Baldus et al., 1990, op. cit., p. 79 fn. 59. For two explanations (one based on Freudian theory, the other on cognitive psychology) of the unconscious nature of racially discriminatory beliefs and actions in American society today, see Lawrence, 1987, op. cit., pp. 329-44.

[122] Gross and Mauro, 1989, op.. cit., p. 113. At least theoretically, the process of victim-based racial identification may apply as well to the white killers of white victims, though white actors in the legal system may show more sympathy for white killers than for black killers. The possibility of offender-based racial identification is a potentially fertile area for future research. For a discussion of "villain identification" by the capital offender, see Bowers, 1988:54. For a review of the extensive literature on the process of identification, see Gross and Mauro, 1989, op. cit., Chap. 7.

[123] Gross and Mauro, 1989, ibid, p. 114; regarding prosecutors, see Baldus et al., 1990, op. cit., p. 184.

[124] The discussion of victim-based racial identification is not intended to imply that intentional discrimination does not operate in the process. It is likely that some combination of the two account for racial discrimination where it exists. Either way, white hegemony in the administration of capital punishment could produce the same results through either process.

[125] See Carmichael and Hamilton, 1967.

[126] See Bohm, 1991, op. cit., p. 120.

[127] Ibid.; Gallup Report, 1989:28.

[128] Gallup Report, ibid.

[129] *McCleskey v. Kemp*, 1987 at 315-16.

[130] Baldus and Woodworth, 1998, op. cit., p. 408.

[131] Ibid.

[132] Hoffmann, 1993, op. cit., p. 125.

[133] Bowers, 1984, op. cit., pp. 131-2; also see Douglas in *Furman v. Georgia*, 1972; Rusche and Kirchheimer, 1968; Baldus and Woodworth, 1998, op. cit., p. 386.

[134] See, for example, Wilbanks, 1987.

[135] See, for example, Van den Haag, 1982.

[136] Ibid.

[137] Apparently this was the position of Justice Scalia, as indicated by a memo he wrote while *McCleskey* was pending in the Court, see Baldus and Woodworth, 1998, op. cit., p. 409.

[138] See Baldus et al., 1990, op. cit.; Baldus and Woodworth, ibid., p. 389.

[139] Bowers and Pierce, 1982:220; also see Gross and Mauro, 1989, op. cit., 1984, op. cit.

CHAPTER 9

Retribution, Religion, and Capital Punishment

Retribution appears to be the primary basis of support for the death penalty in the United States.[1] In a recent Gallup poll, "a life for a life" was the reason given by the largest percentage of death penalty proponents (50 percent).[2] The next–favored reason (19 percent) was incapacitation: "keeps them from killing again." Law professor Joseph Hoffmann claims that the basic principles of retributive justice are now the principal guide by which the Supreme Court evaluates whether the death penalty, either in a single case or in a category of cases, is cruel and unusual punishment in violation of the Eighth Amendment.[3]

Retributive motives or feelings are, at least to some extent, a product of religious teachings. This chapter examines the subjects of retribution, religion, and capital punishment. In the section on retribution, the effects of the death penalty on the families of murder victims and death row and executed inmates are also addressed.

Retribution and Capital Punishment

As a theoretical term, the concept of retribution is imprecise.[4] Philosopher John Cottingham argues that "the term 'retributive' as used in philosophy has become so imprecise and multivocal that it is doubtful whether it any longer serves a useful purpose."[5] Justice Thurgood Marshall, in *Furman v. Georgia* (1972), writes that "the concept of retribution is one of the most misunderstood in all of our criminal jurisprudence."[6] As a result, law professor Margaret Radin notes that "retributivism is espoused by both [political] liberals and conservatives; it is seen as both a new way to limit inhumane practices and to exorcise permissiveness and coddling of criminals."[7]

The different meanings of retribution cause two problems: (1) disagreements over retribution's effects on death penalty opinions, and (2) disagreements about the acceptability of retribution as a justification for capital punishment. Justice Potter Stewart, who voted with the majority in the *Furman* decision, held that retribution was psychologically necessary for maintaining social stability (408 U.S. 238, 308),[8] while Justice Marshall equated retribution with vengeance and argued that neither were compatible with decent and civilized conduct.[9] Did the Justices really have in mind the same definition of retribution?

Meanings of Retribution. Some scholars believe retribution and revenge are virtually synonymous.[10] Others say there is an important difference between the two terms. Professor Radin maintains that "revenge occurs when one person, with the idea of retaliation, injures someone she believes is responsible for an injury either to herself or to someone she cares about."[11] Revenge, for Radin, "is a private act between one person or group and another" and may or may not be justified.[12] On the other hand, she defines retribution as "a public act" or, more specifically, "the formal act of a community against one of its members, and is carried out in the manner and for the reasons that are justified

> *Justice Potter Stewart, who voted with the majority in the* Furman *decision, held that retribution was psychologically necessary for maintaining social stability, while Justice Marshall equated retribution with vengeance and argued that neither were compatible with decent and civilized conduct.*

under the political constitution of the community."[13] The purpose of retribution, argues Radin, is to prevent personal revenge, which she calls "revenge–utilitarianism."[14]

Law professor Herbert Packer describes two versions of retribution: "revenge theory" and "expiation theory."[15] Revenge theory is captured in the idea of *lex talionis* ("an eye for an eye"), while expiation theory is based on the premise that only through suffering punishment can an offender atone for his or her crime.[16]

Criminologist James Finckenauer similarly distinguishes two versions of retribution.[17] In one version (the bad version, in some people's view), the criminal is paid back. This is retribution as revenge and vindictiveness. In a second version (the seemingly acceptable one according to the Supreme Court and some scholars of punishment philosophy), retribution means that the criminal pays back for the harm he or she has done. The desert theorists call this "just deserts." What is confusing, explains Finckenauer, is that in research examining the relationship between retributive feelings and death penalty support, the concepts of desert and retribution have generally been employed interchangeably.[18]

Cottingham has prepared the most exhaustive list of meanings, identifying and critiquing nine "theories" of punishment that have been labeled retributive.[19] First, and the one he argues captures the fundamental notion of retribution is repayment theory. Although ostensibly similar to Packer's expiation theory (with elements of revenge theory), Cottingham claims that there can "not be an atonement theory of punishment; atonement is something voluntarily undertaken, punishment something exacted."[20] Another problem Cottingham has with a repayment theory of punishment is the unexplained question of "how or why suffering something unpleasant . . . should count as payment for an offence?"[21]

A second variety of retribution is desert theory: the idea that punishment is imposed because it is deserved.[22] This theory, taken literally, rests on the idea that an offender receives punishment as a reward for wrongdoing.[23] Recall Finckenauer's assertion that just deserts is one of two versions of retribution, the other being revenge.[24] Finckenauer argues that the principal difference between just deserts and revenge has to do with who repays whom, that is, whether the offender repays society (just deserts) or society repays the offender (revenge).[25] The distinction is specious for at least three reasons. First, just deserts, as Finckenauer defines it, is indistinguishable from restitution. Second, Finckenauer's conception of just deserts appears very similar to Packer's expiation theory and, as Cottingham reasons, as long as punishment is not voluntarily undertaken, it is not atonement. Few offenders volunteer to repay society. Third, Finckenauer proposes that in just deserts the offender is the subject, that is, "the active party," and in revenge the offender is the object, that is, "the passive target of society's actions."[26] It is not clear, however, how the punished offender can be, except perhaps in a hypothetical way, the subject or active party. The offender does not voluntarily seek to be punished to repay society in most cases; the offender is coerced. Moreover, how are the intentions of the offender in regard to punishment to be discerned? In either case, as Cottingham points out, it is not clear why suffering punishment should count as repayment for an offense.

A third variety of retribution is penalty theory, which is associated with the classical Kantian notion that an offender is punished automatically simply because he or she has committed a crime.[27] This idea implies both proportionality and deserts in punishment. In other words, a "punishment must fit the crime and must not be more or other than the person deserves" in order to respect a person's status as an autonomous moral entity.[28] Despite the emphasis on respecting a person's autonomy, penalty theory is still based on repayment, albeit circumscribed repayment.

Fourth is minimalism, which refers to the idea that "no one should be punished 'unless' he is guilty of a crime and culpable."[29] Minimalism is dismissed by Cottingham, who asks, "What on earth is supposed to be distinctly 'retributivist' about [this] thesis?"[30]

Fifth is satisfaction theory, which is similar to repayment theory and rests on a view of reciprocity: "A man is rightly punished because his punishment brings satisfaction to others."[31] However, as Cottingham notes, "if the underlying idea here is that the penal system provides a substitute for private revenge," then satisfaction theory is not a theory of retribution at all but rather one of social utility, furthering the goal of social stability.[32]

A sixth variety is fair play theory, which assumes that "failure to punish is unfair to those who practise self-restraint and respect the rights of others."[33] This theory, however, turns out to be a form of repayment theory as the offender is made to pay "for the unfair advantage he has obtained" by his or her criminal acts.[34]

Seventh is placation theory, which is captured by Kant's famous passage that "even if a civil society were to dissolve itself by common agreement . . . the last murderer remaining in prison must first be executed so that . . . the blood guilt thereof will not be fixed on the people."[35] Cottingham points out that this theory "looks forward to the desired result of appeasing the wrath of God" and, thus, "is unlikely to have much appeal to present-day thinkers concerned to provide a secular justification for punishment."[36]

An eighth variety is annulment theory, which, according to Cottingham confuses retribution with restitution. Annulment theory is based on the idea that "we are obliged to punish because to do so is 'to annul the crime which otherwise would have been held valid, and to restore the right.'"[37]

A ninth and final variety of retribution is denunciation theory, that is, punishment is inflicted to denounce a crime.[38] Cottingham maintains that denunciation theory is not uniquely retributivist since there are other ways, besides punishment, of denouncing crime.[39] At the end of his exercise, Cottingham admits that most of the theories that he has described share much in common with the notion of retribution as repayment. Indeed, one must strain to identify differences.

Sources of Retribution. Because of the presumed universality of retributive emotions, some writers have suggested that retributive motives have a biological basis.[40] Others have argued that retributive emotions are derived from the socialization process and "are the psychological representations of more overt social and socialpsychological processes."[41]

Professors Vidmar and Miller are among those who believe that the socialization process is the principal source of retributive emotions. They argue that retribution "derives from the individual's attachment to the group, internalization of group values, and perception of the offense as a threat to those values."[42] Retribution also may be a means of obtaining social acceptance about the moral rightness of the violated rule.[43] Vidmar and Miller found that retributive punishment reactions increased with the increasing importance of the violated rule and the increasing seriousness of the outcome.[44] Thus, for example, a greater retributive punishment would be expected in a case in which a murderer cannibalized or otherwise mutilated the victim's body than in a case in which the murderer did not.

> *P*rofessors Vidmar and Miller are among those who believe that the socialization process is the principal source of retributive emotions. They argue that retribution "derives from the individual's attachment to the group, internalization of group values, and perception of the offense as a threat to those values." Retribution also may be a means of obtaining social acceptance about the moral rightness of the violated rule.

Problems with Retribution as Revenge. Revenge for death-eligible crimes is an emotional, though quite understandable, reaction. A problem with revenge as a justification for capital punishment is that a decision as important as the intentional taking of a life by the state should be based more on reason than on emotion. Opponents of the death penalty point out that it is largely emotion that makes people want to punish in kind. They add that no other crime is punished in kind; the literal interpretation of the eye-for-an-eye maxim is not imposed for any other offense. For example, the state does not burn down the homes of arsonists, cheat people who defraud, or rape people who rape.[45] Why, then, opponents ask, is it necessary to kill people who kill? Their answer is that it is not. In practice, only a select few among all those who are death-eligible are executed in the name of revenge.

Criminologist Edna Erez claims that the eye-for-an-eye (*lex talionis*) formula has frequently been misinterpreted[46]—that the famous formula was never intended to be taken literally but was meant as a warning against applying punishment in a discriminatory way. The conclusion to the Biblical dictate of "an eye for an eye" is "You shall have one manner of law, as well for the stranger, as for your own country."[47] This has been interpreted to mean that the eye of a peasant is just as worthy as the eye of a noble; thus, the victim and the offender should be treated alike, without consideration of social status. The eye-for-an-eye formula was intended to require monetary compensation and not the trading of body parts.[48] Similarly, law professor Joseph Hoffmann points out that proportional punishment—a goal of retributive justice—does not require payment in kind, but instead needs only to "be defined in terms of whatever the particular society views as appropriate for the crime."[49] The key is that the proportional punishment be applied proportionately and not in a discriminatory way.

Thus, even assuming that revenge is a legitimate rationale, opponents of the penalty argue that there is no reason why revenge could not be served by another noncapital punishment. On this point rests what may be the quintessential difference between proponents and opponents of the death penalty: Proponents sometimes misunderstand that opponents of the penalty do not want capital offenders to escape punishment or justice; indeed, most of them want such offenders to be punished to the severest degree allowed by law. The only difference between the two groups is what the severest punishment allowed by law should be.

Supporters of capital punishment maintain that by allowing the state to seek revenge, relatives and friends of the victim(s) are relieved of the need to do so. An implication is that with the abolition of capital punishment, relatives and friends of a victim are more likely to seek personal revenge. However, as Justice Brennan observed in his *Furman* decision, "There is no evidence whatever that utilization of imprisonment rather than death encourages private blood feuds and other disorders."[50] During the hiatus in capital punishment in the United States between 1968 and 1977, there was no apparent increase in personal revenge, nor do states without capital punishment have elevated levels of personal revenge. This seems proof that a need for revenge can be satisfied by an alternative punishment, such as life imprisonment.

Vindictiveness notwithstanding, the family or the friends of a victim, as well as others, may support capital punishment for the catharsis, finality, or closure it may bring to their loss.[51] Research on capital crime victims' families is meager, but what there is emphasizes their immense suffering and loss.[52] Professor Margaret Vandiver summarizes some of the results of that research:

- The loss of a close relative to homicide is a shatteringly traumatic event. The pain, disruption, and trauma caused by homicide cannot be overstated.

- The trauma and difficulty of adjusting to loss due to homicide is such that survivors often experience Post-Traumatic Stress Disorder-like symptoms. Many survivors report losing their sense that there is any justice or safety in the world; many feel that life itself has lost all meaning.

- Survivors can expect to encounter difficulties in many other areas of their lives, including their marriages, relationships with children, friendships, and work.

- The experience of bereavement moves through several stages, including denial, anger, grief, and ultimately, resolution. These stages are necessarily distinct and do not always occur in the same sequence.

- The process of recovery takes years, if not decades. Expectations of quick grieving and recovery are unrealistic and damaging. Even after survivors resolve their grief, it is unlikely that their emotional lives will ever be the same as before the crime.

- Survivors often are not helped, and sometimes are further victimized, by the criminal justice system. Both formal and informal supports for homicide victims' survivors are dreadfully inadequate.

- The experience of isolation is very common—at the time they most need contact and support, families often feel the most isolated. The opposite situation of intrusion is often a problem as well, with unwelcome contacts from the criminal justice system, the media, and curiosity-seekers.

- There seems to be much potential for advancing the process of healing through nonjudgmental, ongoing, emotionally involved listening, without suggestions as to how the survivors should feel or what they should do.[53]

Some family members do not want their relative's killer executed. Among their reasons are the following:

- a general opposition to the death penalty;

- an execution would diminish or belittle the memory of their relative;

- a desire to avoid the prolonged contact with the criminal justice system that the death penalty requires;

- a desire to avoid the public attention an impending execution bestows on the condemned prisoner;

- a preference for the finality of a sentence of life imprisonment without the possibility of parole and the obscurity into which the defendant will quickly fall, over the continued uncertainty and publicity of the death penalty;

- a desire for the offender to have a long time to reflect on his or her deed, and perhaps to feel remorse for it;

- a hope that someday there can be some sort of mediation or reconciliation between the family and the offender;

- and if the offender is a relative, for obvious reasons.[54]

Some death penalty proponents argue that life imprisonment or a lesser punishment, rather than execution, may not provide the psychological relief deserved by victims' suffering survivors. For some families, anything less than an execution may be taken as a slight, "an indication that society does not value their relative or understand the magnitude of their loss."[55] Opponents respond in two ways. First, they acknowledge that an execution may indeed relieve feelings of profound loss, but assume that, in many cases, the relief may be only temporary. In the long run, they presume (there is no systematic research on the subject), an execution may make the burden more difficult to bear because the desire for revenge appeases only the basest and most primitive characteristics of human beings. Second, they point out that even if an execution did make a loss easier to endure for the relatives of the victim, that advantage would have to be weighed against the effects of the execution on the relatives of the perpetrator. This attempt to balance the death penalty's effects on both families raises two key questions posed nicely by Professor Vandiver:

> Given that the crime cannot be undone, what can the criminal justice system offer to the victim's family? And what kind of sentence can be imposed on a defendant found guilty of first degree murder that is commensurate to the crime, protects society, and yet does not destroy the defendant's family in turn?[56]

There is even less research on the families of death row or executed inmates than there is on victims' families. The research that is available, though, indicates that the effects of capital punishment on death row or executed inmates' families can be as profound as it is for victims' families. Families of death row or executed inmates are different from the families of victims of any other kind of violent death in some important ways. Professor Vandiver lists four of the differences:

- The families of condemned prisoners know for years that the state intends to kill their relatives and the method that will be used. They experience a prolonged period of anticipatory grieving, complicated by the hope that some court or governor will grant relief.

- Their relatives' deaths will come about as the result of the actions of dozens of respected and powerful persons. Their deaths will not be caused by a breakdown in social order but by a highly orchestrated and cooperative effort of authority.

- Their relatives are publicly disgraced and shamed; they have been formally cast out of society and judged to be unworthy to live.

- The deaths of their relatives are not mourned and regretted the way other violent deaths are; rather, the death is condoned, supported and desired by many people, and actively celebrated by some.[57]

In a footnote, Professor Vandiver adds a fifth important difference and its ironic consequence:

> Family members of capital defendants frequently have been victims of violent crime themselves; indeed, it is not unusual for these families to have lost relatives to homicide. Yet, because of class and racial inequities in sentencing, it is unlikely their relatives' deaths were punished with much severity. How ironic for these families that when a relative encounters the criminal justice system as a defendant rather than a victim, the system turns from leniency to severity.[58]

Other problems experienced by families of death row inmates (some of which they share with the families of victims) are stress (both economic and psychological), grief (only the families of death row inmates experience anticipatory grief), depression and other medical illnesses, self-accusation, social isolation, powerlessness, demoralization, and family disorganization.[59] Since the families of both the victim and the perpetrator are usually "innocent," the infliction of pain and suffering on one group to relieve the pain and suffering of the other group is hard to justify.

> *P*roblems experienced by families of death row inmates (some of which they share with the families of victims) are stress (both economic and psychological), grief (only the families of death row inmates experience anticipatory grief), depression and other medical illnesses, self-accusation, social isolation, powerlessness, demoralization, and family disorganization.

The death penalty also affects police officers, attorneys, judges, jurors, witnesses, correctional personnel, and other persons who find themselves involved in the process by choice or by duty. Unfortunately, there is a dearth of research on the death penalty's impact on those people's lives.[60]

Supporters of capital punishment cite retributive grounds in suggesting that legal vengeance is a way of enhancing social solidarity and of sanctifying the importance of innocent life.[61] Assuming the argument has merit, there would seem to be other ways than capital punishment of achieving those ends (e.g., noncapital punishments or, better yet, more positive measures). Moreover, it is difficult to understand how the taking of a life, even of a person guilty of aggravated murder, in any way sanctifies life. Henry Schwarzschild, former Director of the Capital Punishment Project of the American Civil Liberties Union, asked, "How can a thoughtful and sensible person justify killing people who kill people to teach that killing is wrong?"[62]

Recent research shows that the public supports the death penalty primarily for vindictive revenge.[63] This raises two important questions. First, is the satisfaction of the desire for vindictive revenge a legitimate penal purpose? And second, does legitimizing this desire for vindictive revenge contribute to the violent social relationships that pervade our nation? Justice Marshall observed in his *Furman* decision:

Retaliation, vengeance, and retribution have been roundly condemned as intolerable aspirations for a government in a free society. Punishment as retribution has been condemned as intolerable by scholars for centuries, and the Eighth Amendment itself was adopted to prevent punishment from becoming synonymous with vengeance.[64]

A principal source of the desire for vindictive revenge (the eye-for-an-eye variety) is religion; however, religious support for vindictive revenge and for the death penalty is puzzling, since the Bible is ambiguous on both subjects. (This discussion applies only to those religions that use the Bible, either the Old or the New Testament, as their basis of authority.)

Religion and Capital Punishment

The leaders of most organized religions in the United States no longer support the death penalty, and many actually openly favor its abolition.[65] For example, the National Conference of Catholic Bishops has declared its opposition, arguing that capital punishment is "uncivilized," "inhumane," "barbaric," and an assault on the sanctity of human life.[66] Religious leaders have argued that capital punishment is inconsistent with efforts "to promote respect for human life, to stem the tide of violence in our society and to embody the message of God's redemptive love."[67] Capital punishment is believed to institutionalize retribution and revenge and to exacerbate violence by giving it official sanction.[68] Nevertheless, despite the views of their leadership, a majority of people in the United States who profess a religious belief, whether Protestant, Catholic, or Jewish, support capital punishment.[69]

> The leaders of most organized religions in the United States no longer support the death penalty and actually openly favor its abolition.

Capital Punishment in the Old Testament. Religious leaders who oppose capital punishment concede that the Old Testament prescribes the death penalty for many offenses. They are:

- murder (Exodus 21.12-13; Leviticus 24.17; Numbers 35.16ff; Deuteronomy 19.11ff)

- manslaughter (Numbers 35.9-28)

- bearing false witness on a capital charge (Deuteronomy 19.18-21)

- kidnapping or stealing a man (Exodus 21.16; Deuteronomy 24.7)

- cursing God (Exodus 22.28; Leviticus 24.10-16);

- idolatry (Exodus 20.3-5, 22.20; Deuteronomy 13.1-11, 17.2-7)

- disobedience of religious authority (Deuteronomy 17.8-13)

- laboring on the Sabbath (Exodus 31.14-15, 35.2)

- false prophecy in the name of God (Deuteronomy 18.20-22)

- child sacrifice (Leviticus 20.2)

- striking, cursing or rebelling against a parent (Exodus 20.12ff, 21.17; Leviticus 19.3, 20.9; Deuteronomy 21.18-21)

- adultery and unnatural vice (Leviticus 18.23, 20.10-16; Deuteronomy 22.22)

- prostitution or harlotry under certain circumstances (Leviticus 21.9; Deuteronomy 22.20-24)

- sorcery (Exodus 22.18; Leviticus 20.27)

- incest (Leviticus 18.6-18, 20.14; Deuteronomy 27.20, 23)

- sodomy and bestiality (Leviticus 18.22ff, 20.13ff); and

- keeping an ox known to be dangerous, if it kills a person (Exodus 21.29)[70]

Offenders were executed by stoning—the standard method of judicial execution in Biblical times (Leviticus 24.14, 16; Deuteronomy 22.24; 1 Kings 21.13; Numbers 15.35)—and, in some cases, burning (Leviticus 20.14, 21.9; Genesis 38.24), beheading (2 Kings 6.31-32; 2 Samuel 16.9), strangling (not listed in the Old Testament, but contained in the Tractate on the Sanhedrin in the Mishnah), and shooting with arrows (Exodus 19.13). Occasionally, corpses of executed lawbreakers were hung in public as an example to others (Deuteronomy 21.22, 23), and sometimes, the corpse of the executed person was mutilated (2 Samuel 4.12).[71]

More scriptural support for capital punishment in the Old Testament includes Genesis 9.6, which commands, "Who sheddeth man's blood, by man shall his blood be shed," and 25 verses after "Thou shalt not kill," in Exodus 21.12, one finds, "He that smiteth a man so that he may die, shall be surely put to death."[72] Leviticus 24.17 states, "He who kills a man shall be put to death," and in Numbers 35.30-31, "If anyone kills a person, the murderer shall be put to death on the evidence of witnesses. . . . Moreover, you shall accept no ransom for the life of a murderer who is guilty of death; but he shall be put to death. . . ."[73]

It appears that the ancient Hebrews were a vengeful and barbaric people; however, in practice, Hebrew law made it very difficult to execute a capital offender. Some of the legal requirements and procedures were:

- the court was composed of 23 members (as opposed to three members in monetary matters): a majority of one was needed to acquit the defendant, but a majority of two was needed to convict;

- men lacking in compassion and mercy were not to be appointed to the court (among those excluded were the very old, the impotent or castrated, or the childless, all of whom were believed to have good reason for their lack of compassion and mercy);

- adjudication had to begin and be completed in the daytime;

- adjudication could be completed the same day if the defendant were acquitted, but was to be postponed until the following day if the defendant were convicted (to provide the opportunity of discovering favorable evidence);

- two capital cases could not be adjudicated on the same day, to allow enough time to thoroughly present the defendant's case;

- the court was expected to act in the defendant's defense (an adversarial system was not employed in capital cases);

- if members of the court witnessed the capital crime, they could not be involved in the case's adjudication because they could not argue in favor of the defendant;

- if the court began its adjudication process with a unanimous vote against the defendant, acquittal was mandated because such a vote could only mean that the court had not done its job defending the defendant (it was assumed that at least one argument could always be made on behalf of the defendant);

- adjudication began with arguments in favor of the defendant;

- those who argued against the defendant were allowed to change their minds; those who argued in favor of the defendant could not;

- everyone was allowed to argue in favor of the defendant, but only certain people could argue against the defendant;

- the defendant was not allowed to argue against himself or herself (conviction in capital cases could not be based solely on a confession);

- ignorance of the law was a valid defense (the death penalty could not be imposed unless witnesses warned the offender just prior to the commission of the crime that the act was punishable by death *and* the offender acknowledged the warning and admitted knowing the punishment for the crime) (originally this was a means of distinguishing between intentional and accidental murder);

- trustworthy testimony had to be given by two qualified eyewitnesses, who were together at the time and scene of the crime and observed the crime from the same place (witnesses had to be free adults, of sound mind and body, of unquestioned integrity, and have no personal interest in the case);

- evidence from those people related by blood or marriage was not admissible;

- circumstantial evidence was excluded;

- witnesses were warned not to testify to anything that was based on inference or hearsay;

- witnesses were interrogated separately about the exact time, place, and persons involved in the offense, and any material discrepancies resulted in an acquittal;

- witnesses were warned that false testimony would make them liable to the accused's penalty if the accused were convicted.[74]

Further, according to one authority:

> there was a saying that a Sanhedrin [in ancient times, the supreme council and highest court of the Hebrew nation] which put one man to death in seven years might be called murderous. Rabbi Eliezer ben Azarya said that it [the Sanhedrin] would be called murderous if it executed one man in seventy years. And Rabbi Akiba and Rabbi Tryphon said if they had been present, they would always have had some way of making it impossible to pass the death sentence.[75]

Two additional points about capital punishment in the Old Testament relevant to contemporary practice are important. First, the majority of the capital offenses of the ancient Hebrews are not capital offenses today, and few Americans would sanction the death penalty for most of them. Second, rabbis have concluded that the Torah ("the five books of Moses") suggests that different and more appropriate punishments may be used, as historical circumstances dictate.[76]

Finally, there is the Sixth Commandment's admonishment in the Old Testament, "Thou shalt not kill." Death penalty opponents who base their opposition primarily on their religious beliefs cite the Sixth Commandment as a scriptural basis for their position. Proponents of the penalty counter that in the original Hebrew, the Sixth Commandment translates as "Thou shalt not commit murder."[77] Thus, the Sixth Commandment presumably prohibits only murder and not capital punishment or killing in "just" wars. Catholic scholar Father James Reilly indicates that, according to the Roman Catechism of the Council of Trent promulgated by Pope Pius V in 1566, the death penalty is a morally permissible way to punish murderers.[78]

Capital Punishment in the New Testament. The New Testament provides many references that ostensibly argue against capital punishment. Followers of Jesus were asked to love their enemies (Matthew 5.44) and to forgive those who trespass against them (Matthew 6.14–15), and while he was on the cross, Jesus forgave his executioners because of their lack of knowledge and understanding. In Matthew 5.38–40, he provided an alternative to violence: "You have heard the commandment, 'An eye for an eye, a tooth for a tooth,' but what I say to you is: Offer no resistance to injury. When a person strikes you on the right cheek, turn and offer him the other." As evidenced by his ministry to outcasts and his acceptance of sinners, Jesus expressed a love and mercy for all people, regardless of their worth or merit. He was not, however, "soft on crime," but believed that ultimate judgment rested with God (Matthew 25.31–46). As St. Paul warned in Romans 12.19, "Vengeance is mine, says the Lord. I will repay."[79]

During the twelfth and thirteenth centuries (the Middle Ages) when the Catholic Church dominated social life in Western Europe, capital punishment began to be used widely for religious crimes—despite New Testament references seemingly against it. Before then, pre-Christian legal codes listed fewer crimes and milder punishments than those imposed later under religious auspices.[80]

Religious authorities created some of the more barbaric methods of execution. They included the rack, the wheel, the iron maiden, burning at the stake, and impaling in the grave. A primary purpose of those execution methods was to cause prolonged suffering before death so that in the interim, heretics had the opportunity to confess, repent, and receive salvation.[81]

> *R*eligious authorities created some of the more barbaric methods of execution. They included the rack, the wheel, the iron maiden, burning at the stake, and impaling in the grave. A primary purpose of those execution methods was to cause prolonged suffering before death so that in the interim, heretics had the opportunity to confess, repent, and receive salvation.

Thus, even though the official position of the Catholic Church today is against capital punishment, traditional Catholic teaching supported it. Thomas Acquinas cited the following passage from Corinthians:

> Now every individual person is compared to the whole community, as part to whole. Therefore, if a man be dangerous and infectious to the community on account of some sin [crime], it is praiseworthy and advantageous that he be killed in order to safeguard the common good, since "little leaven corrupts the whole lump."[82]

Traditional thinking of the Catholic Church further held that capital punishment is the best deterrent to crime.[83] Paul wrote in Romans 13.4, "It is not without purpose that the ruler carries the sword. He is God's servant, to inflict his avenging wrath upon the wrongdoer."[84] Therefore, if capital punishment is the *only* effective way to protect society from predatory behavior, it is considered both legitimate and necessary. The arguable issue, of course, is whether capital punishment is the *only* effective way to prevent crime.

Protestant scholar and journalist Reverend G. Aiken Taylor states that "most Christians tend to confuse the Christian personal ethic with the requirements of social order . . . we tend to apply what the Bible teaches us about how we—personally— should behave toward our neighbors with what the Bible teaches about how to preserve order in society."[85] This presumed difference between a personal and a social ethic is what may ultimately divide Christians on the subject of capital punishment. But before the ethical division is accepted, several questions must be addressed: (1) "Does God, then, have two different sets of rules by which he wants people to live?" (2) "Does he have one code for individuals as Christians and another for persons acting together, as they do in government?" (3) "Does he have one ethic for Christians and another for rulers and politicians?" (4) "What happens when Christians become part of their society's decision-making process, as in the case of a democracy?"[86] Answers to those questions may enable some Christians to reconcile their differences regarding capital punishment.

Protestant clergyman and scholar Reverend Reuben Hahn writes, "Not to inflict the death penalty is a flagrant disregard for God's divine law which recognizes the dignity of human life as a product of God's creation. Life is sacred, and that is why God instituted the death penalty—as a way to protect innocent human life."[87] The problem with this argument, counters legal scholar Charles Black, is that, "though the justice of God may indeed ordain that some should die, the justice of man is altogether and always insufficient for saying who these may be."[88]

Conclusion

The public's retributive feelings toward capital offenders are what ultimately may sustain the institution of capital punishment in the United States. The reason many people support the death penalty is vindictive revenge—they want to pay back offenders for what they have done. Death penalty opponents ask why capital offenders cannot be paid back with a noncapital punishment such as life imprisonment without opportunity of parole. They point out that no other crime is punished in kind.

A principal source of vindictive revenge is religion: The phrase, an eye-for-an-eye, comes from the Bible. Yet, religious support for vindictive revenge, and for the death penalty, is puzzling because the Bible appears to be ambigious on both subjects. An interesting question is how people, particularly people whose lives are governed by the Bible, can endorse revenge, support or oppose capital punishment, and use the Bible as a basis of their support or opposition, when they know the Bible is ambigious on the subjects.

Religious support for capital punishment may be underestimated because public opinions, established over a long period of time, are difficult to change and probably lag behind changes in the official doctrines of organized religions. Moreover, in certain regions of the United States, religion may have more influence over death penalty opinions than in other regions. In the South, for example, religion may continue to exert an extraordinary influence on support for the death penalty, especially since the Southern Baptist Convention is one of the religious organizations that continues to support capital punishment.[89] Other religious organizations that support capital punishment are: (1) Jehovah's Witnesses, (2) Seventh Day Adventists, (3) the Church of Jesus Christ of Latter Day Saints (Mormons), and (4) certain conservative and orthodox Jewish groups.

Continued support for the death penalty, at least among some Christian groups, may be related to capital punishment's key role in the creation of Christianity. As New York State Senator James Donovan is reported to have asked in a letter to a church group opposed to the state's enactment of a death penalty statute, "Where would Christianity be today had 'Jesus got 8 to 15 years with time off for good behavior'."[90]

Discussion Questions

1. What is retribution?

2. Is retribution an acceptable basis for supporting the death penalty?

3. Why do so many people seek retribution for crimes, in general, and capital crimes, in particular?

4. How or why does suffering something unpleasant count as payment for a criminal offense?

5. How are the intentions of the offender in regard to punishment to be discerned?

6. Why is it necessary to kill people who kill?

7. Given that the crime cannot be undone, what can the criminal justice system offer to the victim's family?

8. What kind of sentence can be imposed on a defendant found guilty of first-degree murder that is commensurate to the crime, protects society, and yet does not destroy the defendant's family in turn?

9. How can a thoughtful and sensible person justify killing people who kill in order to teach that killing is wrong?

10. Is the satisfaction of the desire for vindictive revenge a legitimate penal purpose?

11. Does pandering to or legitimizing the desire for vindictive revenge contribute to the violent social relationships that pervade our nation?

12. Does the Bible (both Old and New Testaments) support the death penalty? Does it matter?

13. How can people, particularly people schooled in the Bible, endorse revenge, support or oppose capital punishment, and use the Bible as the basis of their support or opposition, when they know the Bible is ambiguous on these subjects?

14. Should a religious person support the death penalty?

Notes

[1] Bohm, Clark, and Aveni, 1991; Finckenauer, 1988; Harris, 1986; Lotz and Regoli, 1980; Kohlberg and Elfenbein, 1975; Sarat and Vidmar, 1976; Vidmar, 1974; Warr and Stafford, 1984. Most of the section on retribution is from Bohm, 1992b.

[2] Gallup and Newport, 1991:42.

[3] Hoffmann, 1993:124.

[4] Cottingham, 1979; Feinberg and Gross, 1972; Finckenauer, 1988; Packer, 1968; Radin, 1980.

[5] Cottingham, ibid., p. 238.

[6] *Furman v. Georgia*, 1972 at 342.

[7] Radin, op. cit., p. 1165.

[8] *Furman v. Georgia*, op. cit. at 308.

[9] Ibid., at 332.

[10] For example, see Jacoby, 1983:1.

[11] Radin, op. cit., p. 1169.

[12] Ibid.

[13] Ibid.

[14] Ibid.

[15] Packer, op. cit., pp. 37–8.

[16] Ibid.

[17] Finckenauer, op. cit., p. 92.

[18] Ibid., p. 93.

[19] Cottingham, op. cit.

[20] Ibid., p. 238.

[21] Ibid.

[22] Ibid., p. 239; also see Finckenauer, op. cit.; Gale, 1985; Gibbs, 1978.

[23] Cottingham, ibid.

[24] Finckenauer, op. cit., p. 92.

[25] Ibid., p. 91.

[26] Personal correspondence with the author (1990).

[27] Cottingham, op. cit.

[28] Radin, op. cit., p. 1164; also see Hoffmann, op. cit., on retribution and the death penalty for juveniles.

[29] Cottingham, op. cit., p. 240.

[30] Ibid., p. 241.

[31] Ibid.

[32] Ibid., p. 242.

[33] Ibid.

[34] Ibid., p. 243.

[35] Ibid.

[36] Ibid., pp. 243–44.

[37] Ibid., p. 244.

[38] Ibid., p. 245.

[39] Ibid.

[40] On the universality of retributive emotions, see Heider, 1958; Kelsen, 1943; on the biological basis of retributive emotions, see Trivers, 1971.

[41] See, for example, Vidmar and Miller, 1980: 581.

[42] Vidmar and Miller, ibid., p. 570.

[43] Ibid., p. 571.

[44] Ibid., p. 592.

[45] Amsterdam, 1982.

[46] Erez, 1981:32.

[47] Leviticus 24.22.

[48] Exodus 21.23; Erez, op. cit., p. 37.

[49] Hoffman, op. cit., p. 120.

[50] *Furman v. Georgia*, op. cit. at 303.

[51] Vandiver reports the finding that approximately 16.4 million American adults have lost (1) immediate family members to homicide (5 million; includes vehicular homicide), (2) other relatives (6.6 million), or (3) close friends (4.8 million), see Vandiver, 1998:478–79.

[52] For a more detailed description of the effects of the death penalty on the families of homicide victims, see Vandiver, 1998, op. cit.; 1989.

[53] Vandiver, ibid., p. 480.

[54] Ibid., p. 500.

[55] Ibid.

[56] Ibid., p. 477.

[57] Ibid., p. 486.

[58] Ibid.

[59] Smykla, 1987; Radelet et al., 1983; Vandiver, 1998, op. cit.; Vandiver, 1989, op. cit.; also see Prejean, 1993; Ingle, 1989.

[60] However, on correctional personnel, see Johnson, 1998; Cabana, 1996.

[61] See Van den Haag and Conrad, 1983; Committee on the Judiciary, 1982; Vidmar and Miller, 1980, op. cit.

[62] Schwarzschild in Bedau, 1982.

[63] See Bohm, 1992.

[64] *Furman v. Georgia*, 1972 at 343.

[65] Bedau, op. cit., pp. 305–6.

[66] Gow, 1986: 80.

[67] Religious Leaders in Florida, 1986: 87.

[68] Ibid.

[69] See Maguire and Pastore, 1997:162–3, Table 2.69. Grasmick et al., 1993, discovered that "evangelical/fundamentalist" Protestants were more likely to favor the death penalty than were "liberal/moderate" Protestants. However, Britt (1998) found that black fundamentalists were less likely to support the death penalty than were white fundamentalists. Also see Young, 1992.

[70] Religious Leaders in Florida, op. cit., p. 88; Kehler et al., 1985:5–6.

[71] Religious Leaders in Florida, ibid.; Kehler et al., ibid., p. 6; Erez, op. cit., p. 29. Erez reports that Hebrew law forbade the mutilation of an executed person's body.

[72] Cited in Gow, op. cit., p. 84.

[73] Ibid.

[74] Erez, op. cit., pp. 33–6; Kehler et al., op. cit., pp. 57–8.

[75] Cited in Kehler et al., op. cit., p. 8.

[76] Religious Leaders in Florida, op. cit.; also see Kehler, op. cit., pp. 1-2 for a similar Christian perspective.

[77] Koch in Gow, op. cit., p. 81.

[78] Gow, ibid., p. 82.

[79] Religious Leaders in Florida, op. cit., pp. 88-89; Kehler et al., op. cit.

[80] Bowers, 1984:132-33.

[81] Ibid., p. 133.

[82] Cited in Gow, op. cit., p. 83.

[83] Gow, ibid.

[84] Cited in Gow, ibid., p. 84.

[85] Ibid.

[86] Kehler et al., op. cit., p. 12.

[87] Cited in Gow, op. cit., p. 85.

[88] Black, 1974:96.

[89] Bedau, op. cit., p. 305, fn.2.

[90] Quoted in Bedau, op. cit., p. 305.

CHAPTER 10

American Death
Penalty Opinion[1]

Twenty-five years after the Supreme Court's decision in *Furman v. Georgia* (1972)—the ruling that temporarily halted capital punishment in the United States— about 80 percent of adult Americans indicated that they favor the death penalty for persons convicted of murder. This is the highest level of support in more than 60 years of scientific opinion polling.[2] Since 1966—the year that death penalty support fell to 42 percent, its lowest level ever[3]—support of capital punishment in the United States has increased an average of more than one percentage point per year. In no year for which polls are available has a majority of Americans opposed capital punishment.

Why American Death Penalty Opinion is Important

American death penalty opinion is important because such opinion, perhaps more than any other factor, accounts for the continued use of capital punishment in many jurisdictions in the United States. If most citizens in death penalty jurisdictions opposed capital punishment, it is unlikely the penalty would be employed. Strong public support may contribute to the continued use of capital punishment in at least five ways. First, it probably sways legislators to vote in favor of death penalty statutes (and against their repeal).[4] Few politicians are willing to ignore the preferences of most of their constituents.[5] Support of capital punishment is also a rather easy way for politicians to signal and demonstrate their more conservative "law and order" credentials.

Second, strong public support likely influences some prosecutors to seek the death penalty for political rather than legal purposes in cases where they might ordinarily plea bargain. As Professor White relates from his interviews with defense attorneys:

> Some prosecutors are more reluctant to plea bargain now than they were a few years ago, because they feel that in today's climate failure to seek the death penalty in certain types of cases could have a devastating effect on their political careers.[6]

Third, to retain their positions, some trial-court judges feel public pressure to impose death sentences in cases in which such is inappropriate, and some appellate-court judges may uphold death sentences in cases in which they should not.[7] Among judges recently removed from office because of their unpopular death penalty decisions (that is, judicial politics) were: Chief Justice Rose Bird and two other justices of the California state supreme court, Tennessee Supreme Court Justice Penny White, Mississippi Supreme Court Justice James Robertson, Justice Charles Campbell of the Texas Court of Criminal Appeals, Texas district court judge Norman Lanford, and Washington State Supreme Court Justice Robert Utter.[8]

> *A*mong judges recently removed from office because of their unpopular death penalty decisions (that is, judicial politics) were: Chief Justice Rose Bird and two other justices of the California state supreme court, Tennessee Supreme Court Justice Penny White, Mississippi Supreme Court Justice James Robertson, Justice Charles Campbell of the Texas Court of Criminal Appeals, Texas district court judge Norman Lanford, and Washington State Supreme Court Justice Robert Utter.

Fourth, some governors may be dissuaded from vetoing death penalty legislation and commuting death sentences because of strong public support for the penalty. With regard to commutations, it is instructive to note that prior to 1970, governors in death penalty states "routinely commuted up to a third of the death sentences that they reviewed. . . . Today, however, commutations of death sentences by governors [and review boards] are rare events."[9] Few governors are willing to ignore what they perceive are their constituents' preferences. Further, support of capital punishment generally defines for his or her constituents much of a governor's political agenda—at least the part that concerns crime.

Fifth, and arguably most important, strong public support might be used, at least indirectly, by justices of both state supreme courts and the United States Supreme Court as a measure of evolving standards of decency regarding what constitutes cruel and unusual punishment in state constitutions and under the Eighth Amendment of the United States Constitution.[10] Decline in public support was cited as such a measure in the *Furman* decision.[11]

This chapter is divided into three major sections. First is the history of American death penalty opinion. This section describes what is called here "the too simple and, therefore, misleading death penalty opinion question period." The second section surveys the present period and chronicles what is called "the more complex and revealing death penalty opinion question period." This section begins with a description of research that tested the hypothesis that death penalty support is largely a product of ignorance about the way capital punishment is actually administered. The final section addresses the future of American death penalty opinion and the effect it may have on the practice of capital punishment in the United States.

The History of American Death Penalty Opinion:
The Too Simple and, Therefore, Misleading
Death Penalty Opinion Question Period

The American Institute of Public Opinion, producer of the Gallup polls, conducted interviews for the first scientific death penalty opinion poll in the United States in December 1936.[12] The poll gauged public sentiment about the death penalty in light of the unprecedented media attention given to the execution of Bruno Hauptmann, the alleged kidnapper and murderer of the Lindbergh baby. The poll showed that 61 percent of the 2,201 adults interviewed "believe[d] in the death penalty for murder" and 39 percent did not.[13] The category of "no opinion" or "don't know" was not included as an option. Since that first poll, dozens of surveys of American death penalty opinion have been conducted.[14]

The most recent Gallup poll on death penalty opinion in the United States, conducted in 1995, found that 77 percent of Americans were in favor of the death penalty for a person convicted of murder, 13 percent were opposed, 8 percent responded that it "depends," and 2 percent had no opinion.[15] Note the slight difference in the wording of the questions in the 1936 and 1995 polls. In the 1936 poll, respondents were asked, "Do you *believe* in the *death penalty* for murder?" (In the 1937 and later Gallup polls, respondents were asked, "Do you *favor or oppose capital punishment* for murder?") Respondents to the 1995 poll answered the question, "Are you *in favor* of the death penalty for a person *convicted* of murder?" It is doubtful that the subtle differences significantly altered the resulting opinions, but even a small change in the wording of questions and response categories can make an important difference in the distribution of opinions.[16]

Over the past 60 years or so, support of and opposition to capital punishment have varied substantially.[17] However, when the increases and decreases are plotted over time, a v-shape can be observed. Viewing the v from left to right, in 1936, 61 percent of respondents favored the death penalty; in 1966, only 42 percent of respondents favored it; but, by 1995, 77 percent of respondents supported it. Put differently, between 1936 and 1995, there has been an overall 16 percentage point increase in support and 26 percentage point decrease in opposition to the death penalty. The 10 percentage point difference between overall support and opposition is a function of the 8 percent who respond-

$\mathcal{S}$upport of capital punishment between 1936 and 1966 decreased 19 percentage points, while opposition increased 8 percentage points (the difference is due to the 11 percent of "no opinion" responses in the 1966 poll). On the other hand, between 1966 and 1995, support of the death penalty increased 35 percentage points, while opposition decreased 34 percentage points (again, the difference is attributable to changes in "depend" or "no opinion" responses).

ed that it "depends" and the 2 percent of respondents with "no opinion" in the 1995 poll (the "no opinion" category was not included in the 1936 poll). When the 60-year period is divided into the 1936 to 1966 and the 1966 to 1995 periods, the relatively precipitous decrease-then-increase in support (or increase-then-decrease in opposition) for the penalty is readily apparent. Support of capital punishment between 1936 and 1966 decreased 19 percentage points, while opposition increased 8 percentage points (the difference is due to the 11 percent of "no opinion" responses in the 1966 poll). On the other hand, between 1966 and 1995, support of the death penalty increased 35 percentage points, while opposition decreased 34 percentage points (again, the difference is attributable to changes in "depends" or "no opinion" responses). Note that the increase in support between 1966 and 1995 was nearly twice as great as the decline in support between 1936 and 1966.

A detailed analysis of the 83 percent increase in death penalty support since 1966 has yet to be written. It appears, however, that the *Furman* decision played an important part. As noted, 1966 marked the nadir in death penalty support in the United States, yet by 1967, support for the penalty had risen to 53 percent and opposition had decreased to 39 percent—an 11 percentage point increase in support and an 8 percentage point decrease in opposition.[18] The increase in support was relatively short-lived because by the end of 1971, death penalty support had fallen to 49 percent.[19] The Court's decision in *Furman v. Georgia* was announced on June 29, 1972. Two 1972 Gallup polls asked about death penalty opinions, one before the *Furman* announcement (interviews March 3 through 5) and one after it (interviews November 10 through 13).[20] In the pre-*Furman* poll, 50 percent of respondents favored the death penalty, 42 percent opposed it, and 9 percent had no opinion. The poll conducted post-*Furman* showed that 57 percent of respondents supported capital punishment, only 32 percent opposed it, and 11 percent had no opinion.[21] In short, between March and November, 1972, approximately four months before and four months after the announcement of the *Furman* decision, support for the death penalty increased 7 percentage points and opposition dropped 10 percentage points. Although other factors may have had an effect, it appears that significant public discontent with the *Furman* decision was decisive. Death penalty support has been increasing steadily ever since.

Demographic Characteristics of Respondents. Recent polls have included a greater variety of questions about death penalty opinions, whereas earlier polls focused primarily on the percentage distribution of opinions themselves and the percentage distribution of opinions by demographic characteristics of respondents.[22] Most of the Gallup polls provide information on the following ten demographic characteristics: (1) gender, (2) race, (3) age, (4) politics, (5) education, (6) income or socioeconomic status (SES), (7) occupation, (8) religion, (9) city size, and (10) region of the country.[23]

Between 1936 and 1986, five of the demographic characteristics varied substantially and five of them did not.[24] Characteristics showing greatest variation, in order of the magnitude of that variation, were race, income or SES, gender, politics, and region of the country. In other words, between 1936 and 1986, whites, wealthier people, males, Republicans, and Westerners tended to support the death penalty more than blacks, poorer people, females, Democrats, and Southerners. The characteristics showing much less variation over the 50 years were age, education, occupation, religion, and city size.

A majority of people in all demographic categories, *except race,* supported the death penalty in the 1986 poll, but there was substantial variation within categories for all of the demographic characteristics except religion. City size was not a category in the 1986 poll. Blacks, females, people under 30, Democrats, college graduates, people in the bottom income or SES category, manual laborers, Easterners, and Southerners were less likely to support or more likely to oppose the death penalty than were whites, males, Republicans, high school graduates, people in the top income category, clerical and sales workers, Westerners, and Midwesterners.[25]

In the 1995 poll, support is great in every social category examined with at least 53 percent of the respondents in every demographic category, *including race,* favoring the death penalty for convicted murderers.[26] Nearly 60 percent of blacks have supported the penalty in recent years, although black support in the past has been much lower. A recent study found that black proponents are hardly distinguishable from their white counterparts. Black proponents tend to be male, married, politically conservative, have high incomes, come from middle- and upper-class backgrounds, live in urban areas and the South, are afraid of crime, have never been arrested, and perceive that the courts are too lenient with criminals.[27]

The demographic categories with the next lowest percentage of respondents in favor of the death penalty (with the group and percentage in favor in parentheses) were: race (nonwhites, which included blacks = 56 percent), politics (Democrat = 67 percent), education (college postgraduate—the highest category = 69 percent), age (65 years and older—the oldest category = 71 percent), and income (under $20,000—the lowest category = 71 percent).[28] By contrast, the groups with the highest level of death penalty support (with the percentage in favor in parentheses) were: Republicans (89 percent), people living in suburban areas (83 percent), incomes of $30,000-$49,999—the second to the highest category and $50,000 and over—the highest category (82 percent and 81 percent, respectively), white (81 percent), some college—the next to lowest category (81 percent), and male (80 percent).[29] Based on findings from the most recent Gallup poll, then, it is not much of an exaggeration to state that most Americans favor the death penalty—or so it seems.

The Present: The More Complex and Revealing Death Penalty Opinion Question Period

Little critical scrutiny of the figures presented in various death penalty opinion polls existed prior to the *Furman* decision in 1972. The reported percentages of support and opposition were generally accepted as accurate indicators of public sentiment. One of the first people to question the validity of death penalty opinion poll results, albeit indirectly, while at the same time emphasizing their importance, was former Supreme Court Justice Thurgood Marshall.

The Marshall Hypotheses. Justice Marshall stressed in his opinion in *Furman v. Georgia* the importance of public opinion with respect to the constitutionality of the death penalty. He described four standards by which to judge whether a punishment is cruel and unusual. His fourth standard was: "where a punishment is not excessive and serves a valid legislative purpose, it still may be invalid if popular sentiment abhors it."[30] Thus, wrote Marshall, "It is imperative for constitutional purposes to attempt to discern the probable opinion of an informed electorate."[31] He stressed that the public's choice about the death penalty must be "a knowledgeable choice."[32]

Like many other opponents, Marshall believed that, given information about it, "the great mass of citizens would conclude . . . that the death penalty is immoral and therefore unconstitutional."[33] He assumed that support of the penalty is a function of a lack of knowledge about it, and that opinions are responsive to reasoned persuasion. The one exception to his assumption was that if the underlying basis of support for the penalty were retribution, then knowledge would have little effect on opinions. Though some of his colleagues on the Court disagreed with him, Marshall maintained that retribution "is a goal that the legislature cannot constitutionally pursue as its sole justification for capital punishment."[34] He added, "I cannot believe that at this stage in our history, the American people would ever knowingly support purposeless vengeance."[35]

> *L*ike many other death penalty opponents, Justice Marshall believed that, given information about it, "the great mass of citizens would conclude . . . that the death penalty is immoral and therefore unconstitutional." He assumed that support of the penalty is a function of a lack of knowledge about it, and that opinions are responsive to reasoned persuasion. The one exception to his assumption was that if the underlying basis of support for the death penalty were retribution, then knowledge would have little effect on opinions.

Social scientists did not take long to subject Marshall's assertions to empirical investigation. Two of the first three studies that systematically tested all or part of what have become known as "Marshall's hypotheses" were conducted in the United States; the third was conducted in Canada. A fourth study employing Stanford University undergraduates as subjects, although not a direct test of Marshall's hypotheses, is nevertheless relevant and will be discussed shortly. In one of the American studies, subjects were from the San Francisco Bay area, and the data were collected in 1974.[36] In the other, subjects were from Amherst, Massachusetts, and data were collected in 1975.[37] The Canadian study does not indicate when data were collected.[38] Three of the four studies support all or part of the Marshall hypotheses,[39] although possible problems relating to social conditions at the times data were collected and to methodology render the findings potentially inapplicable to current experience and generally invalid.

Following the *Furman* decision in 1972, there was a flurry of activity as 35 states moved to adopt new death penalty statutes that would meet the Supreme Court's requirements. Thus, at the times the Marshall hypotheses data were being collected in 1974 and 1975, the theory of the death penalty was receiving much media and public attention. A distorting factor in the research, though, was that no one had been executed in the United States since 1967, and no one in Canada since 1962. This moratorium made the issue of capital punishment "abstract" in that the respondents had no recent experience with it. Public opinion about the death penalty is sometimes dramatically different when people consider it in "concrete" situations (at times when people are being executed) rather than in the abstract.

A methodological dilemma for all studies of this type is operationalizing the concept of "informed" or "knowledgeable about the death penalty." According to Justice Marshall, for "the average citizen" (excepting those who base their opinion on retribution), some knowledge is "critical" to an informed opinion and "would almost surely convince [the average citizen] that the death penalty was unwise."[40] For Marshall, an informed citizen would know some of the following:

> that the death penalty is no more effective a deterrent than life imprisonment; that convicted murderers are rarely executed, but are usually sentenced to a term in prison; that convicted murderers usually are model prisoners, and that they almost always become law–abiding citizens upon their release from prison; that the costs of executing a capital offender exceed the costs of imprisoning him for life; that while in prison, a convict under sentence of death performs none of the useful functions that life prisoners perform; that no attempt is made in the sentencing process to ferret out likely recidivists for execution; and that the death penalty may actually stimulate criminal activity . . . capital punishment is imposed discriminatorily against certain identifiable classes of people; there is evidence that innocent people have been executed before their innocence can be proved; and the death penalty wreaks havoc with our entire criminal justice system.[41]

What Marshall fails to stipulate is how much of this information a citizen must know in order to be informed. Must one know all of it or will 50 to 60 percent suffice? Without setting a standard, Marshall leaves unanswered the key question of what it means to be informed or knowledgeable about the death penalty.

Results of the fourth study, the one using Stanford University undergraduates as subjects (wherein the authors did not indicate when their data were collected), differed dramatically from the results of the other three studies. The authors of the fourth study discovered that knowledge or information can have an entirely different effect on death penalty opinions than the one supposed by Marshall.[42] Professor Lord and his colleagues found that information about the death penalty polarized opinions, instead of changing them from in favor to opposed or vice versa.[43] In other words, subjects who initially favored the death penalty tended to favor it more strongly after receiving information about it, while subjects who initially opposed the death penalty tended to oppose it even more after becoming informed. The researchers attributed polarization to biased assimilation, that is, subjects interpreted evidence so as to maintain their initial beliefs:

Data relevant to a belief are not processed impartially. Instead judgments about the validity, reliability, relevance, and sometimes even the meaning of proffered evidence are biased by the apparent consistency of that evidence with the perceiver's theories and expectations. Thus individuals will dismiss and discount empirical evidence that contradicts their initial views and will derive support from evidence, of no greater probativeness, that seems consistent with their views.[44]

Professors Ellsworth and Ross believe that biased assimilation is a probable explanation for the effect of knowledge on opinions in their study:

[We] are tempted to infer that the attitude [opinion] comes first and the reasons second. . . . It looks very much as though our respondents simply went down the list of reasons, checking whatever side of the scale was compatible with their general attitude [opinion] toward capital punishment. The picture that emerges is one of an emotionally based attitude [opinion], tempered by a sense of social desirability.[45]

In short, contrary to expectations held by Justice Marshall and many other opponents, information about the death penalty may not significantly reduce the overwhelming public support that currently exists for capital punishment. Notwithstanding the support for Marshall's hypotheses, if the results of the Lord study are reliable, the effect of exposing people to information about the death penalty may be to polarize them on the issue.

> *P*rofessor Lord and his colleagues found that information about the death penalty polarized opinions, instead of changing them from in favor to opposed or vice versa. In other words, subjects who initially favored the death penalty tended to favor it more strongly after receiving information about it, while subjects who initially opposed the death penalty tended to oppose it even more after becoming informed.

Two other methodological problems with the studies are related to the validity of the experimental stimulus and the experimental manipulation. The first problem involves the form that "knowledge" takes, and the second has to do with the way "knowledge" is imparted to subjects. In the 1976 study by Sarat and Vidmar, the experimental conditions involved reading two 1,500 word essays that described "scientific and other information" about the death penalty. The experimental manipulation was preceded by a pretest and followed by a posttest. The entire operation took only one hour. Sarat and Vidmar are candid about the inadequacies of the manipulation:

> Without question our information manipulations had limited potential for developing truly informed opinion about the death penalty—the issues are intricate and complex while the essays are short and simple; furthermore, exposure to the information took place in a brief interview session without time for reflection, discussion, or clarification.[46]

The experimental manipulation proved somewhat successful, nevertheless. On the pretest, 62 percent of the (181 randomly selected adult) experimental subjects favored the death penalty, 27 percent opposed it, and 10 percent were undecided. On the posttest, 42 percent favored the death penalty, 38 percent opposed it, and 21 percent were undecided. The experimental stimulus did not produce a majority of subjects opposed to the death penalty, but it did decrease support and increase opposition and indecision.

The 1981 study by Vidmar and Dittenhoffer improved the validity of the experimental manipulation in Sarat and Vidmar by increasing the opportunity for subjects to assimilate information about the death penalty. In this study, subjects were asked to read a 3,500 word essay on the death penalty (emphasizing the Canadian experience) and a series of eight articles. The articles contained representative material intended to augment the essay. The subjects also had the option of reading two books—Sellin's *Capital Punishment* (1967) and Bedau's *The Death Penalty in America* (1967)—and were invited to pursue any other related reading. After two weeks, subjects met in small, unsupervised discussion groups to "freely discuss the facts and issues involved in the capital punishment debate and to try to reach a final decision within an hour."[47] The experimental manipulation was preceded by a pretest and was followed by a posttest.

The results of the Vidmar and Dittenhoffer study indicate that the experimental manipulation was effective. On the pretest, 48 percent of the experimental subjects favored the death penalty, 33 percent were opposed to it, and 19 percent were undecided. On the posttest, 24 percent were in favor, 71 percent were opposed, and 5 percent were undecided. Vidmar and Dittenhoffer's experimental stimulus, unlike the one used by Sarat and Vidmar, did produce a majority of subjects opposed to the death penalty.

Despite the improvement of Vidmar and Dittenhoffer's experimental manipulation over the one used by Sarat and Vidmar, the Vidmar and Dittenhoffer study still had serious deficiencies. First, the experimental group consisted of only 21 nonrandomly selected students (18 in the control group). Second, the experimenters had to assume that the subjects did indeed read the assigned material. Third, even if subjects did read the material, it was not possible to determine how much of the material was comprehended. As to the discussion groups, Vidmar and Dittenhoffer are probably correct that discussion should enhance conditions for opinion change, because active learning is presumed to be more conducive to opinion change than passive learning.[48] However, without supervision, the experimenters could not be sure of what happened in the groups. Was the death penalty in fact discussed? Did one member of the group dominate discussion? Were some of the group members intimidated or angered by others? Furthermore, a discussion of only one hour was probably not long enough for such an "intricate and complex" topic. Subjects were not given sufficient opportunity to reflect upon contradictory beliefs or to research information about which they disagreed. A discussion of only one hour also allowed a persuasive speaker to have extraordinary influence. In short, a discussion period of only one hour was probably not long enough to produce the intended effects of the experimental manipulation.

For those and other reasons, Professor Bohm and his colleagues, beginning in the mid-1980s, conducted a series of studies that used an experimental manipulation which provided subjects with more information, provided greater control over the circumstances in which the information was acquired, and allowed subjects more time to evaluate and integrate the information into their own systems of beliefs. The experimental stimulus employed by Bohm and his colleagues was a college class on the death penalty.[49]

A death penalty class generally met a total of 40 hours a semester. Bedau's *The Death Penalty in America*, Third Edition (1982) was the assigned text for the course. Coursework included lectures by the instructor, presentations by guest speakers, videos, and discussion. Topics discussed were the history of the death penalty in the United States, with special emphasis on relevant Supreme Court cases; public opinion; evidence about general deterrence and incapacitation; religious and retribution arguments; and information on the administration of the death penalty (e.g, sources of arbitrariness and discrimination, executions of innocent persons, costs, etc.).

In most of the experiments, subjects completed questionnaires at the beginning and the end of the semester. Although their content varied somewhat from semester to semester, the questionnaires, at minimum, generally sought information about the three principal variables in Marshall's hypotheses: opinions toward the death penalty, knowledge about the death penalty, and desire for retribution. The questionnaires also asked for demographic information about the subjects.

Bohm and his colleagues measured death penalty opinions with four questions because they believed that the general opinion question asked in the Gallup and other polls did not accurately reflect the complexity of public sentiment about the penalty. Each of the questions represented a different type of support or nonsupport for the death penalty. The first question was: "Which of the following statements best describes your position toward the death penalty for *all* persons convicted of first-degree murder?"[50] Only 28.3 percent of less-informed subjects opposed the death penalty for *all* persons convicted of first-degree murder (24.7 percent of males; 31.1 percent of females; 18.3 percent of whites; 37.6 percent of blacks), but 46.6 percent of more-informed subjects were opposed to it (41.2 percent of males; 51.1 percent of females; 32.3 percent of whites; 60 percent of blacks).[51]

A second question asked subjects whether they favored the death penalty for "*some* people convicted of first-degree murder." This question is the one that is most similar to the general death penalty opinion question asked in the Gallup and other polls. Results for this question are similar to those for the previous one: 28 percent of less-informed subjects opposed the death penalty (24.7 percent of males; 30 percent of females; 22.6 percent of whites; 30.6 percent of blacks), but 49.5 percent of more-informed subjects opposed it (49.5 percent of males; 50 percent of females; 40.9 percent of whites; 56.6 percent of blacks).[52]

The third and fourth questions were asked because prior research has found that support for the death penalty is greatly reduced when a distinction is made between support in the abstract and support in concrete situations.[53] The first concrete question was: "If you served on a jury in a trial where the defendant, if found guilty, would automatically be sentenced to death, could you convict that defendant?" Only 22.5 percent of less-informed subjects could not convict (14.4 percent of males; 30 percent of females; 5.4 percent of whites; 23.5 percent of blacks), while 34.4 percent of more-informed subjects could not convict (30 percent of males; 38 percent of females; 21.5 percent of whites; 47.1 percent of blacks).[54]

The second concrete question was: "If asked to do it, could you pull the lever that would result in the death of an individual convicted of first-degree murder?" On this question, 47.2 percent of less-informed subjects (45.4 percent of males; 55.5 percent of females; 37.6 percent of whites; 64.7 percent of blacks) and 49.6 percent of more-informed subjects could not pull the lever (50.5 percent of males; 62.2 percent of females; 40.9 percent of whites; 72.9 percent of blacks).[55]

Another reason for asking subjects four different death penalty questions was to ascertain whether subjects had a "coherent moral position" toward capital punishment. As Professor Radin explains:

> The reason it is often suggested that one ought to look to what people do rather than what they say, or even more pointedly, that those who favor the death penalty should be asked whether they would be willing to pull the switch themselves, is that a person is more likely to have reached a coherent moral position if she is going to be required to transform her beliefs into action.[56]

Although Bohm and his colleagues wondered how people could have a coherent moral position toward the death penalty when they were ignorant about the subject, they nevertheless examined whether responses to the four questions formed a Guttman scale and thus were indicative of a coherent moral position. To their surprise, their findings suggested that their subjects did indeed hold coherent moral positions toward the death penalty, whether they were informed or not.[57] When they used subjects' Guttman scale coefficients as measures of opposition to capital punishment, Bohm et al. found that while only 34.7 percent of less-informed subjects opposed capital punishment, 56.3 percent of more-informed subjects opposed it.[58] This was the only measure that produced a majority of all subjects opposed to the penalty.

In sum, results of this research provided at least qualified support for all three of Marshall's hypotheses.[59] Subjects generally lacked knowledge about the death penalty and its administration prior to exposure to the experimental stimulus but were more informed following it. To the degree that retribution provided the basis for support of the death penalty, knowledge had little effect on opinions. The hypothesis that an informed public would generally oppose the death penalty was supported in one test but not in others. (In some tests, a majority of black males and a majority of black and white females opposed the death penalty.) Thus, even though support for the death penalty might decline after subjects have been informed, the reduction may not be great enough to create a majority opposed to the death penalty.[60] This may hold true even when subjects are asked diverse death penalty opinion questions, such as "personal involvement" questions.[61]

Other findings of this research include the following:

- exposure to death penalty information may result in the polarization of opinions (favoring or opposing more strongly);[62]

- it may be more difficult for subjects to change their positions if they have to publicly announce their death penalty opinions;[63]

- initial beliefs about the death penalty and such issues as deterrence, revenge, and incapacitaton generally are not affected by giving people information about those issues;[64] and

- when opinions about the death penalty do change, it is most likely because of administrative reasons such as racial discrimination or execution of innocent people.[65]

However, when the death penalty opinions of subjects in the 1988 and 1989 classes were examined two and three years later, it was discovered that opinions on the two abstract death penalty opinion questions (that is, "Do you favor or oppose the death penalty *for all* and *for some* people convicted of first-degree murder?") had rebounded to near their initial pretest positions.[66] Opinions on the two concrete death penalty opinion questions (that is, could you convict? and could you pull the lever?) did not change significantly for the 1988 and 1989 classes at any of the three points in time (pretest, posttest, or follow-up).[67] Results of the follow-up study also do not appear to be a function of a loss of knowledge, the irrelevancy of the death penalty class, or the influence of the instructor.[68] Why, then, did opinions rebound? Perhaps it was because death penalty opinions are based primarily on emotion rather than on cognition and that, in the long run, cognitive influences on death penalty opinions give way to emotional factors.

> *W*hen the death penalty opinions of subjects in Professor Bohm's 1988 and 1989 classes were examined two and three years later, it was discovered that opinions on the two abstract death penalty opinion questions (that is, "Do you favor or oppose the death penalty *for all* and *for some* people convicted of first-degree murder?") had rebounded to near their initial pretest positions. Opinions on the two concrete death penalty opinion questions (that is, could you convict? and could you pull the lever?) did not change significantly for the 1988 and 1989 classes at any of the three points in time (pretest, posttest, or follow-up).

Results of the follow-up study suggest that most death penalty opinions may not be significantly influenced by increased knowledge about the penalty or may be influenced only temporarily, at least if that knowledge is obtained in a college classroom.[69] If Justice Marshall had in mind a stimulus like the one employed in the research by Bohm and his colleagues, then Marshall's belief that death penalty opinions can be changed substantially (by increasing knowledge about the subject) may be wrong. This does not mean that the opinions are intransigent. Opinions do change, as evidenced by the more-than-60-year history of public opinion polls on the death penalty in the United States. It means only that classroom knowledge may not be an effective way of changing those opinions.

Asking About Alternatives to the Death Penalty. Perhaps more important than the amount of accurate knowledge a person has about the death penalty is the way in which the death penalty opinion question is asked. A critical problem with the general opinion question (e.g., Do you favor or oppose the death penalty for first-degree murder?) is that there is either no context to the question or the context is ambiguous. For example, when people are asked whether they favor or oppose the death penalty, or, for that matter, whether they favor or oppose the death penalty for all people or for some people convicted of first-degree murder, it is left to the imagination of each individual as to whether that means:

- the death penalty or no penalty at all;

- the death penalty or a too lenient alternative penalty such as five or ten years in prison;

- the death penalty or a severe penalty but with opportunity for parole;

- the death penalty or an alternative severe penalty such as life imprisonment with no possibility of parole; or perhaps

- the death penalty and some other alternative.

With the exception of their latest study, Bohm and his colleagues did not fully anticipate this possibility.[70]

It still appears that many people support the death penalty because they fear an alternative penalty will not be punitive enough or that it may be inappropriate, given the severity of the crime. Several studies show that 25 to 40 percent of the public believes that "the average prison term served by someone sentenced to life imprisonment is less than 10 years," even though the statement is false.[71]

Support of capital punishment drops, though, when the death penalty question is asked and a harsh and meaningful alternative is provided. No more (and many times, less) than one-half of the public supports the death penalty when given the options of it and life imprisonment with absolutely no possibility of parole.[72] When given the options of the death penalty and life imprisonment with absolutely no possibility of parole *and* the payment of restitution by the offender (who would work in prison industry) to the victim's family or the community (LWOP+), even less of the public (only 19 to 43 percent) prefers the death penalty over the alternative.[73] Thus, on the surface, a majority of the public appears receptive to replacing capital punishment with a harsh and meaningful alternative such as LWOP+.

A problem is that the public is also very skeptical about the ability of correctional authorities to keep capital murderers imprisoned for life. A recent national survey shows that only 11 percent of registered voters believed that an offender sentenced to life imprisonment without possibility of parole would never be released from prison.[74] So, although the public might say it prefers the alternative of LWOP+ over capital punishment, in practice it may not want to make the substitution due to fears that the alternative cannot guarantee protection from the future actions of convicted capital murderers.

> Support of capital punishment drops when the death penalty question is asked and a harsh and meaningful alternative is provided.

Asking About Different Types of Death–Eligible Murders. Another ambiguity with general death penalty opinion questions is the type of murder, or first–degree murder, the pollsters have in mind. Not all death–eligible murders are the same. In a recent study, Professors Durham, Elrod, and Kinkade presented people with 34 different murder scenarios,[75] which varied by aggravating and mitigating circumstances. Murders in some scenarios were death–eligible, and murders in others were not. Respondents were asked what they thought was the appropriate punishment.

The researchers found that people's willingness to impose the death penalty may be greater than public opinion polls indicate. Only 13 percent of respondents would sentence all of the murderers to death, but about 95 percent would sentence at least one to death.[76] There was also a huge variation in the willingness of people to impose the death penalty on different types of murderers. For one scenario, more than 90 percent of respondents thought death was the appropriate punishment, while for another, fewer than 25 percent of respondents so believed.[77] Even people in groups historically most opposed to the death penalty were likely to believe the death penalty was appropriate for at least some types of murderers. Although people's willingness to impose the death penalty was generally greatest for first–degree and felony murders, an unexpected finding was that several felony murders drew little death penalty support.[78] Durham and his colleagues also discovered that aggravating circumstances were more influential on sentencing decisions than were mitigating circumstances.[79] Finally, when the researchers compared their data with information obtained from the prosecutor's office, they found that the people they surveyed were more willing to impose the death penalty than was the prosecutor or than the law would have allowed.[80] These data suggest that death penalty support in the United States, for at least some types of murders, may be every bit as strong as recent public opinion polls suggest, and it may be even stronger for specific types of death–eligible murders.

Conclusion: The Future of American Death Penalty Opinion and the Death Penalty

One of the more ambitious attempts to explain death penalty opinion in the United States was based on the results of a 20–year longitudinal study of the development of moral judgment in American males. From that study, Professors Kohlberg and Elfenbein (1975:617) concluded that "nonfactual cognitive components of attitudes [opinions] toward capital punishment are determined by developing moral standards," as opposed to "irrational, purely emotional factors."[81] Since the American public generally is not well informed about the death penalty, then one might assume, following Kohlberg and Elfenbein, that death penalty opinions are primarily the product of "developing moral standards." Kohlberg and Elfenbein posited six moral stages and explained that as society progressed "through the universal, invariant sequence of moral stages," there is "a radical decline in support for capital punishment."[82] At Stage 6, to which society had yet to "progress," no person could support capital punishment.[83]

Kohlberg and Elfenbein observed that:

> A gradual socio–moral evolution is evidently taking place in the United States that can be described and theoretically explained as moral stage development across social institutions and individuals over time. In large part, this evolution takes the form of a movement from Stage 4 to Stage 5.[84]

According to Kohlberg and Elfenbein, then, society is morally developing to a stage where the public will not support the death penalty. This observation, however, was published in 1975 during the hiatus on capital punishment in the United States and after a period of decline in support. Subsequent developments, such as increasing public support for the death penalty and an increase in the number of death sentences and executions, indicate either that Kohlberg and Elfenbein relied on a faulty theory, that they were wrong in their assessment of the moral evolution of American society, or that the American public is regressing in its moral development.

Public opinion about capital punishment, or at least public support, may prove to be irrelevant if and when the penalty is ever abolished in the United States. As Zimring and Hawkins have observed, "Successful and sustained abolition [of capital punishment] has never been a result of great popular demand."[85] Most countries that have abolished the death penalty continued to have a majority of citizens who supported retention at the time of abolition and shortly thereafter. Only gradually did death penalty support decline until opposition dominated public opinion.[86] In short, abolition of capital punishment, where it has occurred, generally has been achieved despite relatively strong public support for retention. Zimring and Hawkins surmise that politicians and other opinion–makers probably will have to lead the public on this issue if capital punishment is ever to be abolished in the United States.

Based on my own analysis of the dramatic reversal in death penalty opinion in the United States beginning in the 1966 to 1967 period, I have concluded that "the key to understanding temporal variations in death penalty opinions probably lies in the fear and anxiety engendered by the social events of an era."[87] The strength of death penalty support and opposition appears to be both a psychological barometer of the level of dread and angst in a society and a symbolic marker of the social landscape. In particular, levels of support and opposition seem to demarcate the threshold level of people's tolerance of media-reported crime, and, at the same time, serve as an indicator of people's threshold tolerance of social change. It seems reasonable to assume "that historical changes, such as a political shift away from the conservative social policies of the last decade [and a half or so], are apt to either produce a dramatic shift in future death penalty opinions or to be marked by changed death penalty opinions as the political shift passes a certain threshold level."[88] Either way, it is unlikely that the practice of capital punishment could be sustained if a majority of American citizens were to oppose it.

Discussion Questions

1. How strongly does the American public support the death penalty?

2. Do you support the death penalty for *all* persons convicted of first-degree murder? Why or why not?

3. Do you support the death penalty for *some* people convicted of first-degree murder? Why or why not?

4. If you served on a jury in a trial where the defendant, if found guilty, would automatically be sentenced to death, could you convict that defendant? Why or why not?

5. If asked to do it, could you pull the lever that would result in the death of an individual convicted of first-degree murder? Why or why not?

6. Would you support the death penalty if the alternative were life imprisonment with absolutely no possibility of parole? Why or why not?

7. Would you support the death penalty if the alternative were life imprisonment with absolutely no possibility of parole *and* the payment of restitution by the offender (who would work in prison industry) to the victim's family or the community (LWOP+)? Why or why not?

8. Should public opinion be used in determining whether capital punishment is an acceptable or a constitutional form of punishment?

9. Does the public's opinion about the death penalty matter? Should it matter?

10. Have the new death penalty statutes and their procedural reforms rid the death penalty's administration of the problems cited in *Furman*?

11. Can death penalty statutes be made constitutionally acceptable?

12. Why do people oppose capital punishment? How could they be so wrong?

13. Why do people support capital punishment? How could they be so wrong?

14. Will the death penalty ever be abolished in all jurisdictions in the United States? If yes, what will cause its abolition?

Notes

[1] A version of this chapter appeared as "American Death Penalty Opinion: Past, Present, and Future," pp. 25-46 in J. R. Acker, R. M. Bohm, and C. Lanier (eds.) *America's Experiment with Capital Punishment: Reflections on the Past, Present and Future of the Ultimate Penal Sanction*. Durham, NC: Carolina Academic Press. Reprinted with permission.

[2] Unless indicated otherwise, figures reported in this chapter are from the Gallup polls, which are the oldest and most sustained effort to measure American death penalty opinion, see Bohm, 1991. However, see the Appendix to Ellsworth and Gross, 1994, for a list of 90 death penalty opinion surveys conducted in the United States between 1936 and July 1993, the text of the questions asked, and the proportions of respondents providing each recorded answer. Although some of those polls measure opinions about the death penalty for certain other categories of persons, such as juveniles and the mentally retarded, for certain other types of crimes, such as rape or kidnapping, and for certain kinds of death sentences, such as mandatory versus discretionary, this chapter focuses primarily on death penalty opinions for capital or aggravated murder. All post-*Furman* executions have involved capital or aggravated murderers.

[3] Erskine cites a Harris Survey released on July 3, 1966, that showed that only 38 percent of respondents favored the death penalty, 47 percent were against, and 15 percent had no opinion, see Erskine, 1970:295.

[4] On Tennessee legislators, see Whitehead, 1998; on Indiana legislators, see McGarrell and Sandys, 1996; but see Sandys and McGarrell, 1994. Evidence indicates that public opinion has affected policymaking in the United States in other areas, such as civil rights, see Oskamp, 1977:241; also cf. Page et al., 1987; Page and Shapiro, 1983; Monroe, 1979; Erikson, 1976; Weissberg, 1976.

[5] See Dieter, 1996. With regard to the death penalty, former New York Governors Hugh Carey and Mario Cuomo and former California Governor Jerry Brown are three notable exceptions. Each governor vetoed death penalty legsislation despite strong public support for the penalty.

[6] White, 1987:17; also see Dieter, 1996, op. cit.

[7] Bright, 1998; Dieter, 1996, op. cit.; Bright and Keenan, 1995.

[8] Bright, ibid., pp. 123-24; Dieter, ibid., pp. 2-4.

[9] Baldus and Woodworth, 1998:388-9; also see Kobil, 1998; Dieter, 1996, ibid.

[10] On state constitutions, see Bedau, 1987, Chap. 8; on the Eighth Amendment, see Marshall in *Furman v. Georgia*, 1972:329; also in *Furman*: Douglas, p. 242, Brennan, pp. 269-70; Burger, p. 383, and Powell, p. 409; *Trop v. Dulles*, 1958:101; *Weems v. United States*, 1910:349, 373; *Robinson v. California*, 1962:666; also cf. *Estelle v. Gamble*, 1976:102; *Roberts v. Louisiana*, 1976:336, 352; *Woodson v. North Carolina*, 1976:301; *Gregg v. Georgia*, 1976:173, 227.

[11] *Furman v. Georgia*, ibid, p. 329.

[12] Bohm, op. cit.

[13] Ibid., p. 115.

[14] See n. 2, supra.

[15] Gallup, 1995:25.

[16] McGarrell and Sandys, 1996, op. cit.; Sandys and McGarrell, 1995; Jones, 1994; Bowers, 1993; Bohm et al., 1991; Williams et al., 1988; Harris, 1986; Ellsworth and Ross, 1983; Sarat and Vidmar, 1976.

[17] The five most volatile short-term periods between 1936 and 1995 were: (1) 1953-1957 (23 percent decrease in support, 5 percent increase in opposition, and 17 percent increase in "no opinions" or "don't knows"), (2) 1960-1966 (11 percent decrease in support and 11 percent increase in opposition), (3) 1966-1967 (11 percent increase in support and 8 percent decrease in opposition), (4) 1971-1976 (16 percent increase in support and 12 percent decrease in opposition), (5) 1978-1995 (15 percent increase in support, 14 percent decrease in opposition, and 9 percent decrease in "no opinions"), see Bohm 1991, op. cit. With the exception of an analysis of the 1966-1967 period, see Bohm 1992a, there have been no attempts, of which this author is aware, to explain the volatile periods.

[18] See Bohm, 1991, ibid., p. 116. For an analysis of the historical circumstances, that is, the social events and economic trends, that contributed to the dramatic reversal in death penalty support and opposition between 1966 and 1967, see Bohm, 1992a, ibid.

[19] See Bohm 1991, ibid.

[20] Ibid.

[21] Ibid.

[22] Death penalty opinion research published prior to 1975, when death penalty support was more moderate than it is today, frequently attributed support of capital punishment to some rather unflattering social psychological characteristics such as dogmatism, authoritarianism, and racism. Proponents of capital punishment were less likely than opponents to approve of gun registration laws or to favor open housing legislation and more likely to favor restrictive abortion laws, approve of the John Birch Society, move if blacks moved into their neighborhoods, and support such things as restrictions on civil liberties, discrimination against minority groups, and violence for achieving social goals, see Vidmar and Ellsworth, 1974; also see Bohm, 1987. However, in light of the dramatic increase in death penalty support in recent years, one might hope that such a distinctive personality profile of death penalty proponents no longer applies. Unfortunately, recent evidence suggests otherwise. Support of capital punishment by many whites continues to be associated with prejudice against blacks, see Barkan and Cohn, 1994; Bohm, 1994; U. S. General Accounting Office, 1990.

[23] Bohm, 1991, op. cit.; also see Longmire, 1996; Fox et al., 1990-1991.

[24] See Bohm, 1991, ibid.

[25] Ibid.

[26] Gallup, 1995, op. cit.

[27] Arthur, 1998; for an interesting and detailed black man's position on the death penalty, see Jackson, 1996.

[28] Gallup, 1995, op. cit.

[29] Ibid.

[30] *Furman v. Georgia*, 1972 at 332.

[31] Ibid., at 362, fn. 145.

[32] Ibid. Elaborating on this point, Marshall wrote that "the question with which we must deal is not whether a substantial proportion of American citizens would today, if polled, opine that capital punishment is barbarously cruel, but whether they would find it to be so in the light of all information presently available," see *Furman v. Georgia*, 1972:362. For Marshall, however, "this is not to suggest that with respect to this test of unconstitutionality people are required to act rationally; they are not [and often do not—author's addition]. With respect to this judgment, a violation of the Eighth Amendment is totally dependent on the predictable subjective, emotional reactions of informed citizens" (at 362). Even if the American people were adequately informed about the death penalty and its effects, Radin is but one scholar who believes that public opinion polls should not be relied on in constitutional adjudication, see Radin, 1978. She argues that public opinion polls should not be used because they (1) "show that the majority of the public favors few of the protections embodied in the Bill of Rights" . . . [and] "the pur-

pose of the Bill of Rights is to protect certain rights of individuals from an overreaching majority", (2) "are subject to methodological errors", and (3) "may record frivolous or ill-considered answers, or answers influenced by intrinsic factors," see Radin, op. cit., pp. 1035-36.

[33] *Furman v. Georgia*, 1972 at 363. In his dissent in *Furman*, Justice Powell disagreed with Marshall, arguing that the public would not oppose the death penalty if it were informed about its administration, see *Furman v. Georgia*, 1972 at 430-46.

[34] *Furman v. Georgia*, 1972 at 363. In *Furman*, Justice Stewart, who voted with the majority, opined that retribution was psychologically necessary for maintaining social stability, see *Furman v. Georgia*, 1972 at 308.

[35] *Furman v. Georgia*, 1972 at 363. Disagreement over the legitimacy of retribution as a purpose of capital punishment may be the product of confusion over what retribution actually means. For a discussion of the different meanings of retribution, see Chapter 9.

[36] Ellsworth and Ross, 1983, op. cit.

[37] Sarat and Vidmar, 1976, op. cit.

[38] Vidmar and Dittenhoffer, 1981.

[39] The study by Ellsworth and Ross, 1983, op. cit., examined only opinions and knowledge about the death penalty. It did not examine whether knowledge about the death penalty would change opinions. Also see Longmire, 1996, op. cit., for the effects of knowledge about the death penalty on the opinions of death penalty proponents, opponents, and undecideds.

[40] *Furman v. Georgia,* 1972 at 362-63.

[41] Ibid., at 362-64.

[42] Lord et al., 1979.

[43] Lord et al. presented 24 proponents and 24 opponents of the death penalty (all subjects were undergraduate students) "first with the results and then with procedural details, critiques, and rebuttals for two studies dealing with the deterrent efficacy of the death penalty—one study confirming their initial beliefs and one study disconfirming their initial beliefs," see Lord et al., op. cit., pp. 2100-2101, for more detail.

[44] Ibid., p. 2099.

[45] Ellsworth and Ross, op. cit., p. 152; also see Roberts, 1984; Tyler and Weber, 1982. The concepts "attitudes" and "opinions" are often used synonymously, especially when discussing the death penalty. However, according to at least one authority, see Oskamp, 1977, opinions should be equated with beliefs, which are primarily cognitive, while attitudes are more emotion-laden. That distinction is ignored in this chapter which employs the concepts "opinion" or "opinions" except in direct quotes (in which case the concepts are bracketed).

[46] Sarat and Vidmar, op. cit., p. 183, fn. 59.

[47] Vidmar and Dittenhoffer, op. cit., p. 49.

[48] Ibid., pp. 45-6.

[49] There are at least two potential problems with Bohm and his colleague's experimental design. First is the use of student subjects. Whether students are representative of the general public with regard to death penalty opinion is questionable. However, in the 1995 Gallup poll, there is not much variation in death penalty support based on education: between 69 percent of "college postgraduates" and 76 percent of respondents with "no college" education favored the death penalty for a person convicted of murder (75 percent of "college graduates" and 81 percent of respondents with "some college" favored the death penalty), see Gallup, 1995, op. cit. Variation in other years, however, has been greater, see Bohm 1991, op. cit., pp. 131-32. In any case, the reason for using student subjects was that it was one of the only ways to employ a prolonged stimulus experimentally. Brevity of exposure to the experimental stimulus was a weakness of previous research (cf. Sarat and Vidmar, 1976; Lord et al., 1979; Vidmar and Dittenhoffer, 1981). A second potential problem with Bohm and his colleague's experimental design is the influence of the instructor. A charismatic teacher could have a significant influence over

his or her students' opinions. The instructor in the death penalty classes was always forthright about his strong opposition to the death penalty but emphasized that his opinion should not influence the opinion of anyone else. Despite his personal opinion, both sides of all issues were presented, and no preference was shown intentionally for either side. Also, the instructor played "devil's advocate" to the positions taken by students to provoke thoughtful consideration of the issues. Students were fully aware from the outset that their grade in the class was independent of their views. Informal feedback from all the classes and results of a two and three year follow-up study of the 1988 and 1989 classes indicate that "demand characteristics" had negligible effects, Bohm et al., 1993:42.

[50] As discussed in Chapter 2, although, in 1976, in the cases of *Woodson v. North Carolina* and *Roberts v. Louisiana*, the Supreme Court rejected mandatory statutes that automatically imposed death sentences for defined capital offenses, a question about the death penalty for all persons convicted of first-degree murder remains instructive. Not only does it give an indication of people's opinions in light of the Supreme Court decisions, but it also serves as a basis of comparison for other questions about the death penalty considered in this research.

[51] Bohm et al., 1991, op. cit., pp. 373-75, Tables 2, 3 &4.

[52] Ibid.

[53] See Ellsworth and Ross, 1983, op. cit.; Jurow, 1971. The distinction made between abstract questions and questions involving concrete situations is somewhat artificial. As is well known, what people say and what people do are often very different. Research indicates that correlations between people's attitudes [opinions] and their behavior are "rarely above .30, and often are near zero," see Wicker, 1969. The largest correlations are typically found when the researcher focuses on a specific attitude [opinion] toward a well-defined situation. Conversely, when the attitude [opinion] is a very general one that is presumed to influence a variety of different situations, much less consistency between attitude [opinion] and behavior is found, see Crespi, 1971. Thus, what people say about the death penalty in general, and what they would do as jurors in a capital murder trial, for example, probably are not the same. For that matter, what people say they would do if they served as jurors in a capital murder trial, and what they would do if they actually served may not be the same. This, of course, is a problem with all survey research.

[54] Bohm et al., 1991, op. cit.

[55] Ibid.

[56] Radin, 1978, op. cit., p. 1041.

[57] Bohm et al., 1991, pp. 368-69.

[58] Ibid., p. 375.

[59] See Bohm et al., 1991, ibid.; also see Bohm, 1989; Bohm, 1990; Bohm et al., 1990; Bohm and Vogel, 1994.

[60] Bohm, 1989, ibid.; Bohm et al., 1991, ibid.; Bohm and Vogel, 1994, ibid.

[61] Bohm et al., 1991, ibid.; Bohm et al. 1993, op. cit.

[62] Bohm et al., 1990, op. cit.; Bohm 1990, op. cit.

[63] Bohm, 1990, ibid.

[64] Bohm et al., 1993, op. cit.; Bohm and Vogel, op. cit., 1994.

[65] Bohm, 1989, op. cit.; Bohm and Vogel, 1994, ibid.; Bohm et al., 1991, op. cit.; Bohm et al., 1993, ibid.

[66] Bohm et al., ibid., 1993.

[67] Ibid. There was some significant change in opinions on the concrete questions in some of the tests.

[68] Ibid., p. 42.

[69] But see Sandys, 1995, for different results.

[70] See Wright et al., 1995.

[71] Bohm et al., 1991, op. cit., p. 371; Ellsworth and Ross, 1983, op. cit.; Wright et al., ibid.; also see Bowers, 1993, op. cit.; McGarrell and Sandys, 1996, op. cit.; Bowers and Steiner, 1998.

[72] See, for example, Gallup and Newport, 1991:44; also see Bowers et al., 1994; Ellsworth and Gross, 1994, op. cit.; Bowers, 1993, op. cit.

[73] See Bowers, 1993, ibid.; Sandys and McGarrell, 1995, op. cit.; McGarrell and Sandys, 1996, op. cit. Bowers notes that there is evidence suggesting that "a majority of the public would also be willing to accept parole after a fixed term of at least 25 years in preference to the death penalty on the condition that it was coupled with a restitution requirement and that the defendant had fully met the restitution requirement," see Bowers, 1993, op. cit., p. 168.

[74] Cited in McGarrell and Sandys, 1996, ibid., p. 509.

[75] Durham et al., 1996.

[76] Ibid., p. 726.

[77] Ibid., p. 727.

[78] Ibid.

[79] Ibid.

[80] Ibid.

[81] Kohlberg and Elfenbein, 1975: 617.

[82] Ibid., pp. 637-38.

[83] Ibid., p. 637.

[84] Ibid., p. 638.

[85] Zimring and Hawkins, 1986:12.

[86] Ibid.

[87] Bohm 1992a, op. cit., p. 539.

[88] Ibid.

References

Acker, James R. (1996) "The Death Penalty: A 25-Year Retrospective and a Perspective on the Future." *Criminal Justice Review* 21:139-60.

Acker, James R. and Charles S. Lanier (1998) "Death Penalty Legislation: Past, Present, and Future," Pp. 77-115 in J. R. Acker, R. M. Bohm, and C. S. Lanier (eds.) *America's Experiment with Capital Punishment: Reflections on the Past, Present and Future of the Ultimate Penal Sanction.* Durham, NC: Carolina Academic Press.

Acker, James R. and Charles S. Lanier (1995) "Matters of Life or Death: The Sentencing Provisions in Capital Punishment Statutes." *Criminal Law Bulletin* 31:19-60.

Amsterdam, Anthony G. (1982) "Capital Punishment," pp. 346-358 in H. A. Bedau (ed.) *The Death Penalty in America*, Third Ed. New York: Oxford University Press.

Ancel, Marc (1967) "The Problem of the Death Penalty," pp. 3-21 in T. Sellin (ed.) *Capital Punishment.* New York: Harper & Row.

Andersen, Kurt (1983) "An Eye for an Eye." *Time* (January 24), pp. 28-39.

Archer, Dane, Rosemary Gartner, and Marc Beittel (1983) "Homicide and the Death Penalty: A Cross-National Test of a Deterrence Hypothesis." *Journal of Criminal Law and Criminology* 74:991-1013.

Arkin, Stephen D. (1980) "Discrimination and Arbitrariness in Capital Punishment: An Analysis of Post-Furman Murder Cases in Dade County, Florida, 1973-1976." *Stanford Law Review* 33:75-101.

Arthur, John (1998) "Proximate Correlates of Black's Support for Capital Punishment." *Journal of Crime and Justice* 21:159-72.

Bailey, William C. (1998). "Deterrence, Brutalization, and the Death Penalty: Another Examination of Oklahoma's Return to Capital Punishment." *Criminology* 36:711-733.

Bailey, William C. (1991) "The General Prevention Effect of Capital Punishment for Non-Capital Felonies," pp. 21-38 in R. M. Bohm (ed.) *The Death Penalty in America: Current Research.* Cincinnati, OH: Anderson Publishing Co.

Bailey, William C. (1990) "Murder and Capital Punishment: An Analysis of Television Execution Publicity." *American Sociological Review* 55:1308-1333.

Bailey, William C. (1984a) "Disaggregation in Deterrence and Death Penalty Research: The Case of Murder in Chicago." *Journal of Criminal Law and Criminology* 74:827-859.

Bailey, William C. (1984b) "Murder and Capital Punishment in the Nation's Capital." *Justice Quarterly* 1:211-233.

Bailey, William C. (1983) "The Deterrent Effect of Capital Punishment during the 1950s." *Suicide* 13:95-107.

Bailey, William C. (1980) "Deterrence and the Celerity of the Death Penalty: A Neglected Question in Deterrence Research." *Social Forces* 58:1308-1333.

Bailey, William C. (1979a) "The Deterrent Effect of the Death Penalty for Murder in California." *Southern California Law Review* 52:743–764.

Bailey, William C. (1979b) "The Deterrent Effect of the Death Penalty for Murder in Ohio: A Time–Series Analysis." *Cleveland State Law Review* 28:51–81.

Bailey, William C. (1979c) "Deterrence and the Death Penalty for Murder in Oregon." *Willamette Law Review* 16:67–85.

Bailey, William C. (1979d) "An Analysis of the Deterrent Effect of the Death Penalty in North Carolina." *North Carolina Central Law Journal* 10:29–52.

Bailey, William C. (1978) "Deterrence and the Death Penalty for Murder in Utah: A Time–Series Analysis." *Journal of Contemporary Law* 5:1–20.

Bailey, William C. (1977a) "Imprisonment v. the Death Penalty as a Deterrent to Murder." *Law and Human Behavior* 1:239–260.

Bailey, William C. (1977b) "Deterrence and the Violent Sex Offender: Imprisonment vs. the Death Penalty." *Journal of Behavioral Economics* 6:107–144.

Bailey, William C. (1974) "Murder and the Death Penalty." *Journal of Criminal Law and Criminology* 65:416–423.

Bailey, William C. and Ruth D. Peterson (1994) "Murder, Capital Punishment, and Deterrence: A Review of the Evidence and an Examination of Police Killings." *Journal of Social Issues* 50:53–74.

Bailey, William C. and Ruth D. Peterson (1989) "Murder and Capital Punishment: A Monthly Time–Series Analysis of Execution Publicity." *American Sociological Review* 54:722–743.

Bailey, William C. and Ruth D. Peterson (1987) "Police Killings and Capital Punishment: The Post–*Furman* Period." *Criminology* 25:1–25.

Baldus, David C. and James W. L. Cole (1975) "Statistical Evidence on the Deterrent Effect of Capital Punishment: A Comparison of the Work of Thorsten Sellin and Isaac Ehrlich on the Deterrent Effect of Capital Punishment." *Yale Law Journal* 85:17–186.

Baldus, David C. and George Woodworth (1998) "Racial Discrimination and the Death Penalty: An Empirical and Legal Overview," pp. 385–415 in J. R. Acker, R. M. Bohm, and C. S. Lanier (eds.) *America's Experiment with Capital Punishment: Reflections on the Past, Present and Future of the Ultimate Penal Sanction.* Durham, NC: Carolina Academic Press.

Baldus, David C., George G. Woodworth, and Charles A. Pulaski (1990) *Equal Justice and the Death Penalty: A Legal and Empirical Analysis.* Boston: Northeastern University Press.

Baldus, David C., Charles Pulaski, Jr., and George Woodworth (1986) "Arbitrariness and Discrimination in the Administration of the Death Penalty: A Challenge to State Supreme Courts." *Stetson Law Review* 15:133–261.

Baldus, David C., Charles Pulaski, and George Woodworth (1983) "Comparative Review of Death Sentences: An Empirical Study of the Georgia Experience." *Journal of Criminal Law and Criminology* 74:661–753.

Barkan, Steven E. and Steven F. Cohn (1994) "Racial Prejudice and Support for the Death Penalty by Whites." *Journal of Research in Crime and Delinquency* 31:202–209.

Barnett, Arnold (1985) "Some Distribution Patterns for the Georgia Death Sentence." *University of California Davis Law Review* 18:1327–1374.

Barnett, Arnold (1981) "The Deterrent Effect of Capital Punishment: A Test of Some Recent Studies." *Operations Research* 29:346–370.

Beccaria, Cesare (1975) *On Crimes and Punishments*. Translated, with an introduction by Harry Paolucci. Indianapolis, IN: Bobbs-Merrill.

Bedau, Hugo Adam (1997) *The Death Penalty in America: Current Controversies*. New York: Oxford University Press.

Bedau, Hugo Adam (1987) *Death is Different: Studies in the Morality, Law, and Politics of Capital Punishment*. Boston: Northeastern University Press.

Bedau, Hugo Adam (ed.) (1982) *The Death Penalty in America*, Third Ed. New York: Oxford University Press.

Bedau, Hugo Adam (ed.) (1967) *The Death Penalty in America: An Anthology*, Rev. Ed. Chicago: Aldine.

Bedau, Hugo Adam and Michael L. Radelet (1987) "Miscarriages of Justice in Potentially Capital Cases." *Stanford Law Review* 40:21-179.

Beyleveld, Deryck (1982) "Ehrlich's Analysis of Deterrence." *The British Journal of Criminology* 22:101-123.

Bienen, Leigh B. (1996) "The Proportionality Review of Capital Cases By State High Courts After Gregg: Only 'The Appearance of Justice'?" *The Journal of Criminal Law and Criminology* 87:130-314.

Bienen, Leigh B., Neil Alan Weiner, Deborah W. Denno, Paul D. Allison, and Douglas Lane Mills (1988) "The Reimposition of Capital Punishment in New Jersey: The Role of Prosecutorial Discretion." *Rutgers Law Review* 41:27-372.

Blankenship, Michael B., James Luginbuhl, Francis T. Cullen, and William Redick (1997) "Jurors' Comprehension of Sentencing Instructions: A Test of the Death Penalty Process in Tennessee." *Justice Quarterly* 14:325-346.

Bohm, Robert M. (1994) "Capital Punishment in Two Judicial Circuits in Georgia: A Description of the Key Actors and the Decision-Making Process." *Law and Human Behavior* 18:319-338.

Bohm, Robert M. (1992a) "Toward an Understanding of Death Penalty Opinion Change in the United States: The Pivotal Years, 1966 and 1967." *Humanity and Society* 16:524-542.

Bohm, Robert M. (1992b) "Retribution and Capital Punishment: Toward a Better Understanding of Death Penalty Opinion." *Journal of Criminal Justice* 20:227-236.

Bohm, Robert M. (1991) "American Death Penalty Opinion, 1936-1986: A Critical Examination of the Gallup Polls," pp. 113-145 in R. M. Bohm (ed.) *The Death Penalty in America: Current Research*. Cincinnati: Anderson Publishing Co.

Bohm, Robert M. (1990) "Death Penalty Opinions: Effects of a Classroom Experience and Public Commitment." *Sociological Inquiry* 60:285-297.

Bohm, Robert M. (1989) "The Effects of Classroom Instruction and Discussion on Death Penalty Opinions: A Teaching Note." *Journal of Criminal Justice* 17:123-131.

Bohm, Robert M. (1987) "American Death Penalty Attitudes: A Critical Examination of Recent Evidence." *Criminal Justice and Behavior* 14:380-396.

Bohm, Robert M. and Keith N. Haley (1999) *Introduction to Criminal Justice*, Second Ed. New York: Glencoe/McGraw-Hill.

Bohm, Robert M. and Keith N. Haley (1997) *Introduction to Criminal Justice*. New York: Glencoe/McGraw-Hill.

Bohm, Robert M. and Ronald E. Vogel (1994) "A Comparison of Factors Associated With Uninformed and Informed Death Penalty Opinions." *Journal of Criminal Justice* 22:125-143.

Bohm, Robert M., Ronald E. Vogel, and Albert A. Maisto (1993) "Knowledge and Death Penalty Opinion: A Panel Study." *Journal of Criminal Justice* 21:29–45.

Bohm, Robert M., Louise J. Clark, and Adrian F. Aveni (1991) "Knowledge and Death Penalty Opinion: A Test of the Marshall Hypotheses." *Journal of Research in Crime and Delinquency* 28:360–387.

Bohm, Robert M., Louise J. Clark, and Adrian F. Aveni (1990) "The Influence of Knowledge for Death Penalty Opinions: An Experimental Test." *Justice Quarterly* 7:175–188.

Bowers, William J. (1995) "The Capital Jury Project: Rationale, Design, and Preview of Early Findings." *Indiana Law Journal* 70:1043–1102.

Bowers, William J. (1993) "Capital Punishment and Contemporary Values: People's Misgivings and the Court's Misperceptions." *Law and Society Review* 27:157–175.

Bowers, William J. (1988) "The Effect of Executions is Brutalization, Not Deterrence," pp. 49–89 in K. C. Haas and J. A. Inciardi (eds.) *Challenging Capital Punishment: Legal and Social Science Approaches*. Newbury Park, CA: Sage.

Bowers, William J. and Benjamin D. Steiner (1998) "Choosing Life or Death: Sentencing Dynamics in Capital Cases," pp. 309–349 in J. R. Acker, R. M. Bohm, and C. S. Lanier (eds.) *America's Experiment with Capital Punishment: Reflections on the Past, Present and Future of the Ultimate Penal Sanction*. Durham, NC: Carolina Academic Press.

Bowers, William J., Margaret Vandiver, and Patricia H. Dugan (1994) "A New Look at Public Opinion on Capital Punishment: What Citizens and Legislators Prefer." *American Journal of Criminal Law* 22:77–150.

Bowers, William J. with Glenn L. Pierce and John F. McDevitt (1984) *Legal Homicide: Death as Punishment in America, 1864–1982*. Boston: Northeastern University Press.

Bowers, William J. and Glenn L. Pierce (1980) "Deterrence or Brutalization: What is the Effect of Executions?" *Crime and Delinquency* 26:453–484.

Bowers, William J. and Glenn L. Pierce (1975) "The Illusion of Deterrence in Isaac Ehrlich's Research on Capital Punishment." *Yale Law Journal* 85:187–208.

Brier, Stephen and Stephen Feinberg (1980) "Recent Econometric Modeling of Crime and Punishment: Support for the Deterrence Hypothesis?" *Evaluation Research* 4:147–191.

Bright, Stephen B. (1998) "The Politics of Capital Punishment: The Sacrifice of Fairness for Executions," pp. 117–135 in J. R. Acker, R. M. Bohm, and C. S. Lanier (eds.) *America's Experiment with Capital Punishment: Reflections on the Past, Present and Future of the Ultimate Penal Sanction*. Durham, NC: Carolina Academic Press.

Bright, Stephen B. (1997) *Capital Punishment on the 25th Anniversary of Furman v. Georgia*. Atlanta, GA: Southern Center for Human Rights.

Bright, Stephen B. and Patrick J. Keenan (1995) "Judges and the Politics of Death: Deciding Between the Bill of Rights and the Next Election in Capital Cases." *Boston University Law Review* 75:759–835.

Britt, Chester L. (1998) "Race, Religion, and Support for the Death Penalty: A Research Note." *Justice Quarterly* 15:175–191.

Bronson, Edward J. (1970) "On the Conviction Proneness and Representativeness of the Death–Qualified Jury: An Empirical Study of Colorado Veniremen." *University of Colorado Law Review* 42:1–32.

Brooks, J. and J. H. Erikson (1996) "The Dire Wolf Collects His Due While the Boys Sit by the Fire: Why Michigan Cannot Afford to Buy into the Death Penalty." *Thomas M. Cooley Law Review* 13:877–905.

Bye, Raymond T. (1919) *Capital Punishment in the United States*. Philadelphia: The Committee of Philanthropic Labor of Philadelphia Yearly Meeting of Friends.

Cabana, Donald A. (1996). *Death at Midnight: The Confession of an Executioner*. Boston: Northeastern University Press.

Camp, Camille Graham and George M. Camp (1994) *The Corrections Yearbook 1994*. South Salem, NY: Criminal Justice Institute.

Canan, Russell F. (1989) "Burning at the Wire: The Execution of John Evans," pp. 60–80 in M. L. Radelet (ed.) *Facing the Death Penalty: Essays on a Cruel and Unusual Punishment*. Philadelphia: Temple University Press.

Carmichael, Stokely and Charles V. Hamilton (1967*) Black Power: The Politics of Liberation in America*. New York: Vintage Books.

Carter, Dan T. (1969) *Scottsboro: A Tragedy of the American South*. New York: Oxford University Press.

Cavender, Gray (1995) "Joining the Fray: An Interview with William J. Bowers." *American Journal of Criminal Justice* 20:113–136.

Cloninger, Dale O. (1977) "Death and the Death Penalty: A Cross-Sectional Analysis." *Journal of Behavioral Economics* 6:87–106.

Cochran, John K., Mitchell B. Chamlin, and Mark Seth (1994) "Deterrence or Brutalization? An Impact Assessment of Oklahoma's Return to Capital Punishment." *Criminology* 32:107–134.

Cole, Richard (1984) "Florida's Execution Lead Is Attributed to History." *The Anniston [AL] Star* (November 22).

Committee on the Judiciary, U.S. Senate (1982) "Capital Punishment as a Matter of Legislative Policy," pp. 311–318 in H. A. Bedau (ed.) *The Death Penalty in America*, Third Ed. New York: Oxford University Press.

Cook, Philip J. and Donna B. Slawson with Lori A. Gries (1993) *The Costs of Processing Murder Cases in North Carolina*. Raleigh, NC: North Carolina Administrative Office of the Courts.

Cottingham, John (1979) "Varieties of Retributivism." *Philosophical Quarterly* 29:238–246.

Cowan, Claudia, William C. Thompson, and Phoebe C. Ellsworth (1984) "The Effects of Death Qualification on Jurors' Predisposition to Convict and on the Quality of Deliberation." *Law and Human Behavior* 8:53–79.

Coyle, Marcia, Fred Strasser, and Marianne Lavelle (1990) "Fatal Defense: Trial and Error in the Nation's Death Belt." *The National Law Journal* 12 (No. 40, June 11):30–44.

Coyne, Randall and Lyn Entzeroth (1998) *Capital Punishment and the Judicial Process: 1998 Supplement*. Durham, NC: Carolina Academic Press.

Coyne, Randall and Lyn Entzeroth (1994) *Capital Punishment and the Judicial Process*. Durham, NC: Carolina Academic Press.

Crespi, I. (1971) "What Kinds of Attitude Measures Are Predictive of Behavior?" *Public Opinion Quarterly* 35:327–334.

Culver, John H. (1985) "The States and Capital Punishment: Executions from 1977-1984." *Justice Quarterly* 2:567–578.

Dann, Robert H. (1935) "The Deterrent Effect of Capital Punishment." *Friends Social Service Series* 29:1–20.

"Death Penalty Fails to Deter Violent Crime, Experts Say" (1997) *The Orlando Sentinel* (January 16), p. D-4.

Death Penalty Information Center, www.essential.org/dpic/

Death Row, U.S.A. (1998) NAACP Legal Defense and Educational Fund, Inc. New York, NY 10013-2897 (99 Hudson St., Suite 1600) (Spring).

Death Row, U.S.A. (1996) NAACP Legal Defense and Educational Fund, Inc. New York, NY 10013-2897 (99 Hudson St., Suite 1600).

Decker, Scott H. and Carol W. Kohfeld (1990) "The Deterrent Effect of Capital Punishment in the Five Most Active Execution States: A Time–Series Analysis." *Criminal Justice Review* 15:173-191.

Decker, Scott H. and Carol W. Kohfeld (1988) "Capital Punishment and Executions in the Lone Star State: A Deterrence Study." *Criminal Justice Research Bulletin* 3:1-6.

Decker, Scott H. and Carol W. Kohfeld (1987) "An Empirical Analysis of the Effect of the Death Penalty in Missouri." *Journal of Crime and Justice* 10:23-45.

Decker, Scott H. and Carol W. Kohfeld (1986) "The Deterrent Effect of Capital Punishment in Florida: A Time Series Analysis." *Criminal Justice Policy Review* 1:422-437.

Decker, Scott H. and Carol W. Kohfeld (1984) "A Deterrence Study of the Death Penalty in Illinois, 1933-1980." *Journal of Criminal Justice* 12:367-379.

DeFronzo, J. (1979) "In Search of the Behavioral and Attitudinal Consequences of Victimization." *Sociological Spectrum* 25:23-39.

Denno, Deborah W. (1998) "Execution and the Forgotten Eighth Amendment," pp. 547-577 in J. R. Acker, R. M. Bohm, and C. S. Lanier (eds.) *America's Experiment with Capital Punishment: Reflections on the Past, Present and Future of the Ultimate Penal Sanction*. Durham, NC: Carolina Academic Press.

Denno, Deborah W. (1997) "Getting to Death: Are Executions Constitutional?" *Iowa Law Review* 82:319-464 (citations are from a draft copy).

Denno, Deborah W. (1994) "Is Electrocution an Unconstitutional Method of Execution? The Engineering of Death over the Century." *William and Mary Law Review* 35:551-692.

Dieter, Richard C. (1996) *Killing for Votes: The Dangers of Politicizing the Death Penalty Process.* Washington, DC: The Death Penalty Information Center.

Dieter, Richard C. (1993) *Sentencing for Life: Americans Embrace Alternatives to the Death Penalty*. Washington, DC: The Death Penalty Information Center.

Dieter, Richard C. (1992) *Millions Misspent: What Politicians Don't Say About the High Costs of the Death Penalty*. Washington, DC: The Death Penalty Information Center.

Dillehay, Ronald C. and Marla R. Sandys (1996) "Life Under *Wainwright v. Witt*: Juror Dispositions and Death Qualification." *Law and Human Behavior* 20:147-165.

Durham, Alexis M., H. Preston Elrod, and Patrick T. Kinkade (1996) "Public Support for the Death Penalty: Beyond Gallup." *Justice Quarterly* 13:705-736.

Ehrlich, Isaac (1982) "On Positive Methodology, Ethics, and Polemics in Deterrence Research." *British Journal of Criminology* 22:124-139.

Ehrlich, Isaac (1977) "Capital Punishment and Deterrence: Some Further Thoughts and Additional Evidence." *Journal of Political Economy* 85:741-788.

Ehrlich, Isaac (1975) "The Deterrent Effect of Capital Punishment: A Question of Life and Death." *American Economic Review* 65:397-417.

Einwechter, Jack E. (1998) Material graciously provided to the author in August. (Major Einwechter is a professor of Criminal Law at The Judge Advocate General's School, Charlottesville, VA.)

Ekland-Olson, Sheldon (1988) "Structured Discretion, Racial Bias and the Death Penalty: The First Decade After Furman in Texas." *Social Science Quarterly* 69:853-873.

Ellsworth, Phoebe C. and Samuel R. Gross (1994) "Hardening of the Attitudes: Americans' Views on the Death Penalty." *Journal of Social Issues* 50:19-52.

Ellsworth, Phoebe C. and Lee Ross (1983) "Public Opinion and Capital Punishment: A Close Examination of the Views of Abolitionists and Retentionists." *Crime and Delinquency* 29:116-169.

Erez, Edna (1981) "Thou Shalt Not Execute: Hebrew Law Perspective on Capital Punishment." *Criminology* 19:25-43.

Erikson, R. S. (1976) "The Relationship between Public Opinion and State Policy: A New Look at Some Forgotten Data." *American Journal of Political Science* 20:25-36.

Erskine, Helen (1970) "The Polls: Capital Punishment." *Public Opinion Quarterly* 34:290-307.

Espy, M. Watt and John O. Smykla (1987) *Executions in the United States, 1608-1987: The Espy File.* Machine-readable data file. Ann Arbor, MI: Inter-University Consortium for Political and Social Research.

Facts on File (1979) *Facts on File Yearbook,* edited by L. A. Sobel. New York: Facts on File, Inc.

Facts on File (1961) *Facts on File Yearbook,* edited by L. A. Sobel. New York: Facts on File, Inc.

Facts on File (1960) *Facts on File Yearbook,* edited by L. A. Sobel. New York: Facts on File, Inc.

Facts on File (1959) *Facts on File Yearbook,* edited by L. A. Sobel. New York: Facts on File, Inc.

Facts on File (1958) *Facts on File Yearbook,* edited by L. A. Sobel. New York: Facts on File, Inc.

Facts on File (1957) *Facts on File Yearbook,* edited by L. A. Sobel. New York: Facts on File, Inc.

Facts on File (1956) *Facts on File Yearbook,* edited by L. A. Sobel. New York: Facts on File, Inc.

Facts on File (1955) *Facts on File Yearbook,* edited by L. A. Sobel. New York: Facts on File, Inc.

Federal Bureau of Investigation (1997) *Crime in the United States 1996.* U.S. Department of Justice, Washington, DC:GPO.

Feinberg, J. and H. Gross (1975) *Punishment.* Encino,CA: Dickenson.

Filler, Louis (1967) "Movements to Abolish the Death Penalty in the United States," pp. 104-122 in T. Sellin (ed.) *Capital Punishment.* New York: Harper & Row.

Finckenauer, James O. (1988) "Public Support for the Death Penalty: Retribution as Just Deserts or Retribution as Revenge?" *Justice Quarterly* 5:81-100.

Fitzgerald, Robert and Phoebe C. Ellsworth (1984) "Due Process vs. Crime Control: Death Qualification and Jury Attitudes." *Law and Human Behavior* 8:31-51.

Foley, Linda (1987) "Florida after the Furman Decision: The Effect of Extralegal Factors on the Processing of Capital Offense Cases." *Behavioral Sciences & the Law* 5:457-465.

Forst, Brian E. (1977) "The Case Against Capital Punishment: A Cross-State Analysis of the 1960's." *Minnesota Law Review* 61:743-767.

Fox, James Alan, Michael L. Radelet, and Julie L. Bonsteel (1990-1991) "Death Penalty Opinion in the Post-Furman Years." *New York University Review of Law and Social Change* 18:499-528.

Frank, James and Brandon K. Applegate (1998) "Assessing Juror Understanding of Capital-Sentencing Instructions." *Crime and Delinquency* 44:412-433.

Freedman, Eric M. (1998) "Federal Habeas Corpus in Capital Cases," pp. 417–436 in J. R. Acker, R. M. Bohm, and C. S. Lanier (eds.) *America's Experiment with Capital Punishment: Reflections on the Past, Present and Future of the Ultimate Penal Sanction*. Durham, NC: Carolina Academic Press.

Friedman, Lee (1979) "The Use of Multiple Regression Analysis to Test for a Deterrent Effect of Capital Punishment: Prospects and Problems," pp. 61–87 in S. Messinger and E. Bittner (eds.) *Criminology Review Yearbook*. Beverly Hills, CA: Sage.

Gale, M. E. (1985) "Retribution, Punishment, and Death." *University of California, Davis Law Review* 18:973–1035.

Gallup, George, Jr. (1995) *The Gallup Poll Monthly*, No. 357. Princeton, NJ: The Gallup Poll (June).

Gallup, Alec and Frank Newport (1991) "Death Penalty Support Remains Strong." *The Gallup Poll Monthly* (June).

Gallup Report (1985) "Support for Death Penalty Highest in Half-Century." Princeton, NJ: The Gallup Report.

Garey, Margot (1985) "The Cost of Taking a Life: Dollars and Sense of the Death Penalty." *University of California, Davis Law Review* 18:1221–1273.

"Georgia Killer Is Granted His Wish to be Executed." (1998) *The Orlando Sentinel* (October 14), p. A-14.

Gibbs, J. P. (1978) "The Death Penalty, Retribution and Penal Policy." *Journal of Criminal Law and Criminology* 69:291–299.

Glaser, Daniel (1979) "Capital Punishment—Deterrent or Stimulus to Murder? Our Unexamined Deaths and Penalties." *University of Toledo Law Review* 10:317–333.

Goldberg, Faye (1970) "Toward Expansion of *Witherspoon*: Capital Scruples, Jury Bias, and Use of Psychological Data to Raise Presumptions in the Law." *Harvard Civil Rights-Civil Liberties Law Review* 5:53–69.

Gorecki, Jan (1983) *Capital Punishment: Criminal Law and Social Evolution*. New York: Columbia University Press.

Gottlieb, Gerald H. (1961) "Testing the Death Penalty." *Southern California Law Review* 34:268–281.

Gow, H. B. (1986) "Religious Views Support the Death Penalty," pp. 79–85 in B. Szumski, L. Hall, and S. Bursell (eds.) *The Death Penalty: Opposing Viewpoints*. St. Paul, MN: Greenhaven.

Grasmick, Harold G., John K. Cochran, Robert J. Bursik, Jr., and M'Lou Kimpel (1993) "Religion, Punitive Justice, and Support for the Death Penalty." *Justice Quarterly* 10:289–314.

Grimes, Ruth-Ellen M. (1996) "Walnut Street Jail," pp. 493–497 in M. D. McShane and F. P. Williams III (eds.) *Encyclopedia of American Prisons*. New York and London: Garland.

Gross, Samuel R. (1996) "The Risks of Death: Why Erroneous Convictions Are Common in Capital Cases." *Buffalo Law Review* 44:469–500.

Gross, Samuel R. (1984) "Determining the Neutrality of Death-Qualified Juries: Judicial Appraisal of Empirical Data." *Law and Human Behavior* 8:7–30.

Gross, Samuel R. and Robert Mauro (1989) *Death and Discrimination: Racial Disparities in Capital Sentencing*. Boston: Northeastern University Press.

Gross, Samuel R. and Robert Mauro (1984) "Patterns of Death: An Analysis of Racial Disparities in Capital Sentencing and Homicide Victimization." *Stanford Law Review* 37:27–153.

Haas, Kenneth C. and James A. Inciardi (eds.) (1988) *Challenging Capital Punishment: Legal and Social Science Approaches*. Newbury Park, CA: Sage.

Hagan, John (1974) "Extra-Legal Attributes and Criminal Sentencing: An Assessment of a Sociological Viewpoint." *Law and Society Review* 8:357-383.

Haney, Craig (1998) "Mitigation and the Study of Lives: On the Roots of Violent Criminality and the Nature of Capital Justice," pp. 351-384 in J. R. Acker, R. M. Bohm, and C. S. Lanier (eds.) *America's Experiment with Capital Punishment: Reflections on the Past, Present and Future of the Ultimate Penal Sanction.* Durham, NC: Carolina Academic Press.

Haney, Craig (1984) "On the Selection of Capital Juries: The Biasing Effects of the Death-Qualification Process." *Law and Human Behavior* 8:121-132.

Haney, Craig and Deana Dorman Logan (1994) "Broken Promise: The Supreme Court's Response to Social Science Research on Capital Punishment." *Journal of Social Issues* 50:75-100.

Haney, Craig, Lorelei Sontag, and Sally Costanzo (1994) "Deciding to Take a Life: Capital Juries, Sentencing Instructions, and the Jurisprudence of Death." *Journal of Social Issues* 50:149-176.

Hans, Valerie P. (1988) "Death by Jury," pp. 149-175 in K. C. Haas and J. A. Inciardi (eds.) *Challenging Capital Punishment: Legal and Social Science Approaches.* Newbury Park, CA: Sage.

Harris, Philip W. (1986) "Oversimplification and Error in Public Opinion Surveys on Capital Punishment." *Justice Quarterly* 3:429-455.

Heider, F. (1958) *The Psychology of Interpersonal Relations.* New York: Wiley.

Heilbrun, Jr., Alfred B., Lynn C. Heilbrun, and Kim L. Heilbrun (1978) "Impulsive and Premeditated Homicide: An Analysis of Subsequent Parole Risk of the Murderer." *Journal of Criminal Law and Criminology* 69:108-114.

Hoffmann, Joseph L. (1995) "Where's the Buck?—Juror Misperception of Sentencing Responsibility in Death Penalty Cases." *Indiana Law Journal* 70:1137-1160.

Hoffmann, Joseph L. (1993) "On the Perils of Line-Drawing: Juveniles and the Death Penalty," pp. 117-132 in V. L. Streib (ed.) *A Capital Punishment Anthology.* Cincinnati: Anderson Publishing Co.

Hoppe, Christy (1992) "Life in Jail, or Death? Life Term is Cheaper." *The Charlotte [North Carolina] Observer* (March 22), p. 12A.

Howard, Jr., R. C. (1996) "The Defunding of the Post Conviction Defense Organizations as a Denial of the Right to Counsel." *West Virginia Law Review* 98:863-921.

Huff, C. Ronald, Arye Rattner, and Edward Sagarin (1986) "Guilty Until Proven Innocent: Wrongful Conviction and Public Policy." *Crime and Delinquency* 32:518-544.

Ingle, Joseph B. (1989) "Ministering to the Condemned: A Case Study," pp. 112-122 in M. L. Radelet (ed.) *Facing the Death Penalty: Essays on a Cruel and Unusual Punishment.* Philadelphia: Temple University Press.

Jackson, Rev. Jesse with Jesse Jackson, Jr. (1996) *Legal Lynching: Racism, Injustice and the Death Penalty.* New York: Marlowe.

Jacoby, Joseph and Raymond Paternoster (1982) "Sentencing Disparity and Jury Packing: Further Challenges to the Death Penalty." *Journal of Criminal Law and Criminology* 73:379-387.

Jacoby, S. (1983) *Wild Justice: The Evolution of Revenge.* New York: Harper and Row.

Johnson, Robert (1998) *Death Work: A Study of the Modern Execution Process,* Second Ed. Belmont, CA: West/Wadsworth.

Johnson, Robert (1990) *Death Work: A Study of the Modern Execution Process.* Pacific Grove, CA: Brooks/Cole.

Johnson, Robert (1989) *Condemned to Die: Life Under Sentence of Death*. Prospect Heights, IL: Waveland.

Jones, Peter R. (1994) "It's Not What You Ask, It's the Way that You Ask It: Question Form and Public Opinion on the Death Penalty." *The Prison Journal* 74:32-50.

Jurow, George L. (1971) "New Data on the Effect of a 'Death Qualified' Jury on the Guilt Determination Process." *Harvard Law Review* 84:567-611.

Kaplan, J. (1983) "The Problem of Capital Punishment." *University of Illinois Law Review* 3:555-577.

Kehler, Larry, Sharon Sawatzky, Harry Huebner, Louise Dueck, Edgar Epp, and Clarence Epp (1985) *Capital Punishment Study Guide: For Groups and Congregations*. Winnipeg: Mennonite Central Committee Canada.

Keil, Thomas J. and Gennaro F. Vito (1995) "Race and the Death Penalty in Kentucky Murder Trials: 1976-1991." *American Journal of Criminal Justice* 20:17-36.

Keil, Thomas J. and Gennaro F. Vito (1990) "Race and the Death Penalty in Kentucky Murder Trials: An Analysis of Post-*Gregg* Outcomes." *Justice Quarterly* 7:189-207.

Keil, Thomas J. and Gennaro F. Vito (1989) "Race, Homicide Severity, and Application of the Death Penalty: A Consideration of the Barnett Scale." *Criminology* 27:511-535.

Kelsen, H. (1943) *Society and Nature*. Chicago: University of Chicago Press.

King, David R. (1978) "The Brutalization Effect: Execution Publicity and and the Incidence of Homicide in South Carolina." *Social Forces* 57:683-687.

King, Glen D. (1982) "On Behalf of the Death Penalty," pp. 308-311 in H. A. Bedau (ed.) *The Death Penalty in America*, Third Ed. New York: Oxford University Press.

Kleck, Gary (1981) "Racial Discrimination in Criminal Sentencing: A Critical Evaluation of the Evidence with Additional Evidence of the Death Penalty." *American Sociological Review* 46:783-805.

Klein, Lawrence R., Brian Forst, and Victor Filatov (1982) "The Deterrent Effect of Capital Punishment: An Assessment of the Evidence," pp. 138-159 in H. A. Bedau (ed.) *The Death Penalty in America*, Third Ed. New York: Oxford University Press.

Kobil, Daniel T. (1998) "The Evolving Role of Clemency in Capital Cases," pp. 531-546 in J. R. Acker, R. M. Bohm, and C. S. Lanier (eds.) *America's Experiment with Capital Punishment: Reflections on the Past, Present and Future of the Ultimate Penal Sanction*. Durham, NC: Carolina Academic Press.

Kohfeld, Carol W. and Scott H. Decker (1990) "Time Series, Panel Design and Criminology: A Multi-State, Mult-Wave Analysis of the Effect of the Death Penalty in Contiguous States," pp. 198-240 in K. L. Kempf (ed.) *Measurement Issues in Criminology*. New York: Springer-Verlag.

Kohlberg, Lawrence and Daniel Elfenbein (1975) "The Development of Moral Judgments Concerning Capital Punishment." *American Journal of Orthopsychiatry* 45:614-640.

Kroll, Michael A. (1989) "The Fraternity of Death," pp. 16-26 in M. L. Radelet (ed.) *Facing the Death Penalty: Essays on a Cruel and Unusual Punishment*. Philadelphia: Temple University Press.

Lawrence, C. R., III (1987) "The Id, the Ego, and Equal Protection: Reckoning with Unconscious Racism." *Stanford Law Review* 39:317-388.

Layson, Stephen K. (1985) "Homicide and Deterrence: A Reexamination of the United States Time-Series Evidence." *Southern Economy Journal* 52:68-89.

Lehner, Patrick (1996) "Abolition Now!!!" http://www.abolition-now.com/

Lilly, J. Robert (1997) "Military Justice: A Neglected Topic." *ACJS Today* 15:11.

Lilly, J. Robert (1996) "Dirty Details: Executing U.S. Soldiers During World War II." *Crime and Delinquency* 42:491-516.

Lilly, J. Robert (1993) "Race and Capital Punishment in the Military: WWII." Paper presented at the annual meeting the American Society of Criminology, Phoenix, AZ, October.

Lilly, J. Robert, Peter Davies, and Richard A. Ball (1995) "Dirty Details: Executing U.S. Soldiers During World War II." Paper presented at the annual meeting the American Society of Criminology, Boston, MA, November.

Longmire, Dennis R. (1996) "Americans' Attitudes About the Ultimate Sanction Capital Punishment," pp. 93-108 in T. J. Flanagan and D. R. Longmire (eds.) *Americans View Crime and Justice: A National Public Opinion Survey*. Thousand Oaks, CA: Sage.

Lord, Charles G., Lee Ross, and Mark R. Lepper (1979) "Biased Assimilation and Attitude Polarization: The Effects of Prior Theories on Subsequently Considered Evidence." *Journal of Personality and Social Psychology* 37:2098-2109.

Lotz, Roy and Robert M. Regoli (1980) "Public Support for the Death Penalty. *Criminal Justice Review* 5:55-66.

Luginbuhl, James and Kathi Middendorf (1988) "Death Penalty Beliefs and Jurors' Responses to Aggravating and Mitigating Circumstances in Capital Trials." *Law and Human Behavior* 12:263-281.

Maguire, Kathleen and Ann L. Pastore (eds.) *Sourcebook of Criminal Justice Statistics 1996*. U.S. Department of Justice, Bureau of Justice Statistics. Washington, DC: GPO.

Mailer, Norman (1979) *The Executioner's Song*. Boston: Little, Brown.

Marquart, James W. and Jonathan R. Sorensen (1988) "Institutional and Postrelease Behavior of *Furman*-Commuted Inmates in Texas." *Criminology* 26:677-693.

Marquart, James W., Sheldon Ekland-Olson, and Jonathan R. Sorensen (1994) *The Rope, The Chair, and the Needle: Capital Punishment in Texas, 1923-1990*. Austin: University of Texas Press.

McFarland, Sam G. (1983) "Is Capital Punishment a Short-Term Deterrent to Homicide?: A Study of the Effects of Four Recent American Executions." *Journal of Criminal Law and Criminology* 74:1014-1030.

McGarrell, Edmund F. and Marla Sandys (1996) "The Misperception of Public Opinion Toward Capital Punishment: Examining the Spuriousness Explanation of Death Penalty Support." *American Behavioral Scientist* 39:500-513.

Mello, Michael (1989) "Another Attorney for Life," pp. 81-91 in M. L. Radelet (ed.) *Facing the Death Penalty: Essays on a Cruel and Unusual Punishment*. Philadelphia: Temple University Press.

Mello, Michael and Paul J. Perkins (1998) "Closing the Circle: The Illusion of Lawyers for People Litigating for Their Lives at the Fin de Siecle," pp. 245-284 in J. R. Acker, R. M. Bohm, and C. S. Lanier (eds.) *America's Experiment with Capital Punishment: Reflections on the Past, Present and Future of the Ultimate Penal Sanction*. Durham, NC: Carolina Academic Press.

Miller, Kent S. and Michael L. Radelet (1993) *Executing the Mentally Ill: The Criminal Justice System and the Case of Alvin Ford*. Newbury Park, CA: Sage.

Monroe, A. D. (1979) "Consistency between Public Preferences and National Policy Decisions." *American Politics Quarterly* 7:3-19.

Montgomery, Lori (1994) "Rising Outrage Over Crime Puts U.S. Back in the Execution Business." *The Charlotte [NC] Observer* (April 3), p. 2A.

Moore, David W. (1994) "Majority Advocate Death Penalty for Teenage Killers." *The Gallup Poll Monthly*, September: 2-5.

Moran, Gary and John Craig Comfort (1986) "Neither 'Tentative' nor 'Fragmentary': Verdict Preference of Impaneled Felony Jurors as a Function of Attitude Toward Capital Punishment." *Journal of Applied Psychology* 71:146–155.

Murphy, Elizabeth (1984) "The Application of the Death Penalty in Cook County." *Illinois Bar Journal* 93:90–95.

Muwakkil, Salim (1989) "The Death Penalty and the Illusion of Justice." *In These Times*, Vol. 13, No. 26 (May 24–June 6), p. 6.

Nakell, Barry and Kenneth A. Hardy (1987) *The Arbitrariness of the Death Penalty*. Philadelphia: Temple University Press.

New York State Defenders Association (1982) *Capital Losses: The Price of the Death Penalty for New York State*. Albany, NY: New York State Defenders Association, Inc.

Niemi, Richard (1989) *Trends in Public Opinion: A Compendium of Survey Data*. New York: Greenwood Press.

Oskamp, Stuart (1977) *Attitudes and Opinions*. Englewood Cliffs, NJ: Prentice-Hall.

Packer, Herbert L. (1968) *The Limits of the Criminal Sanction*. Stanford: Stanford University Press.

Page, B. I. and R. Y. Shapiro (1983) "Effects of Public Opinion on Policy." *American Political Science Review* 77:175–190.

Page, B. I., R. Y. Shapiro, and G. R. Dempsey (1987) "What Moves Public Opinion?" *American Political Science Review* 81:23–43.

Parker, Gary (1991) "Prepared Statement of Gary Parker, Georgia State Senator, Fifteenth Senatorial District, Columbus, GA." Hearing before the Subcommittee on Civil and Constitutional Rights of the Committee on the Judiciary, House of Representatives, One Hundred First Congress, Second Session on H.R. 4618 Racial Justice Act of 1990, etc., May 3 and 9, 1990. Serial No. 125, U.S. Government Printing Office: Washington, DC.

Passell, Peter (1975) "The Deterrent Effect of Capital Punishment: A Statistical Test." *Stanford Law Review* 28:61–80.

Passell, Peter and John B. Taylor (1977) "The Deterrent Effect of Capital Punishment: Another View." *American Economic Review* 67:445–451.

Paternoster, Raymond (1991) *Capital Punishment in America*. New York: Lexington.

Paternoster, Raymond (1984) "Prosecutorial Discretion in Requesting the Death Penalty: The Case of Victim-Based Discrimination." *Law and Society Review* 18:437–478.

Paternoster, Raymond (1983) "Race of Victim and Location of Crime: The Decision to Seek the Death Penalty in South Carolina." *Journal of Criminal Law and Criminology* 74:754–785.

Paternoster, Raymond and AnnMarie Kazyaka (1988) "The Administration of the Death Penalty in South Carolina: Experiences Over the First Few Years." *South Carolina Law Review* 39:245–414.

Pepinsky, Harold E. and Paul Jesilow (1984) *Myths that Cause Crime*. Cabin John, MD: Seven Locks Press.

Petersilia, Joan (1990) "Death Penalty Resolution Debated and Endorsed." *The Criminologist* 15:1.

Peterson, Ruth D. and William C. Bailey (1998) "Is Capital Punishment an Effective Deterrent for Murder? An Examination of Social Science Research," pp. 157–182 in J. R. Acker, R. M. Bohm, and C. S. Lanier (eds.) *America's Experiment with Capital Punishment: Reflections on the Past, Present and Future of the Ultimate Penal Sanction*. Durham, NC: Carolina Academic Press.

Peterson, Ruth D. and William C. Bailey (1991) "Felony Murder and Capital Punishment: An Examination of the Deterrence Question." *Criminology* 29:367–395.

Peterson, Ruth D. and William C. Bailey (1988) "Murder and Capital Punishment in the Evolving Context of the Post-*Furman* Era." *Social Forces* 66:774–807.

Phillips, David P. (1980) "The Deterrent Effect of Capital Punishment: New Evidence on an Old Controversy." *American Journal of Sociology* 86:139–147.

Prejean, Helen (1993) *Dead Man Walking: An Eyewitness Account of the Death Penalty in the United States*. New York: Random House.

Radelet, Michael L. (1981) "Racial Characteristics and the Imposition of the Death Penalty." *American Sociological Review* 46:918–927.

Radelet, Michael L. and Hugo Adam Bedau (1998) "The Execution of the Innocent," pp. 223–242 in J.R. Acker, R. M. Bohm, and C. S. Lanier (eds.) *America's Experiment with Capital Punishment: Reflections on the Past, Present and Future of the Ultimate Penal Sanction*. Durham, NC: Carolina Academic Press.

Radelet, Michael L. and Glenn L. Pierce (1991) "Choosing Those Who Will Die: Race and the Death Penalty in Florida." *Florida Law Review* 43:1–34.

Radelet, Michael L. and Glenn L. Pierce (1985) "Race and Prosecutorial Discretion in Homicide Cases." *Law and Society Review* 19:587–621.

Radelet, Michael and Margaret Vandiver (1983) "The Florida Supreme Court and Death Penalty Appeals." *Journal of Criminal Law and Criminology* 74:913–926.

Radelet, Michael L., Hugo Adam Bedau, and Constance E. Putnam (1992) *In Spite of Innocence: Erroneous Convictions in Capital Cases*. Boston: Northeastern University Press.

Radelet, Michael L., Margaret Vandiver, and Felix M. Barado (1983) "Families, Prisons, and Men with Death Sentences." *Journal of Family Issues* 4:593–612.

Radin, Margaret Jane (1980) "Cruel Punishment and Respect for Persons: Super Due Process for Death." *Southern California Law Review* 53:1143–1185.

Radin, Margaret Jane (1978) "The Jurisprudence of Death: Evolving Standards for the Cruel and Unusual Punishment Clause." *University of Pennsylvania Law Review* 126:989–1064.

Ralph, Paige H. (1996) "Benjamin Rush," pp. 412–413 in M. D. McShane and F. P. Williams III (eds.) *Encyclopedia of American Prisons*. New York and London: Garland.

Rankin, Joseph H. (1979) "Changing Attitudes Toward Capital Punishment." *Social Forces* 58:194–211.

Rapaport, Elizabeth (1993) "The Death Penalty and Gender Discrimination," pp. 145–152 in V. L. Streib (ed.) *A Capital Punishment Anthology*. Cincinnati: Anderson Publishing Co.

Recer, Paul (1994) "Professional Groups Want Doctors Out of Executions." *The Charlotte [NC] Observer* (March 20), p. 17A.

Reckless, Walter C. (1969) "The Use of the Death Penalty." *Crime and Delinquency* 15:43–56.

Reiman, Jeffrey (1998) *The Rich Get Richer and the Poor Get Prison: Ideology, Class, and Criminal Justice*, Fifth Ed. Boston: Allyn and Bacon.

Reinhold, Robert (1982) "Chemical Injection Executes Texas Killer." *The Anniston [AL] Star* (December 7), p. 1A.

Religious Leaders in Florida (1986) "Religious Views Denounce the Death Penalty," pp. 86–91 in B. Szumski, L. Hall, and S. Bursell (eds.) *The Death Penalty: Opposing Viewpoints*. St. Paul, MN: Greenhaven.

Roberts, Julian V. (1984) "Public Opinion and Capital Punishment: The Effects of Attitudes Upon Memory." *Canadian Journal of Criminology* 26:283-291.

Rusche, Georg and Otto Kirchheimer (1968) *Punishment and Social Structure*. New York: Russell and Russell.

Sandys, Marla (1998) "Stacking the Deck for Guilt and Death: The Failure of Death Qualification to Ensure Impartiality," pp. 285-307 in J. R. Acker, R. M. Bohm, and C. S. Lanier (eds.) *America's Experiment with Capital Punishment: Reflections on the Past, Present and Future of the Ultimate Penal Sanction*. Durham, NC: Carolina Academic Press.

Sandys, Marla (1995) "Attitudinal Change Among Students in a Capital Punishment Class: It May Be Possible." *American Journal of Criminal Justice* 20:37-55.

Sandys, Marla and Edmund F. McGarrell (1995) "Attitudes Toward Capital Punishment: Preferences for the Penalty or Mere Acceptance?" *Journal of Research in Crime and Delinquency* 32:191-213.

Sandys, Marla and Edmund F. McGarrell (1994) "Attitudes Toward Capital Punishment Among Indiana Legislators: Diminished Support in Light of Alternative Sentencing Options." *Justice Quarterly* 11:651-677.

Sarat, Austin and Neil Vidmar (1976) "Public Opinion, the Death Penalty, and the Eighth Amendment: Testing the Marshall Hypothesis." *Wisconsin Law Review* 17:171-206.

Savitz, Leonard (1958) "A Study in Capital Punishment." *Journal of Criminal Law, Criminology and Police Science* 49:338-341.

Scalia, John (1997) "Prisoner Petitions in the Federal Courts, 1980-96." U.S. Department of Justice, Office of Justice Programs, Bureau of Justice Statistics. Washington, DC:GPO.

Schneider, Victoria and John Ortiz Smykla (1991) "A Summary Analysis of Executions in the United States, 1608-1987: The Espy File," pp. 1-19 in R. M. Bohm (ed.) *The Death Penalty in America: Current Research*. Cincinnati, OH: Anderson Publishing Co.

Schuessler, Karl F. (1952) "The Deterrent Effect of the Death Penalty." *The Annals* 284:54-62.

Schwarzschild, Henry (1982) "In Opposition to Death Penalty Legislation," pp. 364-370 in H. A. Bedau (ed.) *The Death Penalty in America*, Third Ed. New York: Oxford University Press.

Sellin, Thorsten (ed.) (1967) *Capital Punishment*. New York: Harper & Row.

Sellin, Thorsten (1959) *The Death Penalty*. Philadelphia: The American Law Institute.

Simon, David R. (1996) *Elite Deviance*, Fifth Ed. Boston: Allyn and Bacon.

Smith, M. Dwayne (1987) "Patterns of Discrimination in Assessments of the Death Penalty: The Case of Louisiana." *Journal of Criminal Justice* 15:279-286.

Smith, Tom W. (1975) "A Trend Analysis of Attitudes Toward Capital Punishment, 1936-1974," pp. 257-318 in J. E. Davis (ed.) *Studies of Social Change Since 1948*, Volume II. Chicago: University of Chicago National Opinion Research Center.

Smykla, John O. (1987) "The Human Impact of Capital Punishment: Interviews with Families of Persons on Death Row." *Journal of Criminal Justice* 15:331-347.

Snell, Tracy L. (1997) "Capital Punishment 1996." U.S. Department of Justice, Bureau of Justice Statistics Bulletin (December).

Sorensen, Jon and Robert D. Wrinkle (1996) "No Hope for Parole: Disciplinary Infractions Among Death-Sentenced and Life-Without-Parole Inmates." *Criminal Justice and Behavior* 23:542-552.

Spangenberg, Robert L. and Elizabeth R. Walsh (1989) "Capital Punishment or Life Imprisonment? Some Cost Considerations." *Loyola of Los Angeles Law Review* 23:45-58.

Stack, Steven (1987) "Publicized Executions and Homicide, 1950-1980." *American Sociological Review* 52:532-540.

Steiker, Carol S. and Jordan M. Steiker (1998) "Judicial Developments in Capital Punishment Law," pp. 47-75 in J. R. Acker, R. M. Bohm, and C. S. Lanier (eds.) *America's Experiment with Capital Punishment: Reflections on the Past, Present and Future of the Ultimate Penal Sanction.* Durham, NC: Carolina Academic Press.

Stephan, James J. and Tracy L. Snell (1996) "Capital Punishment 1994." Bureau of Justice Statistics Bulletin, U.S. Department of Justice. Annapolis Junction, MD: BJS Clearinghouse.

Stephens, Gene (1990) "High-Tech Crime: The Threat to Civil Liberties." *The Futurist* (July–August), pp. 20-25.

Stinchcombe, Arthur L., Rebecca Adams, Carol A. Heimer, Kim Lane Scheppele, Tom W. Smith, and D. Garth Taylor (1980) *Crime and Punishment—Changing Attitudes in America.* San Francisco: Josey-Bass.

Streib, Victor L. (1998) "Executing Women, Children, and the Retarded: Second Class Citizens in Capital Punishment," pp. 201-221 in J. R. Acker, R. M. Bohm, and C. S. Lanier (eds.) *America's Experiment with Capital Punishment: Reflections on the Past, Present and Future of the Ultimate Penal Sanction.* Durham, NC: Carolina Academic Press.

Streib, Victor L. (1993) "Death Penalty for Female Offenders," pp. 142-145 in V. L. Streib (ed.) *A Capital Punishment Anthology.* Cincinnati: Anderson Publishing Co.

Streib, Victor L. (1989) "Juveniles' Attitudes Toward Their Impending Executions," pp. 38-59 in M. L. Radelet (ed.) *Facing the Death Penalty: Essays on a Cruel and Unusual Punishment.* Philadelphia: Temple University Press.

Streib, Victor L. (1988) "Imposing the Death Penalty on Children," pp. 245-267 in K. C. Haas and J. A. Inciardi (eds.) *Challenging Capital Punishment: Legal and Social Science Approaches.* Newbury Park, CA: Sage.

Surette, Ray (1992) *Media, Crime, and Criminal Justice: Images and Realities.* Pacific Grove, CA: Brooks/Cole.

Sutherland, Edwin H. (1925) "Murder and the Death Penalty." *Journal of Criminal Law and Criminology* 15:522-529.

Thomas, Charles W. and Samuel C. Foster (1975) "A Sociological Perspective on Public Support for Capital Punishment." *American Journal of Orthopsychiatry* 45:641-657.

Thompson, E. P. (1975) *Whigs and Hunters: The Origin of the Black Act.* New York: Pantheon.

Thompson, William C. (1989) "Death Qualification After *Wainwright v. Witt* and *Lockhart v. McCree.*" *Law and Human Behavior* 13:185-215.

Tifft, Larry (1982) "Capital Punishment Research, Policy, and Ethics: Defining Murder and Placing Murderers." *Crime and Social Justice* 17:61-68.

Trivers, R. (1971) "The Evolution of Reciprocal Altruism." *Quarterly Review of Biology* 46:35-57.

Tyler, Tom R. and Renee Weber (1982) "Support for the Death Penalty: Instrumental Response to Crime, or Symbolic Attitude?" *Law and Society Review* 17:21-45.

U.S. General Accounting Office (1990) *Death Penalty Sentencing: Research Indicates Pattern of Racial Disparities.* Report to Senate and House Committees on the Judiciary. Washington, DC:GAO.

Van den Haag, Ernest (1998) "Justice, Deterrence and the Death Penalty," pp. 139-156 in J. R. Acker, R. M. Bohm, and C. S. Lanier (eds.) *America's Experiment with Capital Punishment: Reflections on the Past, Present and Future of the Ultimate Penal Sanction*. Durham, NC: Carolina Academic Press.

Van den Haag, Ernest (1982) "In Defense of the Death Penalty: A Practical and Moral Analysis," pp. 323-341 in H. A. Bedau (ed.) *The Death Penalty in America*, Third Ed. New York: Oxford University Press.

Van den Haag, Ernest and John P. Conrad (1983) *The Death Penalty: A Debate*. New York: Plenum.

Vandiver, Margaret (1998) "The Impact of the Death Penalty on the Families of Homicide Victims and of Condemned Prisoners," pp. 477-505 in J. R. Acker, R. M. Bohm, and C. S. Lanier (eds.) *America's Experiment with Capital Punishment: Reflections on the Past, Present and Future of the Ultimate Penal Sanction*. Durham, NC: Carolina Academic Press.

Vandiver, Margaret (1989) "Coping with Death: Families of the Terminally Ill, Homicide Victims, and Condemned Prisoners," pp. 123-138 in M. L. Radelet (ed.) *Facing the Death Penalty: Essays on a Cruel and Unusual Punishment*. Philadelphia: Temple University Press.

Vick, Karl (1996) "Delaware Readies Gallows as Rare Form of Execution Draws Near." *The Washington Post* (January 21), p. B4.

Vidmar, Neil (1974) "Retributive and Utilitarian Motives and Other Correlates of Canadian Attitudes Toward the Death Penalty." *Canadian Psychologist* 15:337-356.

Vidmar, Neil and Tony Dittenhoffer (1981) "Informed Public Opinion and Death Penalty Attitudes." *Canadian Journal of Criminology* 23:43-56.

Vidmar, Neil and Phoebe Ellsworth (1974) "Public Opinion and the Death Penalty." *Stanford Law Review* 26:1245-1270.

Vidmar, Neil and Dale T. Miller (1980) "Socialpsychological Processes Underlying Attitudes Toward Legal Punishment." *Law and Society Review* 14:565-602.

Vila, Bryan and Cynthia Morris (eds.) (1997) *Capital Punishment in the United States: A Documentary History*. Westport, CT: Greenwood.

Vito, Gennaro and Thomas Keil (1988) "Capital Sentencing in Kentucky: An Analysis of the Factors Influencing Decision Making in the Post-*Gregg* Period." *Journal of Criminal Law and Criminology* 79:483-508.

Vito, Gennaro F. and Deborah G. Wilson (1988) "Back from the Dead: Tracking the Progress of Kentucky's *Furman*-Commuted Death Row Population." *Justice Quarterly* 5:101-111.

Vito, Gennaro F., Pat Koester, and Deborah G. Wilson (1991) "Return of the Dead: An Update on the Status of *Furman*-Commuted Death Row Inmates," pp. 89-99 in R. M. Bohm (ed.) *The Death Penalty in America: Current Research*. Cincinnati, OH: Anderson Publishing Co.

Vold, George B. (1952) "Extent and Trend of Capital Crimes in the United States." *The Annals* 284:1-7.

Vold, George B. (1932) "Can the Death Penalty Prevent Crime?" *Prison Journal* 12:3-8.

Waldo, Gordon P. (1981) "The Death Penalty and Deterrence: A Review of Recent Research," pp. 169-178 in I. L. Barak-Glantz and C. R. Huff (eds.) *The Mad, the Bad, and the Different: Essays in Honor of Simon Dinitz*. Lexington, MA: Heath.

Warr, Mark and Mark Stafford (1984) "Public Goals of Punishment and Support for the Death Penalty." *Journal of Research in Crime and Delinquency* 21:95-111.

Weissberg, R. (1976) *Public Opinion and Popular Government*. Englewood Cliffs, NJ: Prentice-Hall.

White, Welsh S. (1987) *The Death Penalty in the Eighties: An Examination of the Modern System of Capital Punishment*. Ann Arbor: University of Michigan Press.

Whitehead, John T. (1998) "Good Ol' Boys and the Chair: Death Penalty Attitudes of Policy Makers in Tennessee." *Crime and Delinquency* 44:245–256.

Wicker, A. W. (1969) "Attitudes Versus Actions: The Relationship of Verbal and Overt Behavioral Responses to Attitude Objects." *Journal of Social Issues* 25:41–78.

Wilbanks, William (1987) *The Myth of a Racist Criminal Justice System*. Monterey, CA: Brooks/Cole.

Williams, Frank P., Dennis R. Longmire, and David B. Gulick (1988) "The Public and the Death Penalty: Opinion as an Artifact of Question Type." *Criminal Justice Research Bulletin* 3:1–5.

Wolfgang, Marvin E. and Marc Riedel (1975) "Rape, Race and the Death Penalty in Georgia." *American Journal of Orthopsychiatry* 45:658–668.

Wolfson, Wendy Phillips (1982) "The Deterrent Effect of the Death Penalty upon Prison Murder," pp. 159–173 in H. A. Bedau (ed.) *The Death Penalty in America*, Third Ed. New York: Oxford University Press.

Wollan, Laurin A., Jr. (1989) "Representing the Death Row Inmate: The Ethics of Advocacy, Collateral Style," pp. 92–111 in M. L. Radelet (ed.) *Facing the Death Penalty: Essays on a Cruel and Unusual Punishment*. Philadelphia: Temple University Press.

Wolpin, Kenneth I. (1978) "Capital Punishment and Homicide in England: A Summary of Results." *American Economic Review* 68:422–427.

Wright, Harold O., Jr., Robert M. Bohm, and Katherine M. Jamieson (1995) "A Comparison of Uninformed and Informed Death Penalty Opinions: A Replication and Expansion." *American Journal of Criminal Justice* 20:57–87.

Wyble, D. W. (1985) "Capital Punishment in the Military." *Military Police* (Winter):36–37.

Young, Robert L. (1992) "Religious Orientation, Race and Support for the Death Penalty." *Journal for the Scientific Study of Religion* 31:76–87.

Yunker, J. A.(1976) "Is the Death Penalty a Deterrent to Homicide: Some Time–Series Evidence." *Journal of Behavioral Economics* 5:1–32.

Zahn, Margaret A. (1989) "Homicide in the Twentieth Century: Trends, Types, and Causes," pp. 216–234 in T. R. Gurr (ed.) *Violence in America: The History of Crime*, Vol. 1. Newbury Park, CA: Sage.

Zeisel, Hans (1982) "The Deterrent Effect of the Death Penalty: Facts v. Faith," pp. 116–138 in H. A. Bedau (ed.) *The Death Penalty in America*, Third Ed. New York: Oxford University Press.

Zeisel, Hans (1981) "Race Bias in the Administration of the Death Penalty: The Florida Experience." *Harvard Law Review* 95:456–468.

Zimring, Franklin E. and Gordon Hawkins (1986) *Capital Punishment and the American Agenda*. Cambridge: Cambridge University Press.

Zinn, Howard (1990) *A People's History of the United States*. New York: Harper Perennial.

Index

A

Abolition movement
  colonial times, 3–4
  decline of, 7
  early twentieth century, 6
  nineteenth century, 5
  Progressive Period, 6
  successes of, 4
Abolitionists, question severest punishment, 85
Academy of Criminal Justice Sciences, 90–91
Adams v. Texas, 39
Administration of death penalty. *See* Arbitrariness in administration of; Discrimination in administration of
Administrative Office of the United States Courts, 115
Aggravating circumstances, 12, 36, 47
  constitutional challenges to, 35
  defined, 26–27
  examples of, 27–28
  in favor of women, 151
  in military death penalty procedures, 64, 65–67
  types of, 34–35
"Aggravating only" guided discretion statutes, 26, 28–29
"Aggravating versus mitigating" guided discretion statutes, 26, 27–28
Ake v. Oklahoma, 43
Alternating current, 74–75
American Bar Association, survey of post-conviction appeals hours, 114
American College of Physicians, 78
American Economic Association, 89
American Law Institute's Model Penal Code, 12, 26

American League to Abolish Capital Punishment, 7
American Medical Association, opposition to lethal injection, 78
American Society for the Abolition of Capital Punishment, 4
American Society of Criminology, condemnation of capital punishment, 90
Amsterdam, Anthony, 91, 92, 96, 97, 103–104, 105, 108, 144
"An eye for an eye" (*lex talionis*), 170, 177
  misinterpretation of, 172–173
Andres v. U.S., 21
Annulment theory of retribution, 171–172
Antiterrorism and Effective Death Penalty Act of 1996, 44, 60, 117
Antone v. Dugger, 37
Appeals, frivolous and delaying, 45
Appellate court action, summary of in post-*Furman* capital cases, 45–46
Appellate court, state, options in appeal of death sentence, 44
Appellate process, 38
  acceleration of, 37
  under post-*Furman* statutes, 44
  streamlining, 117
  time involved, 36, 60, 84
Appellate review, automatic, 30–31
Arbitrariness in administration of death penalty
  application of death penalty across jurisdictions, 143–146
  defined, 143
  jurors' misunderstanding of sentencing obligations, 146–147
  justification in post-*Furman* statutes, 146
  plea bargaining, 147–148

About the Author

Robert M. Bohm is a Professor of Criminal Justice and Legal Studies at the University of Central Florida in Orlando. He has also been a faculty member in the Departments of Criminal Justice at the University of North Carolina at Charlotte (1989-1995) and at Jacksonville State University in Alabama (1979-1989). In 1973-1974, he worked for the Jackson County Department of Corrections in Kansas City, Missouri, first as a corrections officer and later as an instructor/counselor in the Model Inmate Employment Program, a Law Enforcement Assistance Administration sponsored work-release project. He received his Ph.D. in Criminology from Florida State University in 1980.

Dr. Bohm has published more than three dozen journal articles and book chapters in the areas of criminal justice and criminology. In addition to being the author of *Deathquest: An Introduction to the Theory and Practice of Capital Punishment in the United States*, he is the co-author (with Keith N. Haley) of *Introduction to Criminal Justice* (Glencoe/McGraw-Hill, 1997; 1999), the editor of *The Death Penalty in America: Current Research* (Anderson Publishing Co., 1991), the author of *A Primer in Crime and Delinquency* (Wadsworth, 1997), and the co-editor (with James R. Acker and Charles S. Lanier) of *America's Experiment with Capital Punishment: Reflections on the Past, Present, and Future of the Ultimate Penal Sanction* (Carolina Academic Press, 1998). He has been active in the American Society of Criminology, the Southern Criminal Justice Association, and especially the Academy of Criminal Justice Sciences, having served as Trustee-at-Large (1987-90), Second Vice-President (1990-91), First Vice-President (1991-92), and President (1992-93). In 1989, the Southern Criminal Justice Association selected him as the Outstanding Educator of the Year, and he was selected as Fellow of the Academy of Criminal Justice Sciences in 1999.